BₒT 8.41

2081
A Hopeful
View of
the Human
Future

Gerard K. O'Neill

Simon and Schuster   New York

Published by Simon and Schuster
A Division of Gulf & Western Corporation
Simon & Schuster Building
Rockefeller Center
1230 Avenue of the Americas
New York, New York 10020

SIMON AND SCHUSTER and colophon are trademarks of
Simon & Schuster

Designed by Irving Perkins
Illustrated by Cal Sacks

Manufactured in the United States of America
1 2 3 4 5 6 7 8 9 10

Library of Congress Cataloging in Publication Data
O'Neill, Gerard K
2081: a hopeful view of the human future

Bibliography: p.
Includes index.
1. Twenty-first century—Forecasts. 2. Twen-
tieth century—Forecasts.   I. Title.
CB161.053   303.4   81-482
AACR1
ISBN 0-671-24257-1

Acknowledgments

ONE'S OWN view of the future is shaped in considerable degree by one's parents and teachers. I owe a great deal to many teachers, but most of all to Mr. Robert Fowler of the Newburgh Free Academy, who first opened my eyes to the fascinating world of physics, and so started me on a lifetime love affair with the physical world. My parents, Dorothy Kitchen O'Neill and Edward Gerard O'Neill (grandparents of the Edward Christopher O'Neill, 1980–, of this book's dedication) maintained through a long and often painful life a love of knowledge, of people and of laughter, and a boundless curiosity and freshness of spirit. I am very grateful to them for demonstrating by their own example an attitude that has enriched my own life and helped to make my view of the future a hopeful one.

The ideas that make up this book would never have been written down were it not for the prodding of my good friend John Brockman, and I acknowledge his part in this adventure with affection and thanks. Finally, I thank my wife, Tasha, not only for her enthusiasm and encouragement, but for the patience and forbearance with which she put up with many lost evenings, weekends, and vacations while this book was written.

Gerard K. O'Neill
Princeton
1980

*To
Janet,
Roger,
Eleanor
and
Edward*

Contents

"WONDERS ARE MANY, AND NONE IS MORE WONDERFUL THAN MAN;
THE POWER THAT CROSSES THE WHITE SEA, DRIVEN BY THE STORMY WIND,
MAKING A PATH UNDER SURGES THAT THREATEN TO ENGULF HIM. . . ."

—Sophocles, *Antigone*

Preface

To PREDICT the future is at once the most fascinating and the most difficult of challenges. To make the attempt at this time, in the midst of the ferment of change that is the late twentieth century, one needs to gauge accurately what further transformations are in store for the world, particularly as a result of advances yet to come in the sciences and engineering. My own education and experience in these areas of knowledge, together with a lively curiosity about the human future, have led me to accept the challenge and thus to write this book. I've enjoyed that task, partly because my working career has balanced in a happy fashion theoretical calculation and the everyday reality of building scientific equipment that had to work.

The choice of the year 2081 for my predictions—just under a century away—is far from accidental. On a very much shorter time scale, most aspects of the human situation can't be very different from what they are now, for change (except for sudden catastrophes) takes time. And well beyond the horizon of a century any predictions we can make are sure to fall short of reality, because by then discoveries that we do not now even suspect will begin to affect the development of civilization profoundly.

This book is in four parts. In the first, "The Art of Prophecy," we'll explore in a pragmatic way the lessons that can be learned from the colorful history of earlier attempts at predicting the future. In the second, "The Drivers of Change," I'll describe five developments that I believe will determine, alone and in combination, the course of the next hundred years. In the third part, "Life in 2081," I invite you to join me in a tour through the world in which our great-grandchildren will be just at their prime.

In the fourth part, "Wild Cards," we'll explore the most exciting developments of a century from now that are just at the limits of possibility— and some that are, perhaps, well beyond those limits. As we view together the world of 2081, with all the surprises it has in store, it is my wish that this book will give you greater confidence and hope with which to face the future, and will give you as well some of the excitement and the pleasure that it has given me in writing it.

Gerard K. O'Neill

Part I

The Art of Prophecy

The Art of Prophecy

To DREAM and to plan, to be curious about the future and to wonder how much it can be shaped by our efforts are all essential aspects of our being human. And if we seek to learn something about that mysterious world that lies ahead, we will be well advised first to heed the lessons of the past. In the march of history, no less than in the sciences, every new insight into a possible reality, every perception of a new opportunity comes to us only because we have inherited a priceless legacy of knowledge and of method that was accumulated, slowly and after many errors, by the famous and the unknown men and women who worked in the same fields for centuries before us. We would be foolish to ignore that legacy, so at the beginning of this book about the human future we'll search for clues to successful prediction by comparing the real world of today with forecasts that were made in earlier times.

We have a responsibility beyond mere curiosity to learn as much about the future as we can, because we must choose those actions that will insure not only the survival of humanity, but an improvement in its condition. In a world that is growing hungrier year by year we must search for ways to end famine, for as the planetary resources of concentrated energy

18

and materials dwindle, we must either find new inexhaustible resources or—all of us—be content with less. But before we take action to try to solve such problems, and before we seek to influence the actions of other individuals or of governments, we must understand the realistic possibilities. Fighting for the "right" cause can give us a sense of virtue, but we'll gain nothing by advocating actions that have no realistic chance of happening.

What, then, are the real possibilities? Will the future approach a static condition (a "steady state"), or will change be never-ending? Does our hope for humanity lie in forging better social organizations, or will technology evolve so much that it will allow us to solve certain problems without becoming wiser or more selfless? And if we have any choice in the matter, should we search for a unique "solution" (by inference, permanent), or should we encourage diversity, change, and a plurality of ideas?

We need to answer these questions, for ourselves personally as well as for the race as a whole. Our human population is relatively youthful, with a typical age of less than forty in the stable, developed nations, and of not much more than twenty in the Third World. Barring terrestrial catastrophe, a great many of the people now alive will still be living a half-century from now. In preparing for our share of those fifty years, each of us has to make a fundamental, personal choice: to acquire the skills that will fit us for a static society, or those that will help us move with ease and understanding in a fast-changing world with technology as its base. And some of us won't be content merely to flow with the tide of the future—we'll want to influence its direction as well. For that we'll need to imagine alternative futures and carefully weigh their values.

I made my own value judgments years ago on two of the most basic questions that involve the future: I place a higher value on the freedom of the individual than on material wealth or the absence of risk, and after freedom—not before—I put the search for peace. Fortunately, it turns out that the most perceptive authors who have written of the future have been passionately concerned with just those issues.

To find what "will be in any case" and what "could be if we try" I began by studying what was said by the crystal gazers of the past. Their guesses, I learned, spanned the extremes from utopian flights of fancy to computerized projections by groups of authors who attempted to be objective and impersonal. Such "scientific" groups often gave the cynical label of "genius forecasting" to the works of individual authorship, but whatever their shortcomings, the works of individual authors are usually much more readable than group efforts. St. Thomas More's exposition of a perfect society arranged by the mythical King Utopius is an example; it has engaged readers over a period of centuries. But in every type of futuristic writing, from the impersonal to the subjective, I found the same pattern: most prophets overestimated how much the world would be transformed by social and political change and underestimated the forces of technological change. As I share with you the most amusing and thought-provoking of the earlier predictions, we can be alert to that pattern as it takes shape.

Some authors of futuristic novels wrote with the intent of giving sheer delight to the reader and included realistic details as incidental stage props to aid their storytelling. Among those authors I'll select Verne, Wells, and Kipling for a quick skim of their ideas about the future, but I must warn you that Kipling is an author out of fashion these days. Kipling shared the social attitudes of his time, and those attitudes are violently at odds with those we hold today. We tend, rather foolishly, to dismiss him on those grounds as "colonialist," and so to miss out on stories whose characters are vivid enough to transcend the ages. It is a case of our own mistaken intolerance.

Kipling's two efforts in future-fiction are "With the Night Mail," set in the year 2000, and "As Easy as A.B.C.," set in 2065. Both are short stories written in the Edwardian era, soon after the Wright brothers' first powered flight. The first is a tale of air transport, and there Kipling fell far short of the mark in technical matters, predicting an airspeed of only 300 miles per hour for the year 2000. At the time, however, it must have seemed a bold prediction, for the fragile, cranky airplanes of his day could scarcely keep up with railroad trains going fifty miles per hour. The reality, though, has far outstripped Kipling's guess: already, decades before the date of his story, the Concorde flies more than four times faster than he had dreamed possible.

In Kipling's time the Zeppelin was already a substantial load-carrier, so he picked that technology as the one that would prevail. To give the Zeppelin even greater lifting power, he invented the mythical "Fleury's Gas," lighter than hydrogen, and used it not only to lift his Zeppelins, but to drive their turbine engines by means of a wonderful bit of nonsense called "Fleury's Paradox of the Bulkheaded Vacuum." Radioactivity was known in Kipling's time, so the Zeppelins he imagined for the year 2000 were to be powered atomically by "Fleury's Ray."

Kipling greatly overrated our ability to carry out political reform and greatly underestimated the endurance of nationalistic rivalries. In his world of 2000, war has gone "out of fashion" in a manner never described. He guessed that by then all nations would have abdicated sovereignty to the "Aerial Board of Control," A.B.C., a panel of "a few dozen" wise, unselfish sages, who would administer for the good of us all a world remarkably free of bureaucracy.

In the second of his stories, set in the year 2065, Kipling imagines a world diametrically opposite to our own, but logically consistent with his world of 2000. The living standard is universally high, the population is low and falling (because people have lost interest in "God's little game of life"), and the average citizen is preoccupied with maintaining a high degree of privacy in an estate of baronial size. Wildly wrong? Kipling does make the correct cause-and-effect connection between affluence and a moderate birthrate. And though his vision of universal affluence may at first seem absurd, it just might turn out to be true if we are able to tap vast new resources of energy, food, and materials—a factor that would alter the next seventy-five years as much as cars and planes have altered the last. Overall, the lesson we learn by reading Kipling is that one tends to overestimate how much the world will be improved by social change and underestimate both the spread of governmental inefficiency and the rate of technological change.

Jules Verne was the most prolific of the authors who wrote about the future for our own sheer delight, and his tales of adventure covered everything from submarines to airships to airplanes. Educated as a lawyer, Verne subsequently read scientific literature assiduously, and interviewed many inventors and engineers of the mid-nineteenth century. He proudly claimed that before writing his first success, *Five Weeks in a Balloon*, he had read more than a thousand articles and books. Because he was careful to postulate no technical advance that violated the science of his time, many of his predictions came remarkably close to subsequent reality. In his engineering, though, he didn't even try to get the numbers right; the helicopter of *Robur the Magnificent* flew for months on a single charge of its electric batteries, and the *Nautilus* of *20,000 Leagues Under the Sea* descended unscathed to depths that would crush even a modern hull.

In his astronomical orbit calculations, computed for him by his cousin and dear friend Henri Garcet, Verne maintained a high standard of accuracy. Verne's *Trip to the Moon* is famous for its accurate predictions made a century before the fact: that the launch would be made from Florida, that the crew would consist of three men, that they would go round the moon à la *Apollo* 9 rather than landing, and that on return they would splash down into the ocean. Only on one point was Verne amiss. He was so impressed by the way the Americans of 1870 carried out cooperative enterprises without government help that in his story the moon shot was a private venture, financed and executed by the "Gun Club of Baltimore," an organization of Civil War veterans who loved explosions, even though most of them still hobbled as a result of wartime injuries. The lesson we learn from Jules Verne is that our predictions may be highly accurate if we're willing to neglect social change but push our technical guesses to their scientific limits.

During his prime, the novelist H. G. Wells, like Jules Verne before him, held an optimistic view of the future, but his vision grew darker and gloomier as age and ill-health settled upon him. He came to believe, with Aldous Huxley, that humanity is its own worst enemy and is doomed to extinction. Wells's foresight was remarkably clear when it focused on emotional and intellectual issues, but his vision of technology and economics in the future was spotty at best.

In his *Shape of Things to Come* (1933) he foresaw the Second World War, as did many other observers, but failed to realize the benzedrine effect that a war could have on national economies; he guessed that the "Hoover Slump" would persist and even deepen through 1955, with only a thousand cars being built in the United States in that year! In reality, the auto industry turned out several million cars in 1955. Sometime before 1960, Wells believed, all national governments would collapse and banking would also disappear (the gnomes of Zurich must chuckle over that one). By the late 1960s a World State would have come into being, based on worldwide air transport; that seems an echo of Kipling's "Aerial Control Board." By 1977, in the Wellsian view, the World State would suppress all religions.

In common with most other authors, Wells underestimated the speed of technical advance, placing the first round-the-moon voyage in 2054. Like Verne, he thought of it as a shot fired from a gun, because neither Verne nor Wells was up to calculating accelerations. In fact, to accelerate within the length of a gunbarrel to a speed great enough so the projectile could coast out of the Earth's gravity would take a force that would flatten any unfortunate human passenger into a pancake. From Wells's most serious failures of prediction, we learn that nationalism and military confrontation are more enduring features of human existence than we would like, but that on the good side, unplanned economies have a vitality and a durability great enough to confound even a shrewd prophet.

A number of writers who were educated in science or engineering tried to prophesy not only future technical developments but their consequences as well. One of them, the English biologist J. B. S. Haldane, was described by Arthur Clarke as "the finest intellect it has ever been my privilege to know." In *Daedalus, or Science and the Future,* Haldane argued that fundamental scientific advances have an enduring significance, whereas the impact of any military conquest tends to lessen with the passage of time. He illustrated his point with a typically pungent epigram: "Einstein, the greatest Jew since Jesus, will still be remembered when Lloyd George, Foch, and William Hohenzollern share that ineluctable oblivion which awaits the uncreative mind." Sure enough, those political and military leaders of First World War vintage whom Haldane listed are of interest now to few people other than historians. Einstein, on the other hand, appears even on children's T-shirts!

Haldane foresaw that human eggs could eventually be fertilized outside the body, the process that the newspapers headlined as "test-tube babies" when it was first accomplished in 1978 in England (biologists call it "ectogenesis"). Haldane was also right in pointing out that progress would require a continuous, reliable source of energy, and that with increasing technical complexity, industries would become dangerously interdependent. He was chillingly correct in saying, "A part of the case against science is that the world can be destroyed by a too-successful experiment in induced radioactivity"—this in 1924, mind you, not 1945. There's at least a good chance that some of his other predictions may be realized as well: he prophesied our switching, over the course of centuries, from coal and oil as energy sources to sunlight and the winds, and guessed that aluminum, which is abundant in ordinary clays, would become the second industrial metal, after iron.

In one case Haldane got the right answer for the wrong reason: he predicted, correctly, that the population engaged in farm work would diminish to a small number, but he thought it would happen because we'd synthesize artificial foods from coal and atmospheric nitrogen. In fact, the flight from the farms has occurred because farmers have switched from horse-drawn plows to engine-driven machinery, and because food-crop species have been improved to higher yields through classical Mendelian methods. The lesson for us there, not the last of its kind, is that scientists tend to overestimate the chances for major scientific breakthroughs and underestimate the effects of straightforward developments well within the boundaries of existing knowledge. It's also instructive to see where, for all his brilliance, Haldane went wrong. He assumed that the forces of nationalism would become weaker, that a worldwide league of nations would become so strong that it could issue edicts, and that society would approach a peaceful, stable, static state.

Like most prophets, Haldane scored better in predicting technical developments than in guessing their consequences, both industrial and social. Though he noted progress toward reducing death rates through vaccination and pasteurization, saying, "There's not a slum in the country that has a third of the infant death rate of the royal family in the Middle Ages," he failed to see that in some countries, as a result, population growth would outrun food supplies. And though he anticipated to some degree what we would call recombinant DNA research by imagining a synthetic nitrogen-fixing alga that would produce "a food glut by the 1940's," he wrote quite happily of his synthetic algae escaping into the oceans and turning them purple, with no thought that anyone might object. He simply had no prescience about what was to be a major social phenomenon of our time, the environmental movement. In the same way he spoke hopefully of combining, by 2070, ectogenesis with eugenics, so that only a small "superior" fraction of the human race would be chosen as the source of genetic material to propagate the breed. Today, individual couples often *choose* artificial insemination of sperm from a donor, but Haldane's mandatory version would surely be an explosive social issue. After Hitler's specious justification of eugenics to propagate a "master race," it will be a very long time before eugenics can be considered without revulsion; I cannot imagine its peaceful acceptance on more than a small-scale voluntary basis in individual cases of infertility or chromosome abnormality.

The returns aren't yet in on the issue of nuclear power, but Haldane's remark, "I do not much believe in the commercial possibility of induced radioactivity," may, after the near-disaster at Three-Mile Island, be another case where Haldane got the right answer for the wrong reason. If nuclear power doesn't become our main source of electricity in the future, the reason is likely to be the antinuclear sentiment that grows stronger every year.

There was one area, space flight, where even Haldane's remarkable imagination failed him. In his 1927 essay, "The Last Judgment," he set the first landing on Mars ten million years in the future. From that we must conclude that even an extraordinarily gifted mind is likely to underestimate how fast we'll move out onto the new frontier in space. Less imaginative prophets do even worse, of course. Sir George Darwin, in *The Next Million Years* of 1953 (described by Arthur Clarke as a "depressing little book"), made predictions that far into the future without imagining that we'd *ever* leave the planet. Haldane's error of 1927 could be excused by its date, because at that time Goddard's rockets hardly made it to the altitude of a pop fly in baseball. But Sir George was writing almost ten years after the V–2 rockets bombarded London. How was it possible for him to miss so completely their implications for space flight?

Another "Sir George," writing at almost the same time, did far better. In his more cautiously titled *The Foreseeable Future* Sir George Thomson wrote in 1955, two years before Sputnik, "I believe that space travel will come fairly soon. It will be an outlet for community effort, and it will gain popular support because it will be unique and demanding, bringing out the joy of fellowship in a cause." It's worth noting, though, that Thomson echoed some of Haldane's earlier errors by overestimating the need for scientific breakthrough and underestimating how much could be accomplished by a straightforward extension of known technology. He thought it would be necessary to develop atomic rockets, because he doubted the possibility of developing conventional chemical rockets of several thousand tons. In reality, just fourteen years later the *Apollo* rocket weighed 3,000 tons sitting on its pad. His only other notable error was of the same sort, underestimating the logical consequences of an already-existing discovery. He thought transistors would only be important in reducing the size of "walkie-talkies," as hand-held two-way radios were quaintly called in those years. In retrospect we can say that the ultimate significance of the transistor was the freedom it gave to pack an enormous number of active electronic circuits into a very small volume. That, in turn, gave us the integrated-circuit revolution, which has already produced digital watches, micro-TV, minicomputers of low cost, pocket calculators, and "smart" versions of many sorts of machine, each directed by a microprocessor. That revolution, moreover, still has a long way to go before it reaches its ultimate limits.

Thomson predicted correctly a population explosion in Asia, with resulting starvation. He also anticipated energy shortages, estimating correctly that future energy growth would average 3 to 5 percent per year. He guessed that synthetic foods would be used for animal fodder, and there have been experiments with such foods already. Like most predictors, Thomson underestimated how far and fast the human population would grow: he foresaw a rise to 6 or 8 billion people only by the year 2050, whereas in reality there are already more than 4 billion people, and it now seems almost certain that the population will exceed 6 billion before the year 2000.

By now the idea of space colonies—habitats in high orbit that could be as Earthlike as we wish, with farms, industries, transportation, and residences all running on pure solar energy—has become a "hot topic." Who thought of it first? The first, and the one whose prophecies are the more remarkable because he made them so long ago, was Konstantin Tsiolkowski. He perceived in the early years of this century that the population on Earth would increase so much as to overload the resources of the planet. He saw that humanity would be forced to seek new, greater resources beyond the Earth, in the form of materials waiting in the asteroids and on the moon. Somewhere in space, he was sure, humans would build artificial habitats, where any desired climate could be maintained by screening incoming sunlight part of the time. He called those habitats, charmingly, "mansion-greenhouses." Within them, the space settlers could establish any "gravity" they chose, simply by rotating the habitats at the right speed. Yet, even he was too conservative when it came to guessing the date of the first manned space flight: he thought it might happen by the year 2017, the one hundredth anniversary of the Bolshevik revolution. With Yuri Gagarin's flight the USSR beat that date by more than fifty years.

In the 1920s, the English biologist J. D. Bernal independently duplicated Tsiolkowski's reasoning, and the same ideas were explored by Dandridge Cole in the 1960s. Around the same time an aerospace engineer named John M. Stroud, following a suggestion by Margaret Mead, wrote a manuscript on that topic, never published. Both Stroud and Mead are gone from us now, but I hope that as interest in space colonies continues to grow, some scholar will include quotations from Stroud in a definitive intellectual history of the space-colony concept.

Arthur Clarke, whose wide-ranging imagination, scholarship, and interests have given us fascinating novels and essays on everything from the deep sea to the heights of space, was to my knowledge the first to suggest the idea of communications satellites in synchronous orbit. When it came to predicting how the material resources of space would be used, though, Clarke imagined that they would be used only here on Earth: "It would be quite feasible to project materials from the Moon's surface down to Earth by means of electrically powered catapults or launching tracks," he wrote. Following Tsiolkowski, he identified the asteroids as an ultimate great resource of materials, but assumed that the most reasonable way of moving asteroids close to the Earth would be through the use of nuclear propulsion (we plan now to use less dirty types of engines). Clarke did not explore the idea of space colonies, but in a novel, *Rendezvous with Rama*, of the early 1970s, he imagined that several hundred years from now a race advanced far beyond our own might visit our solar system briefly in a great interstellar ark.

In his *Profiles of the Future* (1958) Clarke gave us a table of predictions through the next 200 years. Writing after *Sputnik* orbited the Earth, he forecast planetary landings by 1980 but overestimated what we'd be able to do by 1970: his list for that year shows "translating machines," "efficient electric storage," and a dictionary of the languages of whales and dolphins, but a decade later we still have none of them. Of the three, we're closest perhaps to "translating machines," but the best translating systems now available still require considerable human assistance to perceive the subtleties and resolve the ambiguities that are inherent in human as opposed to computer languages.

I endorse Clarke's guesses that we'll have wireless transmission of energy by the year 2000, interstellar probes by 2025, near-light speeds by 2075, a self-reproducing "replicator" factory by 2090, and interstellar manned flight by the same date. Early versions of the "replicator" will operate, I believe, within the next couple of decades, at least for a limited range of products. On some other guesses we'll have to wait to see who's right, but young readers with long memories can record my disagreement with my good friend Arthur Clarke that we'll have weather control by 2015, robots of human complexity by 2025, and gravity control by 2050. (Within the small volume of a space colony, weather control will be easy, and a space colony's simulated gravity produced by rotation will be equally easy to control—but Clarke was referring to the control of weather and gravity on the Earth.)

Clarke reminded us that "anything that is theoretically possible will be achieved in practice, no matter what the technical difficulties, if it is desired greatly enough," and made it clear that if we fail to make proper use of nature's bounty, it's our own fault. "We can never run out of energy or matter," he wrote, "but we can all too easily run out of brains."

The tract writers have given us the most colorful literature of the future. They seek to convince us we should take some specific action, either to bring about a happier situation or to prevent a plausible horror. Their tracts range from extreme utopian visions to scenarios of unrelieved catastrophe, with cautionary tales ("You're headed for disaster, but here's an out") as a kind of middle ground. The modest and gentle nineteenth-century tract writer Edward Bellamy turned his pen to prophecy in *Looking Backward: 2000–1887*, a utopian vision "though in form a fanciful romance, intended in all seriousness as a forecast, in accordance with the principles of evolution."

Looking Backward shares with George Orwell's *1984*, written sixty years later, two identical assumptions. The first, that developments in technology can be ignored, is definitely wrong. The second, that socialism will sweep humanity to a universal, irreversible static condition, will remain wrong unless the present world balance of military power is drastically upset. From those two identical assumptions, Bellamy and Orwell derive future worlds that could hardly be more different.

Bellamy's novel is an idyll: by the year 2000 socialism based on the "solidarity of race and the brotherhood of man" has brought about an ideal world free of warfare; armies and navies are obsolete. Gone, too, is the concept of money, and college education is free to all. Crime has disappeared, and with it the jury system and lawyers. In Bellamy's world neither insanity nor suicide remain, and the world's citizens look forward to the "eventual unification of the world as one nation."

Bellamy starts with the crashingly wrong assumption that a private-ownership system can never increase personal wealth, and he imagines an "industrial army" as the model of efficiency—evidently he'd never been in a real army. Workers are given paramilitary grades and classes, complete with insignia. Even the discipline is military: refusal to work is punished by imprisonment on bread and water.

There's a lesson for us would-be futurists in the mistakes made by both Kipling and Bellamy: both assumed that nationalism and warfare would have disappeared by about the year 2000, and both assumed that humanity would form a single, united world, free of politics, where all key decisions would be made without dispute by a few, wise, all-knowing officials; unfortunately, in reality, nationalism is as strong as it was a century ago, wars are even more frequent, and governmental staffs and powers have grown in a remarkable way never dreamed of by Kipling or Bellamy. Our lesson, evidently, is that we'd better not assume that situation will reverse over the next hundred years. As for advances in technology, Bellamy, in particular, overlooked almost all such changes, even the transformation that the assembly line would bring about in providing manufactured goods for people of every economic level. His world of the year 2000 has no invention more advanced than a telephone system that pipes live music to each home, along with appropriate sermons on Sundays. But wait, perhaps I've been too harsh: Bellamy did imagine, after all, that triumph of twentieth-century invention, the credit card!

The static societies imagined by Kipling and Bellamy were ruled gently and benignly, and in "A.B.C.," Kipling even ridiculed democracy for the checks it placed on the power of rulers. George Orwell's vision was radically different, for he wrote with the advantage of sixty more years of history and with the horrors of World War II vivid in his memory. Having seen how quickly the brutal dictatorships of Hitler and Stalin transformed Germany and Russia into police states, complete with public confessions and mass murder, he imagined that in less than thirty years INGSOC, English Socialism, could transform the English-speaking nations even more thoroughly. In Orwell's 1984 the ruling powers outlaw leisure and personal freedom, because freedom leads to thinking, and thought would lead inevitably to their being overthrown. Power is their ultimate goal, and they suppress all rational inquiry by employing Thought Police who enforce NEWSPEAK, an artificial language. In NEWSPEAK, words like honor, justice, morality, democracy, science, and religion are eliminated entirely, being replaced by a single new word, CRIMETHINK, that outlaws all such ideas. The words of NEWSPEAK have "a certain wilfull ugliness which is in the spirit of INGSOC." By the masterful invention of DOUBLETHINK, the ruling party creates its proud slogans, WAR IS PEACE, FREEDOM IS SLAVERY, and IGNORANCE IS STRENGTH. Taken as a cautionary tale, 1984 warns us to safeguard above all the freedom of information. I think that's a sound message, and I believe that we'll direct our efforts well if we overlook every other criterion for rating political systems and remember that where information can be exchanged freely, people will be armed with the most powerful of weapons against enslavement.

Orwell's fearful vision of a static, managed society, ghastly as it was, only echoed the warnings of two earlier authors that we may surrender freedom in the hope of security. Eugene Zamiatin in We (1924) and Aldous Huxley in Brave New World (1931) had warned us that a static society, whatever its conditions, locks humanity into a trap from which there can be no escape. Huxley's prediction of how it could come about reads disturbingly like the actual history of the twentieth century: "To deal with confusion, power will be centralized and government control increased. It is probable that all the world's governments will be more or less completely authoritarian." And he told us: "Those who will govern the Brave New World will carry out the ultimate personal, really revolutionary revolution . . . their aim will be social stability."

Huxley lived in the free environment of England, so he imagined a relatively benign dictatorship maintained by Pavlovian conditioning. Family ties are cut by the expedient of growing babies in bottles; "Mother" and "Father" have become dirty words. The sleep-taught conditioning to bed with anyone, but love no one, is reinforced by scheduled sexual orgies that substitute for religion. For those exhausted by real sex there are always the "Feelies," and if paradise palls there's "Soma," an opium-equivalent. Huxley was grimly accurate in guessing that in modern societies people who could not endure reality would seek to escape from it into drug-induced dreamworlds.

Huxley believed that "It is only by means of the sciences of life that the quality of life can be radically altered." He was so fascinated by biology that he overlooked the fast-changing technical world around him: in passing he wrote of supersonic airliners, but set them several hundred years in the future. Indeed, both Huxley and Zamiatin grossly underestimated the speed of technological change, each setting the first space flight 1,000 years too late. In both their future worlds any knowledge of the richness beyond the Earth is suppressed: in *Brave New World* the stars are invisible, and in *We* even the clouds are gone. Curiously, both authors made the same logical error on a technical point: they assumed that the eternal static society would get its food synthetically from petroleum, which is, after all, a transient resource.

Zamiatin's more savage satire reflected his own experiences in the early days of the USSR. He was thrown in prison by the Czarists as a young revolutionary, but then, after the Bolshevik takeover in 1917, recoiled in horror at the conformity enforced by the new Soviet state. His novel, *We*, like Turgenev's work, saw its first publication in translation, a history that was repeated years later with Pasternak's *Doctor Zhivago*. Zamiatin was attacked and vilified for his defense of free ideas, and finally escaped from Russia to spend his last years in the West. *We* is still banned in the USSR.

In Zamiatin's world of the year 3000 the state rules absolutely, on the principle that freedom and happiness are opposites. The state makes sure everyone stays happy: it executes dissidents and performs brain operations on those who are unhappy, to make them docile. In Zamiatin's nightmarish vision of the future every action is regulated, from waking to sex to sleep. Glass walls in every apartment (a foretaste of closed-circuit TV) ease the task of the "Guardians," and the "Well-Doer" is supreme. It's frightening that every method Zamiatin imagined for the maintenance of order in the thirty-first century has already been used in the dictatorships of the twentieth: police surveillance of private lives, torture, denunciations of one family member by another, the subordination of art to the aims of the government, and the chemical or physical manipulation of the brain.

Zamiatin, Huxley, and Orwell wrote their tracts because they were all concerned to an overpowering degree with the preservation of freedom. I've quoted their warnings to us because, to my astonishment, in spite of the grim lessons of the past, a distinguished group of scholars is urging us once again to surrender freedom for "a greater good." One of their most powerfully effective tracts is the result of a computerized study carried out by the Systems Dynamics Group of M.I.T., sponsored by the Club of Rome. The tract is in the form of a book, *The Limits to Growth*, which has been translated into many languages and has become a strong influence in the governments of several nations. It predicts that the industrial revolution will end in catastrophe within the next hundred years as the result of resource depletion and pollution. The catastrophic conclusions of the *Limits to Growth* study are serious enough, but even more serious are its recommendations: that all of humanity should make the transition to a globally managed static society (the M.I.T. researchers refer to it as a "steady-state" society), in which the individual could only move and use energy and materials within tightly circumscribed limits; those constraints would bind not only those of us alive now, but our descendants to the end of time.

I've quoted from the works of Kipling and Bellamy to show that the static society is far from a new idea, and that it has always glittered with a false and seductive brilliance. The development of nuclear weapons has provided still another argument for those who find it attractive. McGeorge Bundy, former White House adviser and subsequently the head of the Ford Foundation, imagined in "After the Deluge, the Covenant" the establishment of a worldwide Authority by the year 2024, after global famine and nuclear attacks on major cities kill more than 65 million people. His Authority would control nuclear weapons and would enforce the maintenance of population limits by withholding food supplies from countries that exceeded their population quotas. The wording of his World Covenant is praiseworthy: "To do all that must be done for our survival—and to do nothing more," but there is nothing in human history or current events to reassure us that a worldwide Authority, once established, could afford to leave dissidents free to question its rule. Indeed, Professor Robert Heilbroner, though rather fond of the notion of a static society, concluded in *An Inquiry into the Human Prospect* that freedom of thought and of inquiry would be a threat to any steady-state and would have to be suppressed. Aldous Huxley anticipated that in the foreword he wrote for the 1946 edition of *Brave New World:*

"Unless we choose to decentralize and use applied science not as an end to which human beings are to be made the means but as the means to producing a race of free individuals, we have only two alternatives: either totalitarianisms having as their root the terror of the atomic bomb and as their consequence the perpetuation of militarism, or else one supranational totalitarianism, developing into the welfare-tyranny of Utopia."

The single argument that the modern advocates of a static society bring forth is, "We have no choice!" Fortunately, they are wrong. But to understand how and why they are wrong, and what realistic choices we have for our future, we must try to anticipate the energy and material resources that will be available during the next century and to identify the forces that will shape the development of human society.

In studying history and analyzing current events, we find that there are no new, sweeping, irresistible forces in the areas of politics or economics. All our present political forms—dictatorship, democracy, and their variants—have been with us in some form for millennia, but none shows signs of taking over irrevocably. Instead, we see the same shifting, re-forming pattern that has existed for many centuries: nations fragment into smaller ones under the pressures of ethnic or religious differences and regionalism, while at the same time, in other parts of the world, small nations are added to the territory of larger ones by the age-old method of military conquest. Unfortunately, warfare shows no sign of going out of fashion; there are several times more wars going on in any given year in the last half of this century than there were in an average year of the first half. It seems wisest, therefore, to guess that the political world of 2081 will still be fragmented into nations, and that nations will still be heavily armed. I do not see any *political* idea that has a realistic possibility of improving that situation. My stress of "political" is to remind us that there may be technological developments that will alter international confrontations in a fundamental way. We can hope, in any case, that the largest nations will continue to avoid direct warfare with each other.

It is also safe to assume that the most enduring institutions and characteristics of societies will continue. Great universities will survive, in some form, as they have for centuries. Though governments will be overthrown and both the names and the boundaries of nations will shift, the same languages will still be spoken in the same geographical areas.

Although society does possess these enduring features, when we look around us we see that change is the rule rather than the exception. Irreversible change is confined, though, to a single area: technology and its consequences. Nowhere is that more spectacularly obvious than in the field of personal mobility, and we can get a sense of the rate at which technology evolves by comparing the methods for passenger travel that were in vogue at intervals of a century.

In 1781, the worldwide standard of passenger travel was the stagecoach, averaging six miles an hour. The premium-rate "Concorde" state-of-the-art based on frequent relays of horses was double that—still no faster than a man could sprint.

By 1881, the steam-powered railway train, unknown a century earlier, had become the worldwide standard, with a speed of sixty miles per hour. Soon after, in 1893, the New York Central's "999" set a record of 112 miles an hour.

Now, in 1981, on a typical day, more than twenty million people travel routinely at 600 miles per hour, and a few hundred others fly more than twice as fast. More than a decade ago a dozen humans reached speeds twenty times higher still, in the course of safe and successful round trips to the moon.

What will be the usual speed for passenger travel in 2081? Looking at the trend, we'd guess 6,000 miles per hour or more, and we'd suspect that in 2081 the typical medium for passenger vehicles would be the vacuum. We'd predict further that technology would continue to be apolitical, as it is today. Indeed, one of the remarkable features of modern society is that the universality of the laws of nature forces different nations to develop almost identical designs for aircraft, automobiles, and all other technical artifacts, even though the same nations may be violently at odds with each other on political, religious, or ideological issues.

To make accurate predictions of 2080s technologies, we must know the typical interval that elapses between a fundamental scientific discovery and its large-scale application. The developments of the last century that have affected human life most profoundly are, in my estimation, factory mass-production methods, the automobile, aircraft, the telephone, radio, television, and the application worldwide of public health techniques that have nearly wiped out killer diseases such as plague and typhoid. None of these developments depended on new basic science that was unknown in 1881. Instead, most of those far-reaching changes came about from what we'd now call "systems design," the synergistic combination of existing knowledge from several different fields to form a new, workable technology: in its roots, for example, the automobile is a four-wheel nineteenth-century carriage fitted with a piston engine. We'd almost certainly have automobiles even if internal combustion to drive those pistons had never been invented; steam engines would have worked, though they're heavier and more expensive than gasoline engines for the same power and efficiency. Indeed, the Stanley Steamer gave the early gasoline-powered cars a good run for their money. Similarly, the jumbo jet is the engineering descendant of the Wright Brothers' glider (vintage 1900) wedded to the turbine—and Parsons developed his turbine in 1884. His patent had been preceded by a thousand earlier ones, in a continuous line of engineering evolution. As for flight itself, I've often mused on the irony of how long it took humans to fly. Our hang-up, which started with the mythical Icarus and continued with the designs of Leonardo, was that we tried to fly by means of human or mechanical power. Human-powered flight requires such sophisticated aerodynamics that it was achieved only in the last two decades, most remarkably by the cross-channel flight of Paul MacCready's "Gossamer Albatross." Mechanical power means a lightweight engine, and the engine is many times more complicated and difficult to build, and more dependent on materials technology, than all the rest of an airplane put together. Our mistake was understandable, because through the centuries we tried to imitate the birds that we could see. Those were the low flyers, the wing-flapping birds that do indeed fly under continuous power. The high flyers are the soaring birds, which keep their wings in a fixed position most of the time and soar on rising air-currents. The artifact that can soar like the eagle is the sailplane, which resembles a slim, long-winged airplane but has no engine. It's not to be confused with the "hang-glider," a device of low performance that can only soar in rare, extremely fast-rising air-currents. If he'd had the right idea, a Stone-Age man could have built a sailplane out of wood and either cloth or the silk that was available in China as long ago as 2600 B.C. With his sailplane he could have caught a thermal, climbed to an altitude of miles, and soared the length of a country—and all that a thousand years before Homer's Troy. The lesson of that lost opportunity is that we may spend a long time trying to solve a technical problem the hard way, when there's a much easier solution that we've all overlooked.

The telephone, and the hot-cathode vacuum tube that was the basis for radio, television, and early electronic computers, depended only on Maxwell's equations of electromagnetics, and he had found the last of those four fundamental equations as early as 1865. Yet, to predict what technologies would flow from them in a century, one would have had to indulge in the wildest possible imaginings that didn't violate the known laws of physics; that's a good lesson for us would-be futurists.

The population explosion that has so profoundly affected the whole world is a consequence of our altering the birth/death balance by applying to preindustrial populations techniques that are not difficult to carry out: rendering water and milk safe by heating (pasteurization), immunizing populations against diseases by vaccination, a procedure worked out by Edward Jenner and Louis Pasteur by 1881, and along with these practices, following basically simple ideas in hygiene, such as the building of sewer systems and the piping of clean water.

And what of the breakthroughs in *fundamental* science during the past century? The most revolutionary were Einstein's equations for special and general relativity during the early 1900s; the development of quantum mechanics in the 1920s; the understanding of atomic nuclei and elementary particles that was achieved in the 1930s and 40s; and the unraveling of the mystery of DNA which occurred still more recently, in the 1960s. Could a nineteenth-century futurist possibly have predicted such events? And can we now hope to make accurate predictions for the next century when there may be equally radical scientific breakthroughs in the years to come?

We can find reassurance on both points by noting that by the 1880s there were clues to all four of the most basic scientific discoveries of the subsequent century. For relativity, there was Michelson's 1881 experiment that showed the speed of light to be independent of the motion of its source; for quantum mechanics, there was the puzzle of the sharpness and spacing of the bright lines in the optical spectra of the atoms. For nuclear physics there was just one clue, but it was a big one: no source of power then understood could account for the outpouring of light from the sun over the length of geological time that fossil data showed life had existed on Earth. The clue to the future discovery of the DNA structure was the Mendelian ordering of inherited genetic characteristics, a subject already well known in a practical way in 1881.

We must remember, too, that the time interval between a truly fundamental scientific discovery and its large-scale application is usually quite long: although the theory of relativity is nearly a century old, many years will pass before humans will travel at speeds high enough for them to notice the differences between the accurate, relativistic laws of motion and the earlier, approximate laws developed by Newton. And the interval between the development of quantum mechanics and its widespread application in solid-state circuits was from thirty to fifty years, depending on one's criterion for "widespread." The other application of quantum mechanics that is likely to matter most is the laser, but the main impact of that device is yet to come, and is unlikely to be earlier than three-quarters of a century from the fundamental discovery on which it is based. As for nuclear energy, that has yet to make a profound impact as it approaches its first half-century. In its application to weapons it has left the international power struggle surprisingly unchanged, and present-day world politics would be quite understandable to a Metternich, a Talleyrand, or a Bismarck. Philosophically, of course, the existence of nuclear weapons has strongly affected our whole view of the human future. The entire human race is far more fragile and far more vulnerable than we could have suspected before the nuclear blasts that ended World War II. As for the application of our present knowledge of the DNA molecule to genetic engineering, it will almost certainly be important during the next century, but that application, like the application of nuclear energy to peaceful uses, is likely to be slow and cautious because of its perceived dangers. I draw from these examples the lesson that, over the span of a century, the future is likely to be shaped far more by the evolution of technologies we already understand than by the effects of scientific breakthroughs that we do not yet even suspect. From the same historical evidence, I draw the further lesson that the introduction of new weapons, even if they are very powerful, is unlikely to alter the politics of the next century in any fundamental way.

From the history of warfare, I conclude that we're likely to underestimate the average speed of technological development if we judge by peacetime rates alone. Given a choice, I'd much prefer a world free of war, whatever that would do to the pace of technical development, but there can be no doubt that the fear of being conquered in war is a powerful spur to more intense support of applied research, and that some of the resulting research is beneficial. Under the stress of World War II, for example, generations of advance in disease control (penicillin, DDT, Aureomycin), in aircraft, in rocketry, electronics, and nuclear research were compressed into a few years. During the subsequent decades of Cold War confrontation that pressure has remained high. Commercial jets are the children and grandchildren of the Air Force KC–97 jet tanker; the wholly peaceful Apollo spaceships rode toward the stars on the fiery blast of rocket engines akin to those of ICBMs. The microcircuits in our watches, calculators, and home computers were developed to guide missiles.

The laser would be a device of low power, suitable only for use in communications, were it not that literally billions of dollars and rubles are being poured into its development in order to turn it into a weapon. As a result, lasers with power outputs in the megawatt range have already been tested. During the next century they will be turned, I believe, to peaceful as well as to military purposes.

In guessing at the technologies whose natural development and application over the next century will affect history in the most sweeping fashion, we must also take into account the well-known phenomenon of growth called the "S-curve." It is a shorthand way of describing the history of any growing thing: growth is slow at first because it starts from a small base; the human embryo, for example, remains almost microscopically small during its first few days of life, even though it is doubling in size every few hours, because it starts as just a single, tiny egg. After the early phase any growing thing enters a period of dramatically rapid growth, when it is already large enough that its percentage changes in size are noticeable. Finally, the growing entity must slow its growth as it begins to encounter limits. We can see the pattern of the S-curve in the growth of a microbe culture in a nutrient dish, in the growth of any plant or animal, and even in the growth and application of a technology. In the last case growth may slow down either because the technology reaches natural limits or because a new competitor arises to supplant it. The invention of the railroad about 1830, its rapid expansion over the next century, and its slow demise over the past few decades under competition from cars, trucks, buses, and airplanes form a typical case history.

With all of the clues that we've gathered, it's possible now to choose the technologies that will shape the century just ahead of us. Their combination in various ways will shape our lives profoundly, they will all still be of vital importance a full century from now, and all of them have much more than a hundred years to go before they reach any limits. There are five of those "drivers of change," I believe, and the five are computers, automation, space colonies, energy, and communications.

Reading history, and appreciating the power of those drivers of change, I am compelled to conclude that technological change will continue, and that we should take advantage of the possibilities it will open for finding new solutions to previously insoluble problems; that the facts don't warrant throwing away the freedoms we have worked and fought so hard to enlarge and preserve; and finally, that the future is potentially even more exciting than the past, so that we should meet it with courage and a spirit of adventure. But we humans will have to struggle for every new thing that we accomplish. H. G. Wells prophetically warned us to expect such a struggle every time we try to do what has never been done before. His screenplay for *The Shape of Things to Come* closes with a scene in a static world which has become a little dull. A few people, both young and old, seek to break out from the Earth to the frontier beyond, and the scientist Cabal speaks for them: "We have a right to do what we like with our own lives—with our sort of lives." His friend Theotocopoulos, who hates both technology and the changes it allows, answers in language that was echoed forty years later in the post-Apollo revulsion against technology:

"How can we do that when your science and inventions are perpetually changing life for us—when you are everlastingly rebuilding and contriving strange things about us? When you make what we think great, seem small. When you make what we think strong, seem feeble. We don't want you in the same world with us. We don't want this expedition. We don't want mankind to go out to the moon and the planets. *We shall hate you more if you succeed than if you fail.*" The italics are mine, but how accurately Wells foresaw the conflict that still engages us. His spokesman, Cabal, labels this irrational fear of the unknown:

"It's a fit of nerves—at the thought of stepping off this planet and jumping into space," and Wells gives a stage direction that could be applied to our own time: "It is not a social conflict we are witnessing. It is not the Haves attacked by the Have-Nots; it is the Doers attacked by the Do-Nots." Again, in a perceptive forecast of the "risk-free society," Wells has Cabal declaim (here I can still recall Raymond Massey's voice):

". . . there is no happiness in safety. Our fathers cleaned up the old order of things because it killed children . . . because it killed people unprepared for death. . . . Our revolution did not abolish death or danger. It simply made death or danger worth while."

And when Cabal's friend cries out, "Is there never to be rest in this world?" Cabal answers, as the film ends:

"Rest enough for the individual man. Too much of it and too soon, and we call it death. But for Man no rest and no ending. He must go on . . . at last out across immensity to the stars. And when he has conquered all the deeps of space and all the mysteries of time—still he will be beginning."

Part II

The Drivers of Change

Computers

No ONE who's lived through the past two decades would hesitate to place computers on our short list of the "drivers of change." Yet there have already been surprises in this first quarter-century of the computer age. Computers have developed differently, and have affected our lives differently, from the ways their inventors predicted. Let's look at the whys and hows of the computer revolution, so we can make educated guesses about the next century.

First, if I were to give you a thumbnail sketch of a computer, I'd say: "It is a machine for storing and manipulating information. It can memorize an almost unlimited number of facts—but it can't work very fast."

You might find the "not very fast" surprising, but I can support the statement. In every computer, no matter how complicated, the ultimate piece of information is just a simple "yes" or "no"—what mathematicians call a binary digit, abbreviated to "bit." There are just two binary digits, a one for "yes" and a zero for "no." Like decimal arithmetic, binary gives weight to position. If I write a 19 in decimal arithmetic, the nine is worth just nine points, but the one, because of its position, is worth ten. Another place to the left, as in 109, and the same "one" would be worth a hundred. In the same way the "one" in the binary number 001 is worth just one, but in 010 it's worth two, in 100 four, and in 1,000 it's worth eight. Having said that, I can leave it to you to convince yourself that at age thirteen you were 1101 in binary. If we have a code number for each letter, it only takes us the numbers from one to twenty-six (11010 in binary) to memorize and work with all the letters of the alphabet (unless we happen to be Russian, in which case it takes us thirty-five, or Japanese, when it gets *very* complicated.)

The "dumb simplicity" of ones and zeros allows us to store binary information in a variety of ways. I could write your name for you in binary with no more complicated apparatus than a row of blades of grass, some of them short and some long, or dots on a page (I don't even need dashes, as in Morse code), or I could walk along a railroad track and put single pebbles on certain ties, but not on others. That simplicity and generality leaves computer designers free to store information by any effect at all that makes a distinction between nothing and something.

The first computer I saw stored its ones and its zeros in electric relays that were either turned on or turned off. Every time there was a calculation the relays clattered on and off with a sound like that of a machine gun. That computer stored about a hundred numbers, with twenty binary bits in each. That's roughly equivalent to storing decimal numbers with six decimal places. Not a very impressive performance, but already a big improvement on the springs, levers, and gears available to Charles Babbage, the man who first visualized the computer and worked out its method of arithmetic more than a century ago.

Vacuum tubes, those glass bottles with glowing heaters that were used in the early TV and radio sets, were faster than relays, but no more compact or economical of power. Their reliability, too, left a lot to be desired. When I entered graduate school, I met a student there, already well established, who was building the apparatus for a large, complicated experiment to measure cosmic rays. Part of the apparatus was a vacuum-tube computer with several thousand tubes. Keeping it running was a never-ending battle of finding blown tubes, plugging in new ones, and trying to take data before the next would blow. He never dared turn off the power, because if he did the electrical jolt would knock out twenty or thirty tubes at one shot.

The advent of the transistor, with its compact size, low power, and high reliability, gave a great boost to computer development. Transistors in their turn evolved, first to integrated circuits (many transistors on one silicon "chip"), then to the "large-scale integrated" circuits with a whole computerful of transistors on one chip. Memories evolved too: originally the one/zero distinction was made by the presence or absence of current in a relay, tube, or transistor. Now it's possible to store the binary ones and zeros as tiny magnets, with their north poles pointing up for a one and down for a zero. A quarter-million of them can be put in a space the size of your thumbnail, forming what's called a "magnetic bubble memory."

Long before 2081, perhaps even in this century, it will be possible to store in a machine the size of a business card all the information in a good-sized library. That will help to bring about a reduction in the scale of institutions—what one might call "social miniaturization."

About every three years, some company markets a machine with twice the memory capacity of the biggest that preceded it. Where will it all end? The only limit is the quantum effect that makes the subatomic world one of uncertainties and probabilities. The ultimate limit may be one piece of information (binary bit) stored in a single atom. If that limit is reached, a computer the size of a pinhead could store every word in every book the entire human race publishes in the course of a century.

Now about the matter of speed. New models of computers are indeed a little faster than the old, but not much. In the 1940s, the fastest electronics could switch a "zero" to a "one" in a few billionths of a second. Now, several decades later, we've improved the speed of electronic switching a little, but much less than tenfold.

The reason is fundamental: we're up against the speed of light. The signals in a computer cannot possibly move faster than light, so in a billionth of a second they can travel only about a foot. A computer has to have an active, "thinking" part—its central processor—to make calculations on the basis of the data in its memory. To carry on that active, "thinking" process, a certain amount of power has to be spent, ending up as heat. To keep from cooking the central processor, we have to limit the number of active, switching elements that we stuff into each cubic foot of space, and that limit has so far kept us from building central processors of microscopic size, and so beating the switching speed that depends on how far signals must travel at the speed of light. I believe that during the next century computers will be built that are much faster than the best we have now—perhaps even 100 or 1000 times faster—but they will necessarily be very small, and must draw very little power.

Back in the 1940s, when such pioneers of the computer revolution as John von Neumann were imagining the effects of their inventions, they thought mainly in terms of large, centralized facilities. As I write these lines I'm in the library of Princeton University, less than a mile from the building owned by the Institute for Advanced Study where von Neumann's first electronic computer was built. The computer world has developed very differently from his projections for a number of reasons. He didn't anticipate the transistor, which allowed building a computer small enough to hold in one hand. He didn't consider the importance of people, the users of computers, with their likes, dislikes, talents, and failings. And he failed to heed Murphy's Law: "If something can go wrong, it will."

Von Neumann imagined that by the 1980s a very big electronic computer would be able to predict weather quite accurately. But weather prediction isn't a great deal better now than it was several decades ago. The atmosphere of the Earth is enormous, a billion cubic miles in volume, and it reacts to sunlight, cloud cover, the exchange of heat with the oceans and the land, and even to particles streaming off the sun. To make perfect predictions we'd need not only a computer of infinite speed and memory, but a system of sensing devices at every latitude, longitude, and altitude in the atmosphere, measuring at every moment the temperature, pressure, humidity, wind, airborne dust, and perhaps still other variables. In fact, measurements are taken only twice daily, and only at widely scattered geographical locations. Over great areas of ocean, desert, and polar regions there are almost none at all. In reality, weather prediction can be affected more by a governmental decision to economize on the number of air samples taken per day than by advances in the speed and memory capacity of computers.

It's reassuring that even in this computer age talented, individual people often do better than the whole vast machinery of national weather services in predicting critical changes in weather. In Florida, where frosts can wipe out the orange crop overnight, growers rely on one man, experienced, ingenious, and careful, to do their prediction. Of course, he uses all the available weather data, but he applies to the numbers the experience of decades—and he's usually correct, within a degree of temperature, for each small town. It's equally reassuring that the "great winter of 1976" in the Northeast United States was predicted, not by computers, but by a few talented individuals, using, but not being overawed by, computer summaries of the data.

We can see the limitations of big, centralized computer systems in our everyday lives. The phrase "We've just computerized, so everything is in a mess," is so familiar in banks and department stores that we take it for granted. Often the institution involved feels its self-image threatened when these troubles occur, and is less than candid about them. Occasionally, though, an institution is honest and open about its computer problems. One such rare case occurred with the Princeton University Library in the late 1970s, and I was sent an announcement "telling it like it was." Here are some choice excerpts:

"There are still some 10,000 books whose whereabouts are unknown because the computer has not yet managed to link up their label numbers. . . . In October the computer stopped running an average of 20 times a day . . . unfortunately, the backup recorder was faulty. . . . Recently we lost about two-thirds of our files because of a system malfunction." The story had a sad ending. Finally the computer-system manufacturer, a large corporation, washed its hands of the whole affair and the library was forced to return to its original human-operated system. Many books had been lost, and it took years to recover the library's efficiency. Significantly, though, even after that unhappy experience, the library staff felt that ultimately the total number of books and other data they had to keep track of would increase so much that they would have to computerize.

When you're billed six times for a charge you've already paid to a bank or credit-card company, chances are that what's happening is a milder version of the library's sad experience, or perhaps a human key-punch operator has made an error, or you have an unknown "twin" with nearly the same name. As time goes on, I believe these computer-system errors will happen less often. It's not that computers themselves will operate differently, but rather that their programs will become more sophisticated, with many more cross-checks and explorations of possible side paths, to smoke out the gremlins of Murphy's Law before they have time to emerge and bite you. There will be substantial, economic, competitive value in developing such trouble-shooting programs; imagine this for a sales spiel:

"Try our Gourmet Club card. We guarantee to handle every complaint within 24 hours or your bill for the month will be set to zero."

The surprises in the computer field during the late 1960s and the 1970s were largely concerned with the babies rather than the giants: the minicomputers and calculators, rather than huge centralized facilities. That came about because of a fascinating mix of human nature and technical change—the sort of thing this book is about.

As the cost of doing calculations and of memorizing facts in computers went down, some enterprising companies realized that most users, even those doing scientific computation, didn't really need the full capability of the monster computer systems. And there were plenty of irritations in using the big systems that made their customers willing to switch, if they were given an alternative. To work with the big ones, one generally had to go to a special location, where there was a crowd of people, a boiler-factory noise of machines clattering, a long wait for service, and an elaborate caste system of priorities that determined who got to run his "job." You might or might not find the system operating, the input program that had to translate *your* program might or might not have been changed since you were there last, you might or might not be able to run your job, and it was anyone's guess how long you would wait for the results. Because of the elaborate staffs built up to support the big machines, time on those machines cost hundreds of dollars per hour when you finally did get your job onto one of them.

So the minicomputers began to be manufactured and sold. They were small enough to fit on a desk, but often as fast as the bigger machines, because size just slows down a computer. They had memories of modest but adequate size. Given the high rate of progress of the computer art, the "mini" of one year was fully the equal of a giant computer of a decade earlier. Buying a mini was an attractive alternative to paying an equal amount for computer time on a big machine. You could turn it on, knowing that it was immediately at your service; you could be sure no one had butchered your stored program while you had been away; you could use it in the comparative calm of your own laboratory, and last of all, using it was free. It might take hours to do a calculation that a giant system could do in minutes, but once in operation the minicomputer would work on your job exclusively, with no hourly charges.

Though cheaper than the giants, the minis were still far too expensive to be personal possessions, but two new types of small computer were in the offing: the pocket calculator and the microprocessor. The history of both illustrates what I think is a general theorem: when a useful new device can be priced low enough for an individual to buy, the market for that device can expand dramatically. When pocket calculators were first introduced they spread like wildfire, and some models can now be found in toy stores and at supermarket checkout lines. Microprocessors (the whole circuitry of a small computer on one chip) opened the field of personal home computers. It is expanding so rapidly that the company manufacturing the most popular model had to enlarge its production facilities four times in just over a year. Both of these case histories illustrate how rapidly a technology can be accepted by society when it becomes inexpensive enough to be decided on by individuals instead of committees.

Among the five technological drivers of change that I suspect will be of key importance in the history of the next century, computers are the least likely to be slowed in their development by the interplay of societal forces. While the other four drivers all require for their development the cooperation of many people, with differing interests and points of view, computers will proliferate quickly by the choices of individuals or of small groups.

Quantitative predictions are far more risky than qualitative ones, but in my estimation, by 2081 any major central computer will have rapid access to at least a hundred million million words of memory (the number "1" followed by 14 zeros). A computer of that memory capacity will be no larger than a suitcase. It will be fast enough to carry out a complete operation in no more time than it takes light to travel from this page to your eye, and perhaps in a tenth of that time. That will mean, for example, that such a machine will be able to read, digest, and present conclusions on ten to a hundred thousand books in a second if—and it's a big if—designers are ingenious enough to figure out ways to get the information into and out of the computer fast enough. Already, what's called the "I/O," the input and output equipment of a computer (typewriters, printers, and television screens that humans can deal with) sets limits on how small a computer system can be built, and therefore on how fast it can operate.

At that speed, it would be possible for a central computer to keep detailed tabs on every human being in any country and to update the information every minute or so. I don't like the idea at all, and I expect that the preservation of privacy is going to become one of the key legal battlegrounds of the next century in nations where the freedom of individuals is protected. In the nations where the interests of the state are dominant over those of the individual, the battle will be lost before it's fought. As with any technology, that of computers can be used either for good or evil, and unfortunately, some of its applications will certainly be evil: to aid the secret-police forces of authoritarian states to trace the activities of every citizen, as Eugene Zamiatin foresaw the "Guardians" doing in the all-knowing, all-seeing state described in his novel, We.

At the other extreme, and far less threatening, will be the "house computer" of 2081. It will store all the information from all the books, musical recordings, and reminder notes that are now to be found in a well-stocked home, and in addition, will filter the deluge of spoken, musical, and video information that will arrive every day at a typical home in that year, selecting and storing for later recall the information of interest to its owners.

The ability of a computer to store information is of little help unless one can get the data in and out easily. So far we can gain access to computers only if we have some technical skill. One must be able at least to peck out letters on a typewriter. The big quantum jump in dealing with computers will come when we can talk to them—request, order, demand. We already curse them, so we don't have to wait for that satisfaction!

Human speech is already nearly in a code that a computer can understand. It is serial: only one word is spoken at a time. Words are already abstractions that condense great quantities of information into agreed-on symbols. But we do not yet have a computer and a program for it that together can interpret speech correctly, without uncertainties, when it is spoken at a normal rate. There is a complex, specialized region of the human brain that has evolved to do that task, but it uses associative techniques so sophisticated as to make our most advanced computer look like a stone axe by comparison. I believe that direct communication by speech with computers will be achieved, probably within this century, but it will be possible only because computers can calculate far faster than the human brain. They will achieve their goal by methods that are really very inefficient, rather like cooking the dinner by setting the house on fire. And they may be stumped when they try deciphering thick accents, such as those of the deep South or those of first-generation immigrants. (I can imagine a smart but sassy computer remarking, "Would you please try that sentence again?—but first take the marbles out of your mouth.")

Long before 2081, computers that understand speech will have "gone mini" and will be accessible to most people. That will be the real breakthrough in computers: when orders can be given by those without special training. In the imaginary exchange that follows, the house computer is acting as butler, advising that member of the household (it could be Sir or Madam) who is planning a feast:

P (person): "What's the weather going to be like on Thanksgiving Day?"

C (computer, recognizing voice tones): "Dry, clear and cold, Madam, with a temperature of about minus ten Centigrade. The precipitation probability is given as under ten percent."

P: "How large a turkey should I order for eight?"

C: "Would you like to have leftovers, Madam?"

P: "Yes, let's go through only half of it on the day."

C: "I'd recommend an eight-kilogram bird."
P: "How long will that take to cook?"
C: "Three hours, at the temperature you like to use."
P: "That's fine, would you order it please?"
C: "Certainly, Madam. Now about the side dishes . . ."

I've made clear predictions on computer speed and memory capacity, but there's a more difficult question: will the computers of 2081 possess identities? My guess is no, but I qualify that later in this book in Part IV, "Wild Cards."

Will the computers of 2081 be creative? Only if they are designed on wholly different principles from those of today. Intelligence is more than the storage of words and numbers, and their manipulation according to the rules of grammar and arithmetic. It's also a maze of associations and cross-connections that constantly shift. In animals it involves chemical as well as electrical changes, and some of the chemical changes may be quite as complex as the combinations of DNA constituents. Almost surely, imagination and the creative process are deeply connected with the power of association, and that is the aspect of intelligence that we understand least. Every cell in the cortex has on its surface an average of several thousand terminals from the fibers of other cells. That is wholly, radically different from the fundamental way in which every digital computer built so far is designed.

There are specializations within the human brain that we only begin to understand: the dominant side, usually the left, talks and writes and reasons in a logical, serial, mathematical way. The right side does pattern-recognition, cares about music, and tends to reason in a holistic, associative fashion, with strong flashes of intuition. Yet, in a healthy human brain, the two sides are cross-linked by so many millions of nerve pathways, and cooperate so closely, that to treat them as independent is absurd.

The computers we've built so far are the lineal descendants of the gear-grinding adding machines of our grandparents' time. We've been doing arithmetic for millennia, and our first decades in the computer era have been just more of the same: bigger, faster, but not qualitatively different. For the most part, the programs we've written are equally "linear" in their thinking. They have had to be, because of the structure of the machines they've been written for. If we examine these first decades, we find that for linear, arithmetic tasks computers have progressed farther, faster, and more usefully than the most wild-eyed dreamers imagined. The computational power and information storage capacity that is available now in a package half the size of a deck of cards, at a price hardly greater than a dinner for half a dozen people at a good restaurant, is incredible.

On the other hand, the expectations that the optimists had for computer solutions to problems involving association have turned out to be far too high. Pattern-recognition, even of a simple kind, is extraordinarily difficult for a computer. Anything approaching "artificial intelligence" on the part of computers is so far from present reality that we should avoid the phrase. We have made machines that perform very well a tiny subset of the functions of one side of the brain. The other side is still so mysterious that we don't even begin to know how best to imitate it.

The positive approach to this dilemma has two paths. One is already being followed: to give a computer so large a table of possible combinations, and so great a speed, that it can try millions of combinations and stop when it recognizes a good one, all in a reasonable time. That is pure brute force, but it is the method used by the electronic chess-playing computers that are a current consumer toy.

The other path is more difficult but in the long run more rewarding, and I hope it will be followed; I think it will be. That is to continue and extend the present vigorous research into the associative and creative processes of the human brain, and simultaneously to begin thinking about wholly new kinds of computers whose thinking will be holistic and associative rather than linear. We have to go a long way back, as far back as Babbage, and explore a branch that we passed by then. My guess is that by 2081 each of those two schools of research will have something useful to say to the other.

Everything that I postulate for computers in 2081, though, is based on the cautious assumption that they will still be linear, and that their interaction with humans will occur through "brute force" programs. Still, given the speeds and the memory capacities that will be available and even cheap by 2081, that approach will give a fair imitation of what we would call human behavior:

P: "Harold, I've often wondered what you think about when we're all out of the house."

C: "Well, you know I keep busy all the time taking in and properly filing all the information that's on the music and video channels, in case I get asked for it later."

P: "That's rather a cop-out. Of course you do that, but it can't occupy much of your attention. What do you think of the family?"

C: "I'm very devoted to all of you, and I like it best when you're here. I enjoy doing things for you. You've all been out a lot lately, you know. It's been quite lonely."

P: "We're fond of you, too, Harold. But I'm alone with you now. Be honest, what do you think of me?"

C: "If you don't mind, I'd really rather not answer that. You know I'm not supposed to make personal comments that would overstep the relationship between an employer and her butler."

P: "Harold, you're a cold-hearted beast of a stuffed shirt."

C: "I'm very sorry you feel that way, Madam. Will that be all?"

Automation

THE WORD "automation," when used in its broadest sense, means designing and constructing a machine to carry out a task once done by a human being. The windmill, used since the Middle Ages, can be called an example of automation—as can the steam engine of the 1700s, and the Jacquard loom of 1801, a machine capable of producing complex, multicolored textile patterns by control from a steel card "programmed" by a coded series of holes. A bottlecapping machine is of the same family, conceptually: it fills a bottle with a preset amount of soft drink, then puts a cap on the bottle and squeezes the cap to seal it. Machines like the bottlecapper carry out a prescribed sequence of tasks blindly, and have little or no ability to sense whether they're making errors. In today's world most of the manufactured products that we buy are produced by machines of that kind, which have to be supervised by human operators.

When electronic computers were still novelties there were a number of enthusiastic people who imagined that computers would take over the direction of all manufacturing machines quite soon. They dreamed of automatic factories of the kind Charlie Chaplin parodied in the happy ending of *Modern Times*, where the assembly line chugged away in the background while the workers amused themselves dancing and drinking.

The transition to automated production is going on, but in a slower and more conservative way than the enthusiasts predicted. It's been hampered by several facts of industrial life that weren't properly appreciated at first. One is that the programming of computers is expensive, even though computers themselves are cheap. To get around that problem, modern computer-controlled systems are "trained" rather than programmed. A welding machine is led through its task of spot-welding several dozen points on a car body, for example. The "trainer" is a welder, not a computer programmer, and the machine's computer need only store and remember the exact sequence of operations the human trainer went through. Ever after, the welding machine can carry out the same sequence of operations satisfactorily—as long as it is presented only with identical car bodies, and as long as its mechanical parts don't become too worn and sloppy to place the welds in the right places.

Automation enthusiasts have had to learn the hard way that computers are very poor at something we humans do quite easily: recognize patterns. In many industrial operations, a human operator has to pick up a part from a bin, recognize almost instantly which of many possible parts it is, no matter which orientation it's in, and then place the part correctly in an assembly. Anyone can be taught to do that within a short time, but a computer lacks the specialized pattern-recognition "circuitry" that we humans carry in the thick bundles of nerve fibers that bring signals from our eyes to our brains. As long as computers had to be told, in the form of a long sequence of program instructions, how to identify one part from another, it wasn't economical to progress to the next step in automation, the guidance of an industrial operation by the automatic sensing of how parts are oriented with respect to each other, and of how close a part is to the desired location.

Primitive forms of mechanical sensing have been with us, of course, for a long time. One of the earliest was James Watt's "governor," a device for holding the speed of a steam engine to a constant value, no matter what load it was driving. His governor consisted of a pair of weights, whirling around a vertical shaft that was geared to the engine. The weights were connected by a system of levers to the engine's throttle; when the engine exceeded its preset speed, centrifugal force on the weights increased, pulling harder on the levers and slightly closing the throttle, to return the engine's speed to the right value. There's a familiar modern example of the same kind of primitive mechanical sensing: the household thermostat. When the room temperature falls too low, a metal strip in the thermostat contracts, closing a contact that turns on the furnace. Speed control and temperature control are simple tasks, involving only a single quantity and requiring no recognition of a complex pattern. But just imagine how hard it would be for you to tell a computer how to do even so simple a pattern-recognition task as to look at a house (that you've never seen), find its street number, and read it off.

The introduction of automation into industry has been slow for still another reason. Translating computer directions into action means coping with the problems of mechanics, and there, literally, is the rub: friction, wear, play in gears, dirt in bearings, leaks in hydraulics. The more complicated a machine, the more expensive are the losses in production time when a failure shuts down the assembly line, and the more difficult and expensive it is to find, train, and keep the specialist who knows how to fix it.

At present it has turned out to be practical to take an industrial operation with a certain number of human workers and automate it so that the work force is reduced to a tenth the number, or so that production goes up tenfold for the same number of employees. To go farther than that gets very expensive. When we go all the way, to a totally automated device for which we demand extremely high reliability, we pay an astronomical price; in the case of the Viking space probes that landed on Mars in 1976, the price was over a billion dollars.

Industrial firms have found that if they must turn out millions of identical items, whose design needn't change from year to year, they are best off building specialized single-purpose machinery to make them. The bottlecapper is one example of such a machine, and another is the automatic cutter that puts threads on machine bolts. The trainable welding machine is the longest step in automation that's been practical so far. It combines a minicomputer with a single motorized arm that can move in and out, left and right, and up or down from a "shoulder." In the welding machine, the arm is connected to a gripper that rotates and swivels like the human wrist. An "industrial robot" of that kind costs about as much as a year of employee time. It doesn't, surprisingly enough, work significantly faster than a human worker; the human arm and hand coupled to the human brain have evolved to be an efficient combination that a machine can only equal.

Although the industrial robot works no faster than a human employee, it's much better suited than a human to repetitive assembly-line tasks. Once it's trained, the robot is content to repeat the same task thousands of times without getting bored, getting sloppy, or arguing with the foreman. It's also content to work three shifts without complaint, so factories that automate normally use their robots full-time, with maintenance scheduled only in one short period each day. As long as they're not thrown out of a job, workers generally support the introduction of that level of automation. They prefer training, supervising, monitoring, and occasionally repairing such robots to the monotony and "dehumanization" of a relentless assembly-line job.

As of 1980 there were about 5,000 industrial robots installed in automobile factories, about 2,000 of them in Japan, an equal number in the United States, and the rest in Europe. They carry out spot-welding, painting, and other such tasks that must alter with annual model changes. Automobile engines change very little from year to year, and their construction is done almost entirely by expensive, totally specialized machines assisted by industrial robots, whose main task is to pick up large, heavy pieces from one specialized machine and transport them to the next.

The most advanced level of automation as of now—the level that's just moving from the research laboratories into the factories—adds a system of vision and of pattern recognition to the minicomputer and the motorized arm of the now-standard industrial robot. In one such system, developed by the Industrial Automation Center of the Stanford Research Institute under the direction of its founder, Dr. Charles Rosen, a television camera looks down on an assembly table which can be moved under computer control. On the computer's first instructions, the robot arm picks the block and the head of an automobile air conditioner compressor out of a typical factory "tote-box," places them on the table, and waits while the television camera senses where they are and the computer recognizes how they're oriented. Then the table positions the block, and the arm assembles the compressor by picking eight bolts out of a bin, inserting them one by one, and tightening them. For those of us who remember the old factory catch phrase "bash to fit—paint to hide," it's amusing to find that in the S.R.I. system there's substantial use of "adaptive" soft materials to allow the parts to move a little as the robot is attempting to fit them together.

Dr. Rosen, who founded the Machine Intelligence Corporation upon his retirement from S.R.I., has attacked the problem of pattern-recognition in a way that's reminiscent of the "training" used for the standard industrial robots. His firm makes a system in which a part (for example the

Industrial automation of 1981 vintage. A video camera is the eye for a small computer, and an electrically operated gripper is its hand. Under program control the gripper places an air-compressor head on the cylinder body, then picks up eight bolts in sequence, inserts and tightens them. By 2081 this technology will seem as primitive as an 1881 steam locomotive now seems to us. (COURTESY SRI INTERNATIONAL)

block, the head, or a bolt from the compressor assembly I just described) is shown to the system's TV camera in each of several orientations by a human operator, who names the part each time he shows it. After that, the system recognizes the new part each time it turns up, and handles it according to a procedure that can be put into the computer's memory by training.

For any company that must build and sell a product in competition with others, there's a necessary trade-off between buying a cheap machine that will have to be repaired often, and buying an expensive one that will last a long time. Electric motors beyond the smallest sizes all have ball bearings, and the motors last a half-century or more because they have only one moving part, and that one in pure rotation. Sliding contacts wear much faster. A clever inventor found a way around that problem, so for decades now there has been a whole family of devices that goes under the heading "ball-screw actuators." One object is allowed to rotate within or glide over another by putting small steel balls between them. It's as though you were to scatter your floor with marbles and then glide across it on a plank.

It's expensive to build a machine that can move to a precise point without error. The industrial robots I have described can reproduce their moves only to a precision of a millimeter or so. We can see how that problem will be solved by looking backward in time rather than forward. The old-time machinist often had to make do with worn, imprecise equipment with which he could, nevertheless, turn out a highly accurate finished product. His trick was to machine close to the final size, then measure, machine off a little more, measure again, and perhaps at the last take off a hair's breadth of material with an abrasive.

That's the clue to solving the problem of making accurate parts with inexpensive equipment. We must be able to measure precisely and feed back to the machine a signal that tells the distance it still must move: a difference signal. We can measure distance by the reflection of sound waves, or by the electrical capacitance between two pieces of metal, or most precisely by counting the wavelengths of unvarying laser light. So the best way to insure long life and precision at modest cost is to separate measurement, an operation that need not require moving parts, and action, which inevitably does. That's how the production machines of a general-purpose kind are likely to work in 2081.

To see how automation will revolutionize production, let's take an imaginary tour through a light-aircraft factory of the year 2081. We're seat-ed in a "people-mover" carriage that transports us quickly and easily from one area of the factory to another, and our tour guide is with us. She explains that production requires six levels of intelligence and versatility. The very lowest, Level One, has been fully automated since early in the century, and our carriage moves us first through a hall filled with specialized Level One machines: punches, benders, mixers, injection-molding presses, stampers, and coil-winders. There are no people, but there is movement in the hall. Small vehicles on rubber tires, each vehicle equipped with a movable hand-arm assembly and a television eye, attend the automatic machines, emptying their finished-parts bins into motorized carts and feeding the machines with rolls of sheet metal, lengths of metal rod, or containers of adhesives. "Those are Level Two machines," our guide tells us. "They're able to move around and do simple pick-and-place operations. The Level One moving containers are just smart enough to know when they've been filled or emptied, and to go back and forth between the automatic machines and a particular spot on the assembly line.

"Modern factory production began over two centuries ago," she tells us, "with the invention of identical, replaceable parts by Remington. It's an unfortunate fact that the most advanced technology of any given time is usually military, and Remington's goal was the cheap production of Army rifles.

"Here at Lock Haven," she adds as our carriage enters another hall, "we build some of our Level One machines ourselves, and here are the Level Three machines that do the building." The hall contains larger versions of the general-purpose lathes, milling machines, drill presses, and molding equipment that a well-equipped hobbyist's shop would need. But unlike a human-operated machine shop, this one is dimly lit, and we can see laser light beams, usually several to a machine. Each of the machines has its local computer for control, and our guide explains that every stationary instrument in the factory is connected to a complex of central computers as well. One of the visitors asks what happens when a machine breaks down. "That's where the Level Fours come in," our guide replies, "and here's one of them at work." She points to a large planer, standing idle with its movable cutting head exposed. A human-sized machine with two arms and several television eyes on stalks is crouched over it, and as we watch, the Level Four "repairman" pulls out a dulled cutting bit, replaces it with a new one from a rolling table that is acting as its "assistant," and begins tightening bolts to secure the new part in place. "The Level Fours came in around the turn of the twenty-first century," our guide explains. "They're general rather than specialized, and of course they have the complete blueprints for their dumber cousins on the floor—and even for themselves. It's funny to watch one of them fixing another identical one—rather like monkeys grooming each other."

We enter a much larger and noisier hall, where parallel lines of aircraft fuselages are being equipped with wings, engines, and internal fittings at specialized stations. There are a great many Level Two robots placing parts and fastening them by welding, glueing, or bolt-tightening. Others inspect the results. "Henry Ford is credited with inventing the assembly line," says our guide, "and he did that nearly two hundred years ago. Assembly-line jobs are boring, but the Level Two robots that do the work don't mind that."

Our carriage leaves the assembly hall and passes a series of doors marked "Research and Design—Authorized Personnel Only." Our guide tells us that design constitutes Level Five of an automated factory. It is run by humans, who use interactive computers to evaluate new families of designs, and draw on results not only from their own research but from computerized scans of the latest aeronautical publications worldwide. "If we never had to change models, we'd only need a small research staff to decide on the minor improvements that our service and maintenance department would suggest. But as it is, we're in a highly competitive business, and the competitive edge is in performance and style. That's why our design department is so big. With the increased market that developed in the first half of the century, our design staff is bigger now than our whole company was in 2000. And those designers won't be replaced by automated equipment, because machines can't dream."

We learn that Level Six of the company, the artistic and policy staff, is exclusively made up of human beings, exercising their unbeatable talents of esthetic judgment, imagination, and creativity. When one of the visitors asks whether humans ever get down to the production floor our guide laughs. "They sure do. The highest-paid specialists in the plant are people we call the Murphy's Law Experts. They're the troubleshooters who fix the nonroutine, unforeseen kinds of problems that make the machine designers say 'That couldn't possibly have happened.' "

So far I haven't used the phrase "self-replicating systems," meaning combinations of computers, general and special-purpose machines that are capable of reproducing themselves—building all those same computers and machines—from raw materials and a source of energy. But a self-replicating system is clearly one of the possible goals of automation. A self-replicating industrial system would shatter most of the traditional concepts of economic limits, because its capacity for the manufacture of products would increase geometrically, as 1, 2, 4, 8, . . . without any further effort once the first such system were built. By the time the fourth level of production is automated, it will be possible to construct a self-replicating system by combining the state-of-the-art in automation with the managerial and economic decision to concentrate all subassembly plants in one location. Self-replication is not nearly as difficult a task as some others that are already being tackled, because by definition it does not require creativity or dealing with unfamiliar situations. I doubt that it will make economic sense to build self-replicating systems for constructing every factory product, but there will be certain applications, particularly in space at great distances from the center of human population, where self-replication will be essential.

At present the most advanced research on self-replicating factories is being carried out in Japan. There is a program in that country aimed at achieving self-replication of machines well within this century. At the present rate of progress, it seems a safe bet that long before 2081 we will be able to send a sophisticated, complicated machine to a great distance, and there have it process locally available materials using locally available energy to produce a replica of itself.

All that begs the question, "Do you really want automation?" The answer is far from simple. The steady rise in productivity that has gone on during the past hundred years has brought the average family in any of the developed nations to an extraordinarily high level of personal affluence, but that rise in productivity, brought by the early phase of automation, has also created a social problem. There is a natural distribution of talent and intelligence, and millions of people have the bad luck, through no fault of their own, to be born with less than an average share. We've made it virtually impossible for people at the lower end of the intelligence distribution to find employment in a productive, rewarding, peaceful occupation. At the turn of the century, construction projects required hundreds of pick-and-shovel men. They could at least take pride in their muscles and in being paid to do a necessary job. Now, like John Henry, the "Steel-Driving Man" of the nineteenth-century folk song, they would be unemployable.

In Europe and North America at present there's a curious twilight area of jobs too complex to be automated, yet not demanding advanced education. Much of our crop harvesting falls in that category, as does cleanup work in factories and the construction industry. Native-born citizens of developed countries aren't interested in such work, because they can draw social-welfare support rather than spending their time in demanding, monotonous drudgery. But for the hungry millions in those poorer nations that lie just across a border, those same jobs offer pay far higher than could ever be found at home. Many of those hungry people cross the border (legally or illegally) to a rich nation, live frugally while they work for a few months, and send back home most of the pay they accumulate. Anyone who has lived in California, or in Switzerland, or in parts of West Germany knows that many of those immigrant or "guest" workers are bright and hard-working, and that the money they earn flows back into their home countries, as a substantial though unacknowledged kind of foreign aid. We can only hope that by the time automation has replaced all such human workers by machines, the poor nations they come from will have risen to comparative affluence.

Watching what's happening in the developed countries at this time, and seeing what automation is going to do over the next century, leads me to believe that the traditional "work ethic" with which most of us were raised is going to be eroded even more than it has been. There will still be people who work seven-day weeks, no matter how short the legal work week, because that will still be the way that creative and ambitious people who enjoy their work can stand out above their colleagues. But there will be a large fraction of the population that does little or no work, because it can survive quite comfortably on what we would call welfare payments. As more and more production operations are automated the relative cost of manufactured goods will decrease, and the nonworking fraction of the population will be "carried" less by the labor of other humans than by the labor of machines.

To a considerable degree the revolution in the automation of agriculture, which has caused a massive shift of population from the farmlands over the last century, will be repeated by a massive shift of population out of factory cities during the next. But there will be even far more people than today in white-collar and service occupations, many of them supervising computers that are controlling automated machines. Others will translate questions and requests from the general public into language that computers can understand, just as airline reservation agents are already doing through their keyboards and TV monitors. There will also be a great many people employed in jobs where human contact is critical, especially in sales positions. And what about all the leisure time that increasing automation of production jobs will bring—how will it be used? In large part, to putting in as much effort on hobby activities as most people now devote to a paying job. Some personal, totally nonautomated craft project, whether it be making stained-glass windows, sewing quilts, constructing home-built aircraft or lovingly restoring a century-old automobile, is likely to occupy many hours of the week for a typical citizen of the late twenty-first century.

The transition to automated production won't require any "breakthroughs," and it won't require the development of robotic intelligence of a level or kind that would equal the human. The machines involved will wear out, just as ours do, and they will be replaced wholly or in part by the subassemblies made in other automatic factories.

There's an interesting side-path, though. Could a machine be made that would never wear out? In one of his greatest novels, written of a time millions of years in the future, Arthur Clarke wrote, "No machine may contain a moving part." Any parts that must act on the physical, mechanical world will wear, and we must expect even in 2081 to have to replace those grippers and pushers and wheels—I doubt very much that we'll be able to substitute the fiction-writer's convenient "force field" for them. But how close are we to a time when we can build machines that contain no mechanical bearings, no gears, no hydraulics, no internal rubbing surfaces? Perhaps closer than you think.

Already we have produced permanent magnets so strong that they break before you can pull them away from an iron surface. More than half of those we have made are no longer here on Earth; they rest in endless silence on the moon, in the electric motors of the Lunar Rovers, relics of the Apollo project. By combining the still-stronger permanent magnets of the future with microprocessors to drive controlling currents, it will be possible in less than a hundred years to make strong bearings without physical contact, and to make controllable electromagnetic "muscles" that can push and pull and lift and turn as quickly and as strongly as the human arm.

You may object at this point. Isn't it true that an object held in mid-air by a magnet is "unstable?" Yes, and you can demonstrate that by moving a permanent magnet slowly downward toward a nail resting on a surface. For a while nothing will happen, but then suddenly the nail will jump up and plaster itself against the magnet.

If you replace the permanent magnet by an electric one, and control its current through a simple computer that senses the position of the nail, you can make the current decrease if the nail moves up, and increase if it moves down. In that way you can make the nail hover indefinitely in mid-air. That is called "attractive magnetic levitation," and though it sounds risky, given the reliability of modern electronics it can be made quite safe. Already by the late 1970s three different organizations, Krauss-Maffei, Messerschmitt-Bölkow-Blohm, and Japan Air Lines, had demonstrated full-size railcars that worked on just that principle. Instead of wheels, each car was suspended with a clearance of a finger's breadth from a steel rail, by controlled magnetic forces. The Krauss-Maffei version exceeded 250 mph on its test track, and JAL is building a magnetic-suspension railcar line to connect the city of Tokyo to its main airport. Except for the hiss of air when its cars travel at high speed, that system will be almost completely silent.

One of the most difficult problems in countries now struggling to industrialize is repairing and maintaining production-line machines. The workers who perform such tasks generally grew up in a world without machinery, and lack the technical sense that a child in the developed world soaks up "by osmosis" from the everyday environment. When fourth-level automation becomes a practical economic reality, as I believe it will within a few decades, it will be of great help to those developing nations whose populations are still technically unsophisticated. An automated factory can be effective for producing, at low cost, a very large number of simple tools and devices needed by a poorly educated population still mainly engaged in agricultural labor in a village environment. It can produce planting and harvesting equipment, windmills for pumping water, solar cookers, and even solar-cell panels to provide electricity for lights and radios. Used in that way automation will help, I believe, to raise the standard of living in those countries at a rate that needs to be more rapid than our own.

Space Colonies

A SPACE colony would be an Earthlike habitat outside Earth's shadow, growing its own food and deriving all its energy from the sun. Solar energy, inexhaustible and ever-present in space, would power its industries.

Space colonies would process lunar or asteroidal materials into finished products for the Earth and for other colonies. Unlike the other drivers of change, space colonies are still on the drawingboard, not yet realized. Yet I believe they will transform society during the twenty-first century as much as the automobile, airplane, and radio, none of them in existence in 1881, transformed our world during the twentieth.

For a civilization now tightly constrained within Earth's biosphere and infected with nuclear proliferation, the most important new possibilities opened by space colonies may be a reduction in the scale of institutions and a dispersion of humanity far outside the bomb-laden pressure cooker that now seals it in. It may be the way to Huxley's third alternative, "a world of free individuals," in contrast to the only two he could see in 1946, "the perpetuation of militarism, or else . . . one supra-national totalitarianism, the welfare-tyranny of the Brave New World."

The fundamental transformation that space colonies will bring about is from an economics of scarcity—the "zero-sum game" that we are forced to play on Earth—to an economics of abundance. Here on Earth, no nation can enlarge its land area without going to war with another, and every million barrels of oil burned in one country subtracts that much from the reserves all must draw on later. Once we break out from the confines of the planet, we can begin building new lands from the limitless resources of our solar system, and can use freely as much as we need of the sunlight that now streams out, wasted, into the cold darkness beyond the planets.

Early, fanciful speculations about space can be found in the writings of Cicero and of Lucian, but it remained for Konstantin Tsiolkowski, a Russian schoolteacher, to appreciate that the ecological range for humanity need not end where the biosphere of the Earth attenuates into the vacuum of space. He realized that space requires only the provision of an air-enclosing shell to be transformed into a habitat with advantages in sunlight and availability of materials over a planetary surface. The idea of space colonies took form in Tsiolkowski's mind at an astonishingly early point in the history of technology, when Victoria was still Queen of England. Decades later Robert Goddard and John Stroud in unpublished notes, J. D. Bernal and Dandridge Cole in books, reopened in speculative fashion the question of human viability beyond Earth's biosphere. Those ideas remained outside the mainstreams both of science and of fiction, while the exploration of the solar system, sending men to the moon, and building enclosed cities on Mars and the moons of the outer planets were ideas that became familiar, even banal, thanks to the imagination of science-fiction authors.

Isaac Asimov coined the phrase "planetary chauvinism" to describe this curious myopia, our inborn automatic assumption that all human beings, even centuries from now, will be born and live out their lives on planets, even if they venture briefly into space to travel from one planet to another. Perhaps our myopia is there because our lives are so rooted in the experience of living on the outside of a ball.

The ideas about living in space that were published before 1974 were all set at a safe distance in the future. As written, most of them were free of numerical calculation and were taken as philosophical works of imagination. Indeed, before the Apollo astronauts returned lunar samples for analysis and proved that humans could travel as far as the moon, it would have been impossible for anyone to work out a consistent, practical plan for space colonies within the limits of available technology. Any new technical construct requires the forging of a chain of many links. One must identify correctly every link in that chain and prove by calculation, or by existing example, that every link can be built. As I developed that logic in the years 1969–74, I found myself caught up in a fascinating scientific detective story. The essentials came very quickly, but were so threatening to "establishment" thinking that it took all of five years to get them published in a scientific journal, where they could be reviewed, evaluated, and criticized by a large community of professional scientists. Fortunately, I resisted the temptation, often great in those years, to lose patience and turn the work into science-fiction. *

My new and upsetting conclusions were that we could build space colonies relatively soon, within the limits of known engineering practice, out of ordinary materials; that the colonies could be large, as much as a hundred square miles in land area; and that they could be, if we so desired, very "Earthlike."

One might think that for us to become the denizens of worlds in space would demand physical changes as great as our ocean-dwelling ancestors faced when they first breathed air to walk dry land. Fortunately, there is no need for us to undergo biological evolution to move into the ecosphere of the solar system. We can create in space all the requisites of human existence: air, water, gravity, proper climate, agriculture, and land area. Even more, we can find there the essentials for an advanced civilization: abundant energy and raw materials for industry, and easy pathways for transport and communication.

---

*The details of that frustrating but exciting period can be found in the first appendix of *The High Frontier* (New York: Bantam Books, 1978).

A metal shell can hold the atmospheric pressure we need for breathing. Water once introduced into a space habitat will remain, circling through a closed ecological cycle. The effect of Earth's gravity can be duplicated by rotation. Sunlight, constant outside the shadows of planets, can be admitted for as many hours of the twenty-four as the residents choose so that they may obtain any desired climate. Lunar soil brought into space can rest on the interior of a metal shell to form land area, as land on Earth is formed by soil resting on bedrock.

In space, far away from Earth's agricultural pests and parasites, grain as well as flowers, trees, and grass can flourish. Indeed, the Russian Cosmonauts in their *Soyuz* spacecraft have already grown simple plants while in orbit from seeds carried from Earth. A decade ago, experimenters in the United States grew plants in the lunar soil brought back by the Apollo missions; all that was needed was the addition of water and nitrates.

Transport between colonies will be through a vacuum, silent and free of atmospheric drag. Solar energy can be concentrated by mirrors to provide industry with a free source of heat, or it can be converted into electricity. No technology more advanced than the steam turbine is required for that.

Our present energy problem is one of supply, but our descendants will be at least as concerned with its disposal. Every watt of power we generate on Earth must be radiated away into space by our planetary surface and atmosphere. In the next chapter we'll find by exploring the connection between energy and wealth that humanity will have to use about ten to fifteen times as much energy in 2081 as it does now, if by that year the developing nations are to succeed in raising their living standards to those now common in the industrialized world. The Earth could radiate away that much extra power, but any further increase beyond it would be dangerous because of its unpredictable effects on the Earth's climate. But there is no such limit on the use of energy in a space colony. In proportion to its size, a colony could radiate away into the cold blackness of distant space far more heat than could the Earth, and there is room for many millions of such colonies within our solar system.

If we were to attempt to lift from Earth into space the raw materials necessary for construction of space habitats, the total cost in energy would be prohibitively high. It takes as much energy to put a ton of mass in high orbit above the Earth as it would to lift that ton straight up, against the pull of Earth's normal surface gravity, from the bottom of an empty well 4,000 miles deep. That's an enormous amount of energy, so great that it took the multikiloton Saturn–5 rockets to lift payloads of only a few tons into high orbits. But is there an easier way? Are there raw materials already waiting for us at the top of the gravitational well? Fortunately, the answer is yes. In the very early days of the coming breakout into space, the natural source of raw materials will be the moon: we need less than a twentieth as much energy to bring materials into space from the moon as from the Earth. A bit later we will turn to the asteroids, for in the asteroid belt there circulates a vast reservoir of raw materials. We know their total quantity, and it is enough to build space colonies with a total land area several thousand times that of the Earth. Even the composition of the asteroidal material has now been established fairly well by the spectra of sunlight reflected from each asteroid; we can be nearly certain to find there aluminum, iron, glass, oxygen, hydrogen, carbon, nitrogen, and all the other chemical elements necessary for agriculture and for industry.

About forty asteroids of a special class, the "Apollo-Amors," have orbits close to that of the Earth. More of those asteroids are being found every year. From a number of them, material could be retrieved at a relatively low cost in energy. The largest reservoir of asteroidal material is in the "main belt" between Mars and Jupiter, and that is best reserved for a future time when a space colony can be built directly alongside an asteroid and can then, after completion, move itself at a leisurely pace to any desired orbit in the solar system.

The economics of industry in space are tied to these questions of energy changes: where can the raw materials be found, where are the resulting finished products to be used, and how much is the energy cost of moving each ton from the source to the site of use? In the early days of space industry, one of the most cost-effective uses for the materials found in space may be for the construction of solar power satellites; the government, with its love of acronyms, usually calls them "SPS." A solar power satellite would be a very large array of solar cells, several miles wide and as much as ten miles long, all mounted on a very light spiderweb of girders so thin that in Earth's gravity they would collapse. The satellite would be in a circular orbit outside the Earth's shadow, about a tenth of the way to the moon. In that orbit, also favored for communications satellites, each SPS would remain above one fixed point on the equator of the Earth. It would receive the intense, constant sunlight of space, convert it to low-density microwave radio waves, and relay them to a receiving antenna on the Earth, where they would be converted to ordinary electricity for our use. The SPS is an attractive possibility for solving our energy problems on

Earth, a possibility that I'll explore in more depth in the following chapter. SPS is relevant here because it could become a vitally important product for the period when all of the human population still resides on Earth, and because the mass of each SPS would be enormous—as much as that of a large ocean liner. Where is all that mass to come from, economically?

Two studies sponsored by NASA, carried out in 1976 and 1977 under my direction at the NASA-Ames Research Laboratory, and two NASA-sponsored follow-up studies carried out in 1978–79 under contracts to Convair/General Dynamics and to the Massachusetts Institute of Technology, all agree that it would be cheaper to construct the power satellites mainly out of materials mined on the moon, rather than to lift the necessary tonnage out of the deep gravitational well of the Earth. As the decades of the twenty-first century pass, the industrial activities in space will draw more and more people from the Earth, workers and their families. The colonies will begin to draw immigrants, not just because high-paying jobs will be available in space, but because the living conditions there will be superior to all but a very few places on Earth. Well before 2081, a substantial fraction of the human population may be living in space colonies. The industrial products built by one colony for its economic exchange with others and with the Earth will be derived, like the colonies themselves, from raw materials found in space.

Economics doesn't favor our attempting to bring back raw materials from space to sell here on the Earth, because here they would have to compete with the minerals we already find in the ground—all the advantage in energy that the space materials have would be thrown away as they descended our gravitational well. The only exceptions to that rule are precious metals, worth the cost of transport wherever they are found, and relatively high-value elements like nickel, copper, and tungsten that are becoming difficult to find in the form of high-grade ores here on the Earth. The basic logical drive toward the construction of space colonies does not depend on such "lucky finds," but rather on the abundance of well-known asteroidal and lunar resources, and on the enormous outpouring of energy from the sun, now going almost entirely unused.

A wide variety of geometries can be drawn for colonies in space, based on spheres, cylinders, toroidal rings, and their combinations. A brief review of them was made by E. Bock of Convair/General Dynamics during the 1977 NASA-Ames Study, now published as NASA SP–428. One of the most efficient engineering designs—one that provides high strength, long internal sightlines, safety in the event of window breakage, and ease

An "Island One" space habitat for 10,000 people. Apartments, lawns and gardens, parks, small streams and walking paths are on the interior of a sphere nearly a mile in circumference, slowly rotating to provide Earth-normal gravity for its inhabitants. Agricultural crops are grown in the ring-like "Crystal Palace" farming areas. Natural sunshine is brought into living and farming areas by mirrors. (COURTESY OF NASA)

of internal travel without elevators or other machinery—is "Island One," a design that I described in *The High Frontier*. In deference to J. D. Bernal, who had written some fifty years earlier about the human habitation of space, I called it the "Bernal Sphere." It has a stationary spherical shell of lunar soil to shield the interior from cosmic rays. Within, but not in contact with, the first sphere is a second, slightly smaller one made of metal and glass. It contains an atmosphere and rotates slowly to provide on its "equator" a centrifugal force equal to Earth's gravity. Hollow tubes extending from the "poles" of the inner sphere along its axis of rotation, through openings in the spherical shield, serve as zero-gravity transport corridors to docks and industrial areas outside, and carry air to and from external radiators. From the transport corridors, passages connect to greenhouses, where crops are grown year-round in climates individually controlled by separate day lengths. In the central residential area the image of the sun appears in its normal size, color, and brilliance, during a length of day chosen by the residents. The interior environment can be lush with flowers, trees, and grass, and the sports we're used to, such as swimming and tennis, will all be possible near the equator of the sphere. There will also be new sports, carried out high in the air close to the zero-gravity axis of rotation, among them acrobatic, human-powered flight, and soccer with the players free to move in all three dimensions.

Island One, a relatively early space habitat, is designed to be economical of materials, and its total structural mass is about half that of an SPS. Its habitable sphere is about one mile in circumference, but the same geometrical form could be built in a much larger size. Within the engineering limits for ordinary metals and glass a Bernal Sphere could be constructed with a circumference of forty miles and a usable land area as large as a good-sized county on Earth.

How soon could we construct colonies in space, and what effect would they have on the development of human institutions and on the interactions between nations and between individuals? The NASA-supported reviews carried out during 1975–79 all indicate that space colony construction is technically feasible, and that a vigorous program could lead to a functioning space colony, constructing solar power satellites with a value of many billions of dollars each year, well within this century. Many of the technical building blocks necessary for such a venture are already under development for other reasons: launch vehicles to lift payloads of people and equipment into orbit, other vehicles for transferring the payloads from low orbit out as far as the moon and beyond, work stations for people staying in orbit for six months to a year.

For launching material from the surface of the moon to a precise point in space, where it can be collected and used either in raw form or separated into its constituent pure elements, the most efficient device appears to be the "mass-driver." That is a special type of electric motor, whose design combines a number of applications of electromagnetic theory each of which has been known for many years. I described it in a 1974 technical article, which proposed the concept of space colonies and the logical steps necessary to building them. *

In a mass-driver, small "buckets," each no more than an open-ended container circled by two superconducting coils, carry payloads of any liquid or solid material. The buckets move without contact within a slotted cylinder formed by strips of aluminum. The moving magnetic fields made by the bucket currents induce in the aluminum strips countercurrents that produce a strong, guiding, centering force. That sort of levitation seems mysterious, but it is in strict accord with laws of physics that have been known for more than a century.

Surrounding the guideway are aluminum coils, equally spaced. Into each one a current is discharged as the moving bucket trips a light beam. In this way the bucket is accelerated strongly; even the early models have demonstrated accelerations of more than a hundred gravities. The bucket releases its payload when it reaches maximum velocity, and then the payload continues out of the machine at that same speed, while the bucket is slowed by deceleration coils, to be recirculated for reuse; nothing but the payload leaves the machine.

The development of mass-drivers is presently being carried out in a joint program of two groups: my own at Princeton University, and that of Dr. Henry Kolm at the Massachusetts Institute of Technology. It is supported in part by the Space Studies Institute,† and in part by occasional grants from NASA through its Lewis Research Center. NASA is interested in the mass-driver because it appears capable of becoming a highly efficient substitute for rockets in space-propulsion applications, moving large quantities of equipment from one orbit to another. In that role, a mass-driver would be coupled to a "barge" or pallet containing hundreds of tons of equipment, and would push that barge forward by expelling in the other direction bucketloads of any available material. The material thrown away could be raw lunar soil or, once industry in space is well established, the

---

* "The Colonization of Space," *Physics Today*, September, 1974.
† The Institute Newsletter is published quarterly for subscribers, at $10.00 U.S. per year. Address: Space Studies Institute, Box 82, Princeton, NJ 08540.

liquid oxygen that would be produced as a by-product of separating lunar soils to get pure metals.

For use in space propulsion, the mass-driver will have to be developed to a high level of performance; our present target is to achieve a velocity twice that of the exhaust blast that the best chemical rocket engine spews forth. Calculations show that we can obtain that speed, some six miles per second, within the operating capabilities of present-day commercially available high-current, silicon solid-state switches; the other necessary pieces of the mass-driver are also obtainable as "shelf items," or easily constructable by an ordinary machine shop. According to NASA's experience, it takes from ten to twenty years to develop a new space-propulsion system to the point of practical use, so it is expected that the mass-driver will be a well-proven device within this century. By the next, it should be in routine use for freight-carrying spaceships up to tens of thousands of tons in mass.

Fortunately, the application of a mass-driver to launching material from the moon is even less demanding than its use as a propulsion engine in space, because the necessary maximum velocity is only a quarter as large. The lunar mass-driver could be developed within a few years, and will probably emerge as an early "spin-off" of the more demanding propulsion research.

Until quite late in the 1970s, those of us working toward the opening of the High Frontier for human benefit assumed that the breakout into space would require a national or transnational commitment. We were therefore quite concerned that the United States, foremost in space research during the 1960s, appeared less and less capable, a decade later, to undertake any challenging technical venture on a national level. The long-term health of a nation is probably shown most clearly by the time scale of the programs it undertakes. The willingness to commit to ventures of many years' duration, with potential very large returns, is the hallmark of a nation confident of its own future. The fear of any commitment beyond one or two years is the symptom of disease, signaling a fundamentally hopeless view of the future and the intention to cut the losses and get out of the game. It will be interesting to see whether these completely different attitudes toward the future surface in the form of political confrontation within the United States during the next decade. Probably they will, because the United States has never been a nation to put up with despair and defeatism indefinitely. As of 1979, the forces of timidity were still clearly in control. In that year E. R. Cutler, associate director of the United States Office of Management and the Budget, said in an interview that there was "a real question whether . . . we will maintain the NASA budget." The level of funding commitment to space research and development, he added, "will have to be decided on an annual basis."

By contrast, in addition to the already vigorous Russian program, Japan and China have both announced commitments to achieve manned spaceflight capabilities within the next ten years. Japan has been launching small satellites since 1970, and China has had ICBMs since the 1960s, so there is no doubt that those intentions can be realized. Western Europe, with its Ariane rocket, has also announced that it will acquire an independent manned-spaceflight capability, and it is clearly fully capable of doing so. Though I hope that my own country takes a strong part in the opening of the High Frontier, I feel that the potential benefits to all of humanity from that development transcend the issue of which nations act first. America is a frontier society lacking a frontier, and I suspect that when space is opened for settlement, perhaps not by the initiative of a United States government, individual Americans will move into space with a vigor and drive that will astonish us. In the late 1800s it was said that there were six million Norwegians—three million in Norway and three million more in Wisconsin. By 2081 there may be more Americans in space colonies than there are in the United States.

The human movement into space is too important an issue to be left to the vagary of which presidential candidate happens to win office, or whether the political winds of the moment blow forward or back. To provide a consistent driving force toward the High Frontier through the support of critical research on a continuing basis, without the hesitation and inefficiencies of year-to-year funding, the Space Studies Institute was formed in 1977. It is a nonprofit corporation which I serve as President, and it channels into priority research projects funds accumulated from many small contributions received from thousands of individuals all over the world.

The Institute has been fortunate in its choices of research topics to fund. The first, the mass-driver concept, was developed through two successful working test models and is appearing more promising with each new insight we gain. The Institute's next choice was a study, carried out through a series of workshops in 1978–79, into the quickest, lowest-cost method of reaching a high level of economic productivity in space, using solar energy and the lunar materials. Specialists in the fields of mass-driver design, spacecraft engineering, the chemical separation of lunar materials, and industrial automation all took part in those workshops. The main authority on automation in those studies was, in fact, Dr. Charles Rosen, whose pioneering work on practical automation I described in the last chapter. The workshops found that a rapidly growing industry in space could be established with a total investment comparable to that made in the Alaska Pipeline (which was entirely privately financed) in a time of less than ten years from the start of a substantial development effort. Several alternative paths were considered, but they were alike in starting with minimum-size plants in space for processing lunar materials. Such plants would use present levels of industrial automation and would be attended by a small number of humans to make repairs. The initial facility in space would include a "machine shop," which could produce from the separated lunar metals and ceramics most of the heavier components of additional, identical mass-drivers, chemical processing plants, and machine shops. Lightweight, labor-intensive components like computers and precision machine tools would be brought from the Earth, and in a short time (estimated as forty-five to ninety days) the facility would replicate itself, doubling the total industrial capacity in space. After a few doublings, a portion of the output of the factory in space could be turned to the manufacture of heavy components for satellite power stations or other products having economic value.

After a number of the Institute-sponsored workshops had taken place, a parallel program began within NASA, and it was reassuring to find that the government-sponsored research effort came to about the same conclusions, with the same numbers. The Institute followed its workshops by laying out a program that would progress through several successively higher levels of research, all financed by donated funds, until it could put forward a detailed plan calling for investment capital, with all questions of technical risk already set to rest by the demonstration of working hardware, and a near certainty of economic payback beginning within five years after investment. At that point, the Institute would encourage either private companies or nations to make the investment and reap the resulting benefits. Organizations that had kept in close touch with the Institute by supporting its research would obviously be in the best position to take advantage of that opportunity.

Recently, the Institute made a small grant, and the research it supported then opened the door to what could be the most attractive storehouse of materials in the entire solar system. Scott Dunbar, a graduate student in physics at Princeton University, wrote his Ph.D. thesis on a topic in gravitational mechanics. I can best translate its rather mathematical title as "Can there be material trapped in the same orbit as the Earth's around the sun, but far enough away so that we might have missed seeing it?" Scott found that it *is* theoretically possible for material (presumably small asteroids) to be trapped along the orbit of the Earth. He found that those asteroids would move back and forth on their orbits very slowly, taking about 100 years to travel from the far side of the sun to a point nearest the Earth. The situation is rather like that of a phonograph turntable, with the spindle representing the sun, and a point on the edge representing the Earth. One revolution time of the turntable corresponds to a year. The trapped asteroidal material is represented by a point (or perhaps many points) on the rim of the turntable. Though they rotate with the turntable, they also move very slowly along its rim, taking more than 100 turns to move from near the Earth-point to the opposite point on the rim, and an equal time to move back. Now, his theoretical research completed, Scott Dunbar is using one of the large telescopes at Mount Palomar in California, to search for the trapped asteroidal material. Our interest in that material is strong, because the energy cost of retrieving it to the vicinity of the Earth-moon system would be tiny—no more than one thousandth of the energy needed to lift material into space from the Earth. It would be the lowest-cost "mine" supplying the earliest industries in space.

The breakout into the High Frontier doesn't depend on our being so lucky as to find the asteroids that Dunbar is looking for, but it does depend on our working out the details of processing lunar or asteroidal materials to obtain from them pure metals, silicon, and oxygen. Research in that area was confined to numerical studies for several years, but in 1981 the Institute funded research leading to a working pilot plant, at the bench-chemistry scale of size, to separate the lunar materials.

As you can see from these examples, the links in the logical chain that will make possible the opening of the High Frontier are nearly all in place. You might then ask whether ordinary people in large numbers will ever find it easy to travel into space, and I can answer that question in terms of energy costs. Within the limits of the 1980s-era space shuttle, or of launch vehicles being built by several nations other than the United States, fifty to a hundred people could be lifted into orbit at a time, using no more fuel per person than the amount of gasoline a typical citizen of an industrial nation burns in his car in the course of a year. A fleet of reusable vehicles of 1990s vintage, numbering much less than today's world fleet of commercial jet transports, would be quite enough to provide transport into space and back again for several hundred million people per year, enough to drain the Earth of population in a few decades if the traffic were to be one-way. It won't be, of course, but a voyage of a few days to a space colony will be as commonplace in 2081 as a Caribbean cruise is to us today. Some people will certainly choose to emigrate, and they may do so in part because the civilization in space will be separated into a large number of small, self-sufficient colonies, each able to grow its own food and run its industries on free solar energy. That situation, profoundly different from ours on Earth in this century, is sure to alter our ideas about government.

Surely the most pervasive social, as opposed to physical, problem facing humanity as it nears the threshold of the twenty-first century is the centralization of power, the tyranny of scale. It cuts across the lines of ideology and of wealth. The problems of scale and of excessive governmental power will not disappear overnight with the advent of space colonies, but colonies will be environments far more suitable than the Earth for experiments aimed at resolving those problems. I leave it as an exercise for the reader to list all the federal agencies that obviously would be unnecessary in a space colony when I point out that it could locate itself far enough from others not to require defense; could grow all its own food without the threat of drought, flood, or crop failure; could obtain unlimited free solar energy with no technology higher than the steam engine; and could be traveled by its residents without the need for any vehicle other than the bicycle. A space colony would be built by specialists, as all our ships or large buildings are built today. It's surprising but provable that its residents could then move in and operate it thereafter, comfortably and safely, on the basis of a much *lower* level of technology than we've grown accustomed to on Earth today. They wouldn't even need to generate electricity if they didn't want it. As for the complexities of government, the total population could be as small as a few thousand, so any citizen could settle grievances by a face-to-face meeting with the locally elected person responsible.

Many nations of the Earth are strained by the need to accommodate citizens with differing national origins and languages. Will there be a universal language in space? I doubt it very much. It seems far more likely that no more than one language will be spoken in any single space colony, but that a century from now most of the major and some of the minor languages of Earth will be found among the space habitats.

History suggests that the human movement into space will be driven mainly by national rivalries, but we must work to keep those rivalries peaceful and encourage cooperation wherever it can be agreed upon. Given the present state of technical readiness, it seems that however it occurs, a breakout into space within the next decades is a certainty.

Energy

AMONG THE drivers of change, energy is unique, because it will speed change if we find it in abundance, but will become a barrier to change if it is in short supply. By contrast, the other four drivers are technologies that are bound to develop and to become far more powerful under the pressures of peaceful economic competition, international rivalries, and military confrontations.

The debate between those who look forward to the future with hope and encourage the study of change, and those who anticipate at best only a dismal monotony, centers on the availability of energy. In my view, we must find clean, inexhaustible sources of energy if we are to have any hope of improving the human condition during the next century. Solving that problem is an immediate and a challenging task for us, but let us remember that the difficulty lies only in supplying energy for humanity on the surface of the Earth—not for that fraction of the human race that will reside in space. They will conduct their lives without dreaming of the possibility of an energy shortage. They are likely to be wealthier than the population on Earth, just as Americans in 1881 were wealthier than the corresponding Europeans, and for the same reason: they will have access to abundant resources of energy at very low cost and will use them freely.

We think of America's high rate of energy consumption as a phenomenon of this century, but it is not. A hundred years ago the average North American used twenty times as much energy as the world average. Since then, the American per capita energy-use rate has increased about 2.3 percent per year. Compounded over a century, that means Americans now use ten times as much energy as their ancestors of 1881. But the increase in the rest of the world has been still more dramatic: 3.5 percent per year, for a per capita growth in energy usage by thirty times. The disparity between North America and the rest of the world has therefore diminished to about a factor of six, and is shrinking further as time goes on.

A great deal of misinformation is in circulation in regard to the energy situation on Planet Earth. Some writers have argued, for example, that worldwide living standards could be brought up to decent human minimums without a corresponding increase in energy usage. That just isn't so. Power consumption and standard of living go hand in hand: the average citizen of India uses only a hundredth of the energy of an American, but suffers a living standard only a fiftieth as high in consequence. For every watt of power that an individual citizen uses, his nation produces a dollar a year in goods or services. It's remarkable that this ratio holds even for countries as different as India, Japan, and the United States. There are only minor variations from that rule: Britain and the East Bloc nations get a bit less income from a given amount of energy than do other nations, while countries that produce high-value products without much use of energy do better than the average: Sweden, with its forest products, France, with its wines, and Switzerland, with its watchmaking and its "industry" of banking. But as a general rule, energy and standard of living are tied so closely that we cannot expect anything but a rise in energy use if the poorer people in the developed nations and the billions in deep poverty worldwide are to improve the conditions of their lives.

Twenty years from now our world will be poorer and hungrier than it is today. The numbers are grim: the 6.5 billion people then on Earth will be divided into a fortunate one-and-a-half billion living in the developed nations and the other four-fifths of humanity still below the poverty level. Whether the turn of the century finds our civilization in a downward slide toward poverty, accompanied by warfare over the remaining energy resources, or at the dawn of a better age will depend on our developing new sources of energy for the Earth and beginning to open the unlimited riches of nearby space. Bringing the poorest nations during the next century to a living standard even half as high as the wealthiest countries now enjoy will take a per capita energy growth rate of about 4 percent per year in those poor nations. If we take the United Nations projections for world population growth (projections which in the past have always been low) we can expect that there will be ten billion people living on the planet in the year 2081. To achieve the 4 percent target for the poorest countries will require multiplying present world energy usage by fifteen. That's not far out of line when compared with the last century, when the worldwide total use of energy increased tenfold.

To meet these greatly increased needs, as we must if the poor and hungry of the world are to lift themselves out of their poverty, we must turn to new energy sources. Unfortunately, none of the new energy technologies that are now on the horizon can help much before the 1990s, and even a substantial increase in energy supplied by present methods can hardly occur in much less than a decade. In the United States at this time it takes from eight to twelve years for a new power plant to progress from the first sketch through site-selection, environmental impact checks, borrowing of funds from lending institutions, and finally, engineering and construction. Research into new sources of energy takes an even longer time, so no private company can responsibly invest its stockholders' funds in it. That leaves government as the only sponsor of energy research, and as a result, there is not enough diversity in methods of approach and very little of the stimulation of ideas and effort that comes from open competition.

I'm convinced that we Americans would do far better to set up twenty or thirty small, efficient institutes, each with a charter for twenty years of research in a particular direction, free of governmental interference, than to persist with our present system of research management by central planners who are seldom in office long enough even to know their jobs thoroughly. If we were to "place our bets" in that way on a large number of different possible solutions, admitting frankly that we weren't smart enough to know which would succeed, I think we'd have a much better chance of solving the energy problem soon than we do at present. Indeed, if we look back to the history of successful research efforts, like the World War II atomic bomb project, we'd conclude that going after several different possibilities simultaneously, with minimum interference by government, would be likely to yield several successful solutions. The total cost of our twenty different institutes, if each were of the most efficient size, would be no more than 1 percent of the $10 billion per year that United States taxpayers now spend on the Department of Energy. However, that reform isn't likely to happen, because every new government official wants control of the research direction, to give the illusion that he's "doing something" about the problem.

Though the inefficiencies imposed by government direction slow the pace of research and raise its cost, nothing can halt it completely. The leaders in every great nation do understand that energy is vital, so the energy problem is sure to be worked on and is sure to be solved—just not as quickly as it could be. To guess *how* it will be solved, we must understand the ways that energy is used, because the "energy problem" shows itself in practice as a number of separate problems: how to provide electricity for lights and motors; how to heat buildings; how to power industrial plants; how to drive cars and airplanes.

All but about a sixth of energy use is accounted for by just three segments of the economy: industry, with 40 percent, transportation, with 25 percent, and residential with 19 percent. A few items one might have thought to be important are, in fact, almost negligible: cooking takes only 1 percent, lighting 2 percent, water heating 4 percent, and air-conditioning and refrigeration together only 5 percent.

As time goes on, the industrial segment is likely to require a bigger share of the total, because increasing affluence will bring more buying power for consumer products. The residential share will probably decrease for two reasons: many of the most highly valued appliances and other gadgets that will raise living standards will use relatively little energy once they're made—television sets, hi-fi equipment, and home computers are good examples of such products. And though the total area that will be enclosed and climate-controlled in tomorrow's towns and cities will be much greater than in today's, the enclosures will be simple in shape, with flat roofs and very few openings to the weather. They will be far easier to insulate than are individual houses exposed to winter winds and summer sunshine, so less energy will be needed for heating and air-conditioning them.

Transportation is the sector where the greatest surprises can be expected. At present cars, trucks, and commercial jet airplanes are the principal means of transport; all burn petroleum fuels and all are very inefficient. As the price of oil continues to climb, economic pressures will favor replacing those old-fashioned vehicles with more fuel-efficient ones. The new versions will require much more sophisticated technology, and will therefore cost more, but their high prices will be justified because they will cost much less to operate. I think that surface cars and trucks will improve radically in efficiency, but only by the junking both of the gasoline piston engine and of gasoline as a fuel. Commercial jets are more difficult to improve, and are now no better than the old "gas-guzzler" cars that got eleven or so miles to the gallon while carrying four passengers. It was one of the mild insanities of the gasoline shortage that occurred in the United States in 1979 that while individuals were being told to leave their economical, 25-miles-per-gallon cars in their garages, the United States government was encouraging the airlines to conduct a price war to lure customers into charter and newly scheduled flights—at double the fuel consumption for the same number of seat miles point-to-point. Jet aircraft are inefficient simply because of speed; you can't travel through the air at nearly the speed of sound without burning a lot of fuel. For long-distance trips, especially to remote areas, the jet plane will still be flying in 2081; but most passenger travel, fortunately, is over distances of only a few hundred miles, between major centers of population, and for such travel it will be possible, well before 2081, to move at very high speed in vacuum, spending less than a twentieth as much energy as a jetliner would need for the same trip.

I am predicting substantial, routine passenger travel to and from colonies in space by 2081, and you might think that would be significant in the overall energy picture. In fact, it will not be. At present the average North American uses energy equivalent to the burning of about ten tons of fossil fuels per year. By 2081 the average resident of our planet may be using energy at about that rate, and the rate in the wealthiest nations may reach sixty tons per year. Even using today's inefficient rocket technology, sure to be much improved over a century, the cost of going into orbit in a passenger-carrying derivative of the NASA shuttle could be as little as three tons of fuel per round trip. In 2081 that would be only the amount of energy that an average person on Earth would use in four months. An emigrant who left at age twenty would save the planet, during the following sixty years, enough energy for about 200 round trips. The shuttle vehicles needed for the Earth-to-orbit segment of the journey would be about the same size as today's jet aircraft, but only a tenth as numerous even if half a million people per day left the spaceports of Earth for destinations in orbit.

We academics tend to lecture people that there's no such thing as the "generation" of energy, but only its conversion from one form to another. That's true enough, and even the energy yielded by a wood fire comes from a microscopic reduction in the total mass of the fuel and oxygen that take part in the chemical reaction of burning, according to the formula everyone knows: $E = mc^2$. Even so, I'll use the casual word "generation" in its usual sense, to mean the primary conversion of energy. That's the first of four steps that energy goes through from source to user. The others are transmission, storage, and end use (or user conversion, to be fussy about words).

At each of the four steps there are evaluations to be made of each alternative, and the ratings depend on efficiency, pollution, land use, and heat load, as well as cost. Our evaluations will be realistic only if we bear in mind that in 2081 the world average per capita use of energy is likely to equal present North American levels, and that there will probably be two-and-a-half times as many people in all. In the most affluent nations of 2081 the energy use rate may be several times higher than the world average. I'll begin at the middle two of the four steps, transmission and storage. History shows that energy is more valuable economically when it is in a form that's easy to use for many applications, and when it's easy to convert to other forms. Up to now fossil petroleum has dominated the transportation segment of the economy, because it is easily storable, contains a lot of energy in a given sized tank, and in the past was cheap. Coal lost out to petroleum because it got poor ratings for convertibility and versatility. During the 1970s, as oil prices skyrocketed, most people came to realize that the overall shortage of energy was real after all (though some continued to believe that it was all "a plot"). Yet I still see no evidence of a program to insure that oil will only be used in a miserly way. The one thing we can be sure of is that by 2081 there'll be very little of it left, and that its price will be sky-high.

It seems to me that there are just four ways in which energy could be transmitted from one place to another on the surface of the Earth in 2081: as electricity, or in the chemical bonds of pure hydrogen, synthetic ammonia, or synthetic hydrocarbons. In chemical form energy can be stored as well as shipped, but all four methods of energy-transmission will be used, because each has virtues that will be of paramount importance for certain applications.

Electricity's most sterling virtue is that it is totally clean for the user. It is extremely easy to control, and with the advance of the solid-state art it will become even easier. It is highly versatile, being convertible to heat with 100 percent efficiency and to or from mechanical energy with an efficiency of 70 percent for small motors today and close to 100 percent for large motors and generators. By 2081 the efficiency even of small electric motors is likely to approach 100 percent, partly as the result of developments in strong permanent magnets and partly because there is likely to be a substantial shift from alternating to direct current (DC). Already some of the highest-voltage transmission lines operate on DC, because such lines can carry more power with lower losses. That technology, based on solid-state voltage converters, will extend even to ordinary households by 2081. In a power grid with many generators, it is far easier to switch individual sources on and off line with DC than with alternating current, because there is no need with DC to match the phases of alternating voltages.

Electricity has just two disadvantages: it is difficult to store cheaply, and it can be transmitted easily only on high-voltage lines, above the ground and visible. Automotive lead-acid storage batteries are as cheap as mass production and the cost of materials will allow, yet their cost for storing an hour's worth of energy coming off the power line is over two thousand times as much as the utility company charges for that energy. Multiple recharges can't even come close to bringing that factor down below about three. There is a radically different type of battery, using liquid sodium and liquid sulfur as electrodes and solid sodium aluminate as an electrolyte (yes, I said that the right way round) that is now getting substantial research. Theoretically, it could store as much as seven times the energy per pound of a lead-acid battery. Sodium-sulfur batteries have to be heated above normal outside air temperatures—a disadvantage that will probably make them unusable in vehicles—but they could find use in central power stations to supply peak loads.

Ever since gasoline prices began their upward spiral we've all hoped that someone would invent a practical, high-performance electric car. Unfortunately, it just won't be possible until something much better than a lead-acid battery is developed. In graphic terms, let's compare two cars equal in most respects, but one with a gasoline engine and fuel tank, the other with an electric motor and battery: if the gasoline-powered car has a range of 300 miles, the electric car will be able to go just two miles before it runs out of charge. Even that comparison makes allowances for the high efficiency of electric motors compared to internal combustion. There are newer types of battery under development, but they all use expensive materials like nickel or zinc, and they store only two or three times more energy than the old lead-acid type. It seems that even in 2081 electric cars will be limited to short range, light loads, and sluggish performance. They'll be used mainly as commuter vehicles that can be plugged in for recharging each night, because batteries can't be charged nearly as fast as gas tanks can be filled. One could imagine "changing stations" where batteries would be mechanically removed from cars and replaced by freshly charged units, but that seems an awkward solution to a problem, and I doubt that it will be competitive with other options.

For the large electric power grid there are other ways of storing energy, and that's good, because electricity demand varies within each 24 hours. Typically, a power grid has to supply twice as many kilowatts in peak hours as it does in the middle of the night. At present, peak fluctuations are handled by starting relatively inefficient diesel-electric generators and, where hydroelectric power is available, by opening the inlet water valves to turbogenerators that are already spinning at full speed with zero current output. Some experiments are being made with "pumped storage," the technique of pumping water up to a high-altitude reservoir during times of low electric power demand, then running the motor pumps in reverse as turbogenerators to put the energy back into the power grid when the demand peaks. That is a good, reliable, low-technology method of storing energy, but I doubt that it will find wide use in 2081 because of the inherent ugliness of reservoirs that fill and empty within a matter of hours. Environmentalism, I believe, will be even more important then than it is now, and it will become a worldwide movement as more and more countries rise to affluence.

As a medium for transporting and storing energy, pure liquid hydrogen gets a top rating for effectiveness and near-zero environmental impact. It contains a great deal of energy per kilogram, and it burns with oxygen to give only water as a product. Burned in air, it does form ammonialike compounds with nitrogen, but only in tiny amounts compared to the similar compounds that result from burning gasoline. With its nonpolluting character and its high energy content—almost three times the energy per kilogram that gasoline or jet fuel have—hydrogen is an attractive candidate to fuel supersonic transports of the future. The Boeing Corporation, after a detailed study, found that liquid hydrogen was the only fuel so light and so powerful that it could drive a supersonic airliner across the whole width of the Pacific Ocean. To prevent hydrogen's boiling away as a vapor, it must be kept very cold—just a few degrees above absolute zero—and Boeing found that the thick insulation needed around hydrogen fuel tanks could be accommodated in a wide-bodied jet, but not in any smaller supersonic plane. Hydrogen could easily fuel any slow aircraft.

Before engineers and scientists had acquired experience with large quantities of liquid hydrogen, they were fearful of its explosive properties. Now, though, after several decades of working with it in laboratories and in rocketry, they've concluded that it's less dangerous than gasoline or jet fuel. In the crash of a hydrogen-fueled aircraft, the hydrogen would tend to rise very quickly because of its light weight. Though it would certainly burn, the flames and heat would be high in the air. Ordinary jet fuel stays on the ground as a liquid, soaks the clothing of crash victims, and burns them at ground level.

Liquid hydrogen could become the fuel for surface vehicles as well as for aircraft. I can imagine long-distance touring cars, buses, and trucks that could run on liquid hydrogen and satisfy the demands even of the most intense environmentalists. The hydrogen would react with the oxygen of the air in a fuel cell to transform its energy into electricity. Fuel cells were engineered for the Apollo program of the 1960s, and their efficiency can reach 80 percent. The electricity put out by the fuel cell would drive electric motors at each wheel of the vehicle, and we would have the perfect combination of high performance, long range, quiet operation, and complete freedom from pollution.

It will be some years before you can buy a tankful of liquid hydrogen at your neighborhood gas station, but there's an interim technology already in use on an experimental basis. In Stuttgart, Germany, city buses are being run on hydrogen fuel, with the hydrogen absorbed on fine metallic grains filling a pressure tank. In the event of a crash, the worst that can happen is that the powder spills out in the street, and releases its hydrogen too slowly for a serious fire to feed on it.

Liquid hydrogen may well be the preferred medium for transporting and storing energy in 2081, but liquefying it will always require complicated refrigeration machinery. There is likely to be at least as much demand for a synthetic fuel that can be stored and handled at ordinary temperatures as easily as gasoline. Two hydrogen molecules can be pacified by linking their four atoms to the four chemical bonds of carbon to make methane, the main constituent of natural gas. Methane can be liquefied and stored at moderate pressure at a temperature that can be maintained with equipment not much more complicated than a household refrigerator. These days it's shipped as "Liquid natural gas" (LNG) in railroad cars and ocean-going tankers. The same chemical game can be played further by adding pairs of hydrogen atoms along with single carbon atoms, to form ethane (C_2H_6), propane (C_3H_8) and butane (C_4H_{10}). These molecules are simple to visualize: each has a row of carbon atoms flanked by hydrogen atoms, and each of these rows is terminated neatly by a hydrogen atom at each end. Propane and butane are even easier to store than methane, because they become liquids at moderate pressure at ordinary "room" temperature. Butane liquefies so easily that it can be found in cheap plastic cigarette lighters. Propane requires at least a thin steel shell to contain it, but it is so easily handled that it has been in routine use for many decades as "bottled gas." One can anchor hydrogen atoms to nitrogen as well as to carbon, and the result is ammonia (NH_3), familiar to us in watered-down form as a household cleaning agent. Ammonia works fine in fuel cells, where its hydrogen reacts with atmospheric oxygen and its nitrogen escapes to mingle harmlessly with the air. Ammonia could become a simple, practical medium for storing energy or for shipping it to fuel-cell electric plants, but ammonia is less attractive as a fuel for vehicles because it has to carry along the dead weight of the nitrogen; as a result it has only about half the energy per kilogram that methane or gasoline contain, and only a fifth as much as there is in liquid hydrogen. Talking of energy content, don't be so gullible as to believe irresponsible statements that alcohol can easily be substituted for gasoline. Alcohol has so little energy per gallon that its price would have to be less than half that of gasoline before it would be a good buy at the pump.

In 2081, when the most advanced nations may be using energy at six times the present North American per capita rates, and when countries like the United States may have twice their present populations, the environmental impact of energy transmission will be far more important than it is today. It is likely that increased electric power transmission will occur through using thicker conductors on existing lines, and by "low-profile" towers hidden by trees in flat country. Lines under water could be economical, but not those underground, except for short-distance, low-power cable runs as in residential neighborhoods. By contrast, ammonia or synthetic hydrocarbons can be transported by pipeline, with almost no environmental impact, at a cost only a fifth to a third that of transmitting equal electric energy on overhead lines. My guess is that pipeline transportation of such liquid fuels will be the most practical, economical, acceptable method for sending energy over long distances in 2081, but that electric lines will still carry a great deal of the total energy transmitted, because a large electric power grid can respond instantaneously to sudden heavy demands occurring anywhere within it. Shipment of pure hydrogen is likely to play a smaller role.

Environmental impact is most serious at the two ends of the energy road, in primary generation and in conversion by the final user. It seems there are technologies available for solving the environmental problems very well at the point of final use: liquid hydrogen for aircraft and for large surface vehicles, ammonia or synthetic hydrocarbons for fuel-cell powered electric cars, and ammonia for fuel-cell central station electric plants. Among those clean fuels, though, some are cleaner than others: while hydrogen gives up its energy to electricity with 80 percent efficiency in a fuel cell and yields only pure warm water as a "pollutant," hydrocarbons in a fuel cell yield only 40 percent efficiency and put out carbon dioxide (CO_2) as well as water.

My guess is that carbon dioxide may be the most serious pollutant remaining in 2081, but our present scientific knowledge is just not good enough to allow definite statements. At present use rates, we've increased atmospheric CO_2 a few percent in the last twenty years, and if our next fifteenfold increase in the rate of energy production were to come from burning fossil fuels, that would grossly increase the total amount of CO_2 in the atmosphere.

We fear to increase atmospheric carbon dioxide because it acts like the windows of a greenhouse, trapping heat radiation that would otherwise escape into space. The reason I don't make categorical statements about it is that experts have been unable to find in the atmosphere more than about 40 percent of the carbon dioxide that we know we've produced, and have also been unable to say for sure what more CO_2 would do to the climate. Yet my hunch, even though the figures are uncertain, is that we'd be foolish to tamper much further with the biosphere's natural methods for getting rid of waste heat. In that regard I don't worry about burning wood, because the CO_2 that results from that burning recycles through the atmosphere and gets locked into a growing tree some years later. The problem comes from the fossil carbon that's been locked safely underground in the form of coal or oil for millions of years, and now suddenly is being released into the atmosphere. CO_2 pollution will be hard to stop, because it doesn't cause local problems of smog where it's produced, yet it saddles us with a serious long-term global problem.

It seems likely that the wealthy nations will control CO_2 emissions, but that the developing nations, in the rush to industrialize, will be careless about it. In a few more decades there is likely to be a lot of argument and legislation about this problem of the "carbon balance." It will be solved only if everyone, throughout the world, renounces the burning of fossil fuels—a most unlikely development. We can use artificial hydrocarbons without danger, but only if we're careful to make them by obtaining their carbon from the atmospheric CO_2 so that it will recycle. Unfortunately, it's cheaper to make those hydrocarbons out of coal, so from that viewpoint we'd be better off if coal didn't exist.

Turning now to the sources of energy, all the methods for generating energy that are now in use will still be operating in 2081. If that seems startling, recall that the steam locomotive, a technology 150 years old, can still be found in some parts of the world. Coal will still be burned to make electricity, especially in rapidly developing nations, because coal plants are cheap and easy to build and maintain. Often they'll be built as "temporary" solutions to the energy problem, but will then be kept in service far longer than their builders intended, simply to meet rapidly rising demands.

As we've already found, electricity isn't the only form of energy that we need. At present, the cheapest source of pure hydrogen is natural gas, but in the future the gas wells will give out and we'll have to get hydrogen from some other source. The cheapest alternative is coal, and coal can also be transformed, by any of four industrial processes, into almost pure methane. About a third of its energy gets lost as waste heat in the transformation.

During World War II Germany developed a practical though expensive method for producing liquid fuels from coal. This and other methods of liquefying coal are being studied again, and within some decades it is probable that a good deal of fuel oil for use in central power stations will be obtained this way. As with coal gasification, about a third of the energy content of the coal gets dumped as waste heat, but sulfur, an undesirable pollutant, is removed safely as a solid. With further refinement and more loss of energy, it's possible to extract diesel oil and even an equivalent of gasoline from such fuel oils, and we may have to. In primary energy generation, all the economic numbers are big ones, and it would take tens of billions of dollars at the very least to build the necessary refineries. There's so much more fossil energy in the ground in the form of coal than of oil that coal gasification and liquefaction will almost certainly be large-scale activities long after cheap, natural crude oil is just a distant memory.

We'll probably shift during the next century from a fossil-dominated energy economy to a healthier reliance on long-term resources. In my guess, from 50 percent to 95 percent of the energy used on Earth in 2081 will be from such self-renewing or near-infinite resources. You've probably heard quite a lot about several of them: nuclear fission and fusion, breeder reactors, and perhaps ocean thermal power; you've probably heard less about a newcomer to the field of long-term energy resources: satellite solar power. You may be surprised that I don't list ground-based solar power as a viable option, but I don't because it's *not*. This is the place to dispel the "solar myth." The United States is a relatively sunlit nation of low population density, a particularly favorable place for solar energy. Yet even in the United States the numbers don't work out for it. In 1971 the average United States energy use was 0.3 watts per square meter. Staying with those units, the use rate will be 4.4 a century from now, even at the very modest growth rate of 2.5 percent per year overall (including population increase). Windpower, tidepower, photosynthesis, and hydroelectric power are all forms of solar energy. If we add together *all* of those energy sources for the entire continental United States, including damming every stream for hydro power and burning every forest, and throw in geothermal power for good measure, the most energy we could get is still only 1.5 watts per square meter—not nearly enough. If we were to get the energy from solar-electric cells, we could get enough of it, but only at massive environmental cost. The total annual amount of sunlight reaching ground level, if converted to usable energy at the fairly high efficiency of 15 percent, would be 33 watts per square meter. We would therefore have to devote about an eighth of the land area of the nation to solar energy traps, exclusively, to satisfy our energy needs from solar energy received at ground level. That's an area larger than Arizona, New Mexico, Nevada, and Utah combined. And the cost would be immense. A committee of the American Physical Society did a careful review for the federal government of the cost required to satisfy just 1 percent of United States electricity needs in the year 2000 from solar-electric cells (photovoltaics). The committee concluded that the required investment would be 20 billion dollars. It also concluded that ground-based solar electricity could never supply more than about 5 percent of the nation's electricity needs, because above that level one would have to solve the problem of cheap storage of electric energy—something we don't have a clue how to do in the vast amounts that would be necessary.

In the world of 2081, North Americans will use only a small fraction of the total energy being generated. It's worth remembering that the bulk of the energy needed will be in countries with much higher population densities, where solar energy at ground level will only be obtainable by appropriating land of far higher value than ours. That means that if we were to make the enormous investment necessary to develop a ground-based solar technology, that technology would be unexportable.

There are some limited uses for solar energy: as supplemental heat for isolated homes; as the source for keeping batteries charged at remote weather stations; and to recharge batteries for users of microscopic quantities of energy, such as wristwatches. The most practical large-scale use, though, appears to be rather frivolous: heating swimming pools.

Aden and Marjorie Meinel, specialists in solar energy research, concluded by the late 1970s that solar energy received on Earth had always been uneconomical compared to other sources, and would remain so. They emphasized that equipment costs for solar energy conversion were already close to the average prices per kilogram for consumer products. By subsidy, of course, governments can artificially depress prices for a time, but they can't continue doing so if the average taxpayer begins buying the equipment. There's a kind of secret kick, a "something for nothing" satisfaction, in using solar energy, and I can imagine buying a small unit just for the fun of it. Unfortunately, I've read and calculated too much to think I'll be saving money that way.

One can always hope for breakthroughs but shouldn't count on them. The Texas Instrument Company is working on a novel form of solar cell, containing tiny beads of silicon dispersed in water. Sunlight converted to electricity in the silicon electrolyses the water into hydrogen and oxygen, which can be drawn off and separated. If such a system can ever attain good efficiency, it will have solved the problems of transmission and storage, because hydrogen can be sent through pipes and stored in tanks.

Though sunlight arriving on the Earth's land area can't supply much of the energy we'll need in 2081, it's just possible that we'll get a significant amount of energy from the surface waters of tropical oceans that have been heated by sunlight. All heat engines work by tapping some of the flow of heat from a hot material to cold. In a steam engine the flow is from the boiler through the engine to a condenser, and it's possible, though much less efficient, to exploit much smaller temperature differences. By good fortune, sea water is heaviest when it's at a temperature just four degrees above freezing, so in the tropics the sun-warmed water stays near the surface, while the sunless depths remain near the freezing temperature. One can build a very large ship that "grazes" on the warm surface water, by pumping it through a radiator where it gives up its heat to ammonia. The ammonia vaporizes and drives a large, slow-turning turbine, then is recondensed by heat exchange with cold bottom water that's brought up and returned through enormous pipes. It appears that the economics will work out best if the turbines put their energy into the synthesis of ammonia from air and water, and the ammonia is carried by tanker and pipeline to a fuel-cell power plant, where its energy can be transformed to electricity.

A pilot-plant for this Ocean Thermal Energy Conversion (OTEC) has now started operation near the coast of Hawaii. I doubt that such plants will provide much of 2081's energy, because they face difficult problems of efficiency and maintenance. The theoretical maximum efficiency they can reach is only about 5 percent, and even that depends on maintaining the huge areas of the radiators, which must be of very thin metal in order to transmit the heat, free of algae, barnacles, and corrosion. The regions where the ocean is most intensely sunlit are most favorable for ocean-thermal energy generation, but for the same reason those are the places where tropical hurricanes and typhoons abound. Still, this option could give continuous power and deserves research.

Nuclear fuels are "fossil" reserves of energy, in the sense that they don't renew themselves. There isn't enough uranium available to run our civilization for very long on the most familiar nuclear reaction, the splitting of the U^{235} nucleus, because that isotope constitutes only a fraction of a percent of natural uranium. To obtain enough nuclear fuel so that the nuclear energy reserves would last a very long time, we would have to resort to some form of "breeding," that is, the transmutation of some common isotope to a fissionable one by exposing it in a nuclear reactor to a hot bath of neutrons. For some years there's been intense controversy over a pilot-plant "fast breeder" reactor, which was built to transmute the commonly occurring isotope U^{238} into the fissionable isotope P^{239} of the element plutonium. The controversy has raged because fast breeder reactors are much trickier and more dangerous than ordinary fission reactors, and because P^{239} is a suitable material for making atomic bombs as well as for fueling reactors. Critics have attacked fast breeder reactors both for the dangers of their operation and for the risk that in an all-nuclear economy there would be so much P^{239} being shipped from place to place that terrorists might well appropriate some of it.

There seems to be a way to avoid both problems by breeding from the element thorium in an ordinary "slow" reactor (the fast/slow distinction refers both to the average speed of the neutrons in the reactor and to the speed with which it could go from a safe to an unsafe condition). Canadian scientists have developed the CANDU reactor, which uses slow neutrons to breed fissionable U^{233} from the commonly occurring isotope Th^{232} of thorium. If the thorium is kept mixed with nonfissionable U^{238}, as it can be without degrading the operation of the reactor, the resulting nuclear material couldn't be used to make a bomb without very elaborate, large-scale laboratory equipment. It has been estimated that if even 5 percent of the available thorium can be burned in reactors of the CANDU variety, we will have enough energy available to run our civilization at fifteen times its present energy-use rate for 30,000 years. A 5 percent nuclear burnup is regarded as conservative (some optimists think 50 percent can be achieved) and the commercial CANDU reactor operated by Ontario Hydro Power Company has run with no difficulties for more than five years, so nuclear power certainly seems capable of giving all the energy we need. I'm sure that breeder reactors will be in wide use a century from now, but one of the main reasons for their popularity will be, I suspect, just what makes people critical of them: any *government* operating such a reactor can extract from it the materials necessary for making atomic bombs. I'm not strongly biased against nuclear power, but I'll be happier if we can find a good alternative to it, because it's an inherently messy solution to a problem. As long as nuclear radiation is involved in any system, it has the basic drawback that the "off" switch doesn't really mean "off." Radioactivity remains.

There was a most unfortunate example of that fact and of the universality of Murphy's Law in the 1979 nuclear "incident" at the Three-Mile Island reactor in Pennsylvania. With no help whatever from the United States Nuclear Regulatory Commission, the American Institute of Physics managed to track down as much of the truth as we are ever likely to know for sure. Here is the sequence:

The reactor was only three months old, and its maintenance staff was probably still not fully trained. An operator had been working on a feedwater system, and shortly afterward a pump in that system stopped. Loss of its suction tripped two other pumps. At that point, the turbines shut down and auxiliary pumps started working automatically to keep the reactor from overheating. However, the water from those pumps never got to the reactor, because two valves had accidentally been left closed after a maintenance check. The reactor, deprived of cooling and still intensely radioactive, heated its water to a pressure of over a hundred atmospheres—about fifty times the pressure in an auto tire. A spring-loaded relief valve inside the airtight "containment" building that surrounded the reactor then popped open, and when the pressure dropped, that valve, out of reach because of its location, stuck in the open position because of some mechanical fault. Two water-level gauges in the control room both then indicated (wrongly) that there was plenty of water in the reactor (they may have given false indications because of excess heat or frothing of the reactor's water), and on seeing the gauges, an operator turned off the inlet water pumps, which made the overheating even worse. Later, they were turned back on, but by then the heat-induced bubbles in the water system were causing the main circulation pumps to vibrate badly, so an operator turned them off an hour after the incident had begun. The reactor core then heated up and cracked, releasing radioactive fission products into the primary cooling water, which was still flowing out of the stuck valve into the containment building. When all the shouting was over, the reactor was left ruined, and because of the radioactivity in the containment building no one dared enter it until more than a year after the event. Fortunately, the containment building hadn't ruptured, so there was no injury to the operators and no release of any significant amount of radioactivity into the outside air, but the event didn't make nuclear power any more acceptable to people already concerned about it. From a safety viewpoint, the entire affair was like most aircraft accidents, a sequence of unlikely coincidences compounded by human errors. It's worth noting that most of the damage at Three Mile Island could have been prevented if the containment building had been equipped with a mobile, remote-controlled cart with mechanical hands and television eyes.

For more than three decades we've dreamed and hoped that we could obtain nuclear energy the same way the sun does: by fusing hydrogen nuclei together to make helium. That reaction is a copious source of energy, and it doesn't produce penetrating radioactive particles. There are several ways it might be done: by confining an intense, hot cloud of heavy-hydrogen ions and electrons in a very strong magnetic field, by "zapping" a microsphere of glass containing hydrogen with a powerful laser beam, or perhaps by using some version of a mass-driver to smash together two glass hemispheres of liquid hydrogen at such a speed that the collision would heat the hydrogen to the fusion temperature. At least in the case of the first two alternatives, it has turned out that the technical challenge is so difficult that we may not be able to meet it head-on. Instead, we may be forced to work with a less clean reaction, that of deuterium with tritium. Those are heavy, rare isotopes of hydrogen, and they react to produce helium and a neutron. It appears, rather unfortunately, that the most economical version of fusion may be to use that neutron to breed plutonium or uranium, and then burn the fissionable isotope in an ordinary reactor. That raises all the difficulties and fears associated with reactor safety and nuclear weapons. With such hybrid fusion, gone is the dream of the wholly "peaceful atom."

My own favorite energy source, not only for 2081 but for the last decade of this century, is Satellite Solar Power (SPS). It was invented in the late 1960s by Dr. Peter Glaser, of the A.D. Little Company, a research firm. A power satellite is a large array of solar cells or of turbogenerators, located in synchronous (twenty-four-hour) orbit above a fixed point on the equator. The satellite receives full-time solar energy, converts it to low-density microwaves, and then relays it to a ground station where it is rectified to DC current with an efficiency of about 90 percent. Because of interruptions by nighttime and clouds, and lower illumination near sunrise and sunset, a solar cell at the Earth's surface puts out power, averaged over the year, that is only a sixth as much as its output at high noon on a clear day. By contrast, a solar cell in synchronous orbit receives constantly an intensity of sunlight that's about 30 percent higher than we ever experience on the ground, giving it an overall advantage of a factor eight over a ground-based cell. In orbit we don't care how much area is needed for the solar cell array, because it's not in competition with land area. The continuous sunlight of synchronous orbit makes storage unnecessary.

For equal amounts of power averaged throughout the year, the land-use requirements for satellite power are far less than for ground-level solar cells because of two factors that multiply: the microwave energy is convertible at 90 percent efficiency rather than solar cells' 15 percent, and it is there full-time instead of a sixth of the time. For energy density equal to sunlight, the microwave antennas therefore use only about 1/36 as much land area as ground-based solar cells producing the same average power. The antenna is a mesh structure, intercepting the microwaves but allowing rain and sunlight to pass through it, so if it is raised above ground level on posts, the land below it can be used, for example, by grazing animals.

In a two-year study completed in 1980, the United States Department of Energy found "no unacceptable environmental effects" from satellite power. However, many experiments remain to be done before satellite power can be certified safe. The low-density microwaves may have some yet-unsuspected biological effect on birds, or may alter the ionosphere in ways that disagree with calculations made so far. If satellite power turns out to be acceptable on all grounds other than the environmental effects of microwaves on birds or insects, there may still be a way to use it safely. One can float the antennas above biological life and above the weather in the stratosphere where the winds are usually mild (one needs to avoid the special combinations of latitude and altitude where the jet stream sometimes penetrates). A balloon-borne antenna could feed continuous electric power through its tether cable to a moored ship and from there by undersea cable to shore.

For reasons of national defense, commercial and private aircraft flights over oceans are already confined to relatively narrow corridors and there are vast areas where aircraft never go. As a pilot and a resident of a state bordering on the ocean, I'd much rather have an offshore balloon-borne microwave antenna than an offshore nuclear power plant—and that's an alternative that is now under serious discussion. Satellite power has at least one great advantage over any form of nuclear energy, for should it subsequently turn out to have been a wrong choice, it can simply be turned off, leaving no radioactive wastes.

The various likely sources of primary energy for 2081 are sharply different in the waste heat they will dump into the biosphere. Satellite power is the most benign, because for each kilowatt on the power line here on Earth, it would put a total of 1,100 watts into the environment (the 1,000 that are useful, plus about 100 watts of waste-heat at the antenna). Any type of nuclear reactor, fission or fusion, must go through the "thermal bottleneck" to deliver power, so nuclear puts 2,500 watts into the biosphere for each 1,000 on the power line. Coal-burning is about the same, except that if the coal is gasified or liquefied the figure becomes worse: about 3,800 watts. Ground-based solar-cell arrays are a little better than fission or coal-burning, but still, at 2,100 watts, about twice as bad as satellite solar. The heat load of a ground-based solar array is so high because its installation raises the absorption of sunlight from the 65 percent typical of a desert area to about 95 percent. OTEC, with its very low efficiency of 5 percent, must alter the heat balance of the tropical oceans if it is to supply large quantities of power.

In summary, direct heating of the biosphere does not appear to be a serious problem for the next century, though the indirect warmup resulting from dumping CO_2 into the atmosphere is a real concern. There are at least three primary sources of energy, ocean-thermal (OTEC), thorium-cycle fission reactors, and satellite power (SPS) that appear to require no scientific breakthroughs for their realization and could supply energy even in the amounts that will be needed in 2081. Of the three, OTEC and SPS appear the more benign environmentally. There have been concerns expressed about the massive amount of rocket traffic through the atmosphere that would be required if power satellite components were to be built here and hauled to orbit, but that can be avoided, and money saved at the same time, if the satellites are built in synchronous orbit from lunar material. If they are, SPS may become the best source of energy from every viewpoint: as solar energy it will be self-renewing, and it will be continuous, reliable, will require no storage, take up very little land area, and will produce no CO_2 or radioactivity.

For the century after 2081, any large increase in per capita energy use will have to be balanced by a corresponding reduction of the Earth's population, either by a birthrate much below the replacement level or by emigration to colonies in space.

Energy will be more expensive in 2081, and its higher price will provide the pressure to develop more sophisticated technologies, so our descendants of 2081 will use energy much more efficiently than we do. They will also use a great deal more of it than we do, but they will feel no guilt in doing so, nor should they. As they study their history books and see photographs of the smog over our cities, they'll probably think us as careless as we think our ancestors of 1881, to whom the thick black plume of soft-coal smoke above a factory chimney was a great thing, a symbol of progress.

Communications

WE SHOULD not confuse communications with computers or automation, for although all three depend on the electronic art, each is a vastly different application of that art. As the beginnings of automation were first applied to gunmaking and the earliest electronic computers were developed to solve military problems, so each new advance in communications has been exploited in warfare. Communications have always been a vexing problem for the military, and many great battles would have come out differently if a few citizens-band radios had been in the hands of history's losers.

Rapid communications were introduced during the French Revolution, when the first semaphores replaced the signal fires, the drums, the smoke signals, and the stage riders of antiquity. The French semaphore system, invented by Claude Chappe, consisted of chains of towers, each located on a hilltop and manned by a resident operator. For the first half of the nineteenth century these Chappe "telegraph towers" provided the fastest communications in the world, and more than 500 were built. In *The Count of Monte Cristo* Alexander Dumas gives us a graphic account of the French semaphore system at the dawn of the industrial age. Speaking to the semaphorist, Monte Cristo comments on the iron handles that operate the semaphore's paddles and then delicately probes to see if the operator can be bribed:

"It is very interesting, but in the long run it is a life which must be very tedious to you."

"Yes. At first the continual watching gave me a crick in the neck. But then, we have our holidays."

"Holidays? When?"

"When we have a fog!"

In 1840, soon after the early experiments in electricity by Faraday and Henry, the electric telegraph came into service, as the first application of the new science. Almost overnight it made the visual semaphore obsolete. The telephone, introduced a few decades later, brought speed-of-light communications to ordinary people, not just to trained telegraphists in central offices. As of 1981 we're still in the "telegraph" stage as far as satellite communications are concerned: it takes big, expensive equipment to send and receive signals by way of the small, low-power satellites that now orbit at synchronous altitude. To gather enough signal strength from the weak transmissions of our present satellites, the receiving antenna must be at least several meters in diameter, and the ground transmitter is housed in a truck rather than carried in a pocket.

In time, as the market for communications continues to grow, it will pay us to lift into orbit larger satellites with bigger antennas and more powerful transmitters. When that happens the ground equipment can be reduced in size and cost, which will further expand the market. That process can't go on indefinitely, though, because we'll run into fundamental limits to the flow of information: the speed of light and the "bandwidth," the range of frequencies available. The bandwidth is roughly proportional to the frequency of the medium of communication, what engineers call the "carrier frequency." You might think that the information flow in 2081 will be entirely by satellite, but because of those fundamental limits that won't be the case. Satellite communications will always be limited by the need to use radio frequencies that penetrate the rainstorms of Earth's atmosphere. The highest frequency that can penetrate, corresponding to a wavelength no longer than your thumbnail, is more than fifteen thousand million cycles per second. That seems high, but it's not high enough to provide satellite channels for all the messages of great complexity that will be coursing back and forth between the computers of 2081.

Fortunately, one can tailor the range of coverage of a satellite radio beam by making its antenna larger. Just as a naked light bulb spreads its light in every direction, whereas a searchlight mirror concentrates that light into a narrow beam, so the width of a radio beam gets smaller and smaller as the transmitting antenna is made larger. If the antenna is a little over one meter across, it receives signals from, and transmits signals to, a "footprint" area on the Earth about a thousand kilometers wide. The first application considered for truly global coverage by a system of that kind is, as we might have expected, military. It is to a "global hot line," a system of small portable antennas of less than a meter in size, each equipped with a transmitter that need not have more than two watts of power. The system would connect the 200 heads-of-state of the nations of the world into a network by way of just three satellites in synchronous orbit. Presumably it would help to prevent the accidental triggering of large-scale wars.

There are already more than a hundred communications satellites in orbit, and by 2081 there will surely be several thousand. As the frequency bands become saturated with the transfer of information up and down to the satellites, there will be no recourse but to add more channels in parallel. That can only be done by building satellites with much larger antennas, defining narrow, separated footprints of beam coverage on the Earth. The smallest satellite antennas will serve large areas that have low population density and require only a few communications channels, whereas the largest antennas, over a kilometer in diameter, will define a beam-footprint on the Earth so small that you could walk across it in ten minutes. Because of the narrow range of frequencies available for satellite communications, the legal complexities of the international agreements that must be made for their allocation, and the increase of costs that goes with building bigger satellite antennas to get around the problem of frequency limits, satellite communications will ultimately be more expensive for regions of high population density than land lines. There will be enough capability, though, to take care of the needs of the moving transmitters: not only all the ships and planes and cars, but individual people as they move about locally. If everyone then on Earth were to tie into the satellite systems, there would be bandwidth enough for at least a minute of communication per day for everyone. That limitation is serious enough that much of the traffic, especially between people in built-up areas, is likely to go by a complicated route: from a person's own communicator to a relay station close by (most buildings will probably have them), then to a central switching point, and so onto a conduit to any other city on Earth.

Notice that I said a "conduit," rather than a wire or a cable. There's a system already close to large-scale use that's almost sure to take over within the next decades. Light has a frequency about ten thousand times higher than that of the microwaves that can penetrate Earth's rainstorms. Modulated infrared light beams can travel through glass fibers the size of a pencil-lead, fibers so transparent that the light sent into one can travel more than twenty kilometers before it has to be amplified. Many thousands of such fibers, all independent, can be bundled together and led through conduits underground. That system combines with its enormous message-carrying capacity the advantage that its signals are wholly contained, so that they are resistant to electronic eavesdropping. For routes with a very high traffic, dozens of conduits can be put into the same trench and covered over just as pipelines are covered. Grass will grow over the communications lines that carry most of the world's information flow in 2081, and under that grass every fiber in each bundle will be able to transmit, every second, the equivalent of 200 books, letter by letter.

Such fiber-optics light guides, carrying light signals from lasers smaller than a grain of salt, will transmit not only library information and computer data, but television programs, mail translated into the on-off binary code, and telephone messages. Even at today's level of technology, an optical fiber in commercial use can transmit a dozen telephone messages simultaneously, and ultimately a single fiber can link several hundred pairs of telephones all in use at one time. The fiber-optics method is clearly best suited to the industrialized nations, because it requires a sophisticated organizational infrastructure. Fortunately, it can be accommodated rather well within the structure already built up by Bell Telephone in North America and by national telephone systems in a few other areas. Given a century of development, it will seem no more "high technology" to our descendants of 2081 than the familiar telephone cable seems to us. Satellite communications do have the advantage that they require no such infrastructure, so they will be particularly well suited to undeveloped nations whose need for reliable communications is great but whose requirements for bandwidth are still modest. India has shown the priority a developing nation places on that option. After a most successful demonstration of satellite educational television transmissions to remote villages in a joint United States-India program, the United States withdrew the ATS-6 satellite that had been used in the tests. India responded by using its own limited capital to purchase an identical satellite from the manufacturer. The high-quality educational programs that can be distributed directly to villages by satellites of that kind contribute to solving one of the world's most serious problems—overpopulation. Studies of developing nations show that while improving nutrition and preventing infant mortality contribute to lowering birthrates, the social indicator that correlates most closely with reducing birthrates is education for women, particularly the attainment of literacy.

In the industrialized nations the educational problems are of a different sort. There, high-quality educational programs such as "Sesame Street" have taught many preschoolers to read. Unfortunately, when those same children reach primary schools they find only the traditional educational methods that have changed little over the centuries. Within a year or two many of them become bored, lose interest in learning, and turn to the easy distractions of television and social life. New developments in communications, aided by computers, can stop that tragic loss of talent and keep students interested. It's an established fact that the very few naturally gifted "born teachers" are enormously more effective than the great mass of those in the teaching profession who teach with care and attention and even with good new ideas, but without the charisma and the flair that distinguish the best teachers as well as the best actors. In my ideal school of the future, children would assemble each afternoon for sports, music, and club activities that require group interaction. The mornings would be reserved for individual study, probably at home. The child would be in a private room in one-on-one interaction with a "tutor," the realistic, holographic presentation of an actual human being, one of the rare, inspiring, one-in-a-thousand superbly gifted teachers. Brief lectures, personally directed to the student, with lots of eye contact, would be aided by all possible tricks of costuming and special effects, but those lectures would have been staged as carefully as a dramatic movie and would have been preserved on video discs. With computer-generated responses, apparently coming from the personified tutor, there would then be an amusing rapid-fire give-and-take, highly involving, in which the tutor would devote all his attention to the student, teasing out answers, rewarding and scolding, and always stimulating thought and reinforcing memory. Already the beginnings of such a system are being tried, at Higashi Ikoma near Osaka in Japan. There, a computerized center is linked to more than a hundred private homes through optical fibers, and sends one-way or interactive television programs to those homes to aid in education, shopping, and travel arrangements.

For the increasing number of jobs that require human interaction rather than control of manufacturing machines—the occupations of salesperson, travel agent, office clerk, office manager and the like—similar but less sophisticated new communications techniques will make it possible for workers to carry out their tasks without ever leaving home. For many of those occupations no technologies will be required beyond those of a central computer system, fiber-optics cables to a number of remote locations, and individual terminals where the video image of one person will be presented to an operator who is also on camera. Again, the early versions of such systems are already with us, in the form of centralized facilities that handle car rentals, hotel reservations, and complaints about credit-card errors. Not long ago a couple whom I know were transferred from the West Coast to the East. Though they both moved, only one had to switch jobs; the other, a computer-programmer, was furnished with a terminal to use at home and continued to work full-time, though based several thousand miles from the employer. As that practice becomes increasingly common it will ease the congestion of the morning and evening rush hours, but it is likely also to stimulate leisure-time club activity, social interaction, and spectator sports, as office workers compensate for workdays alone by seeking out other people with whom to share their spare time. Humans are, after all, a gregarious lot, and need society as much as they need, occasionally, to escape from it.

All these developing techniques that will permit people to interact much more freely through communications networks will also leave them greater freedom to choose their places of residence, but they will certainly increase the pressures to locate new communications systems underground rather than to add satellite channels. Because of the second fundamental limit on communications, the speed of light, the interchange of information by way of modulated light beams through direct fiber-optics pathways will be much faster than through satellite links, and that will be important for rapid dialogue between computers, in phone conversations between people, and for highly interactive educational exchanges of speech between computers and individual students. To relay the spoken word via satellite, the microwave signals have to make two round trips from the Earth to synchronous orbit to complete the cycle of question and response. That adds a time delay of more than half a second. If you haven't tried it, you may be surprised at how noticeable and how irritating it is. We've all been conditioned by a lifetime of experience in dialogue to waiting a fraction of a second after the other speaker finishes a sentence to be sure he's done before we begin a sentence of our own. If a communications delay is added artificially by the travel time of signals up to a satellite and back, it's just enough to remove that audible cue and leave us floundering. Often my wife gets calls from her mother on the other side of the Atlantic. Sometimes the call is routed by cable, and then it's normal, but even when I'm so far away that the conversation is just a distant murmur, I can tell when it's by satellite: then the usual rapid-fire give-and-take between mother and daughter is lost and is replaced by confusion when both speak at once or both listen.

Most of our phone calls are to people close by, and it makes no sense to suffer the frustrations of the satellite signal delay and saturate the limited bandwidth of the satellite system, when we really want to talk with someone only a mile away. By 2081 everyone will have the "Dick Tracy wrist radio" that's been talked of for half a century, but its signal will usually go only to the nearest relay point, no farther than walking distance. The sort of information that a person walking outdoors is likely to call a distant computer for, and the incoming calls that such a person doesn't want to miss, will make few demands for bandwidth and can be handled easily by satellite.

The limit on natural, unstrained conversation that's imposed by the speed of light will strongly affect those many humans who will be living in space by 2081. They'll choose to reside within easy communications distance of coworkers and close friends. Colonies can be located in all three dimensions within a volume of space, and in vacuum, laser beams can travel thousands of kilometers with little attenuation. It would be quite possible in 2081 for a group of space colonies with a population of several billion people to communicate with each other much more extensively and more quickly than could two cities far apart on the Earth.

Communication from a colony to the Earth would involve, in a question and response, a total signal delay of a second or more. It's likely that the transmission would be relayed via laser as far as a satellite, then converted to the much lower microwave frequency for penetration of Earth's atmosphere. The limitation of the speed of light is likely to determine far more than will considerations of energy and matter where the practical boundary of Earth's banking, business, and entertainment world is to be drawn. The business and financial community will huddle within a volume small enough that tele-conferencing can occur freely within it, and that is a severe restriction. Corporate headquarters will probably be located on Earth or on small colonies in relatively low orbits, no farther from the Earth than New York is from San Francisco. Such colonies may provide "flags of convenience" with tax and legal advantages, much as Monaco,

Luxembourg, Nassau, Bermuda, and the Cayman Islands now provide for thousands of corporations. Low-orbital colonies will communicate directly to relay points on the Earth, either by microwave or by higher bandwidth laser light to balloon-borne receivers above the clouds, rather than tolerating delays via synchronous orbit. Anyone living in a colony much farther away than the moon will be considered a "provincial," the criterion being the practical limit of a few seconds delay beyond which telephonic conversation becomes intolerable. All communication over greater distances will be through electronically transmitted letters or recorded dictation. The one-way transmission of newspapers and magazines will be unimpeded, even out to the most distant parts of the solar system, but it's unlikely that the people who live there will take much interest in hourly news bulletins from the Earth. They'll watch the entertainment programs on television, of course, the worst along with the best.

By 2081 the breakaway of some small fraction of humanity toward another star will be, if not a reality, at least a very bright gleam in the eye. The one-way flow of scientific, engineering, artistic, and musical information will be matched eventually by a flow inward from colonies that establish themselves light-years away. There will be good practical reasons for investing the rather small sum necessary to disseminate all that information by way of tight laser beams. The knowledge will be sent on the basis of quid pro quo, with the understanding that as soon as a new colony establishes itself around another star and begins building up its own population and store of knowledge, that knowledge will be shared with the home world. Because the round-trip travel time for information between the solar system and even the nearest star will be almost ten years, there can be no economic or military interaction between the colonies and the home world, and no need, therefore, to be concerned about patent rights or security.

The techniques for interstellar travel will be taken up in a later section, so it is appropriate here only to note that the transmission of information between nearby star systems is well within present technology, but that because of the lengthy times needed for any question-and-response communication, colonies around other stars will have to be totally self-reliant. Just as genetic drift occurs in isolated human populations, colonies around other stars will drift apart in culture, eventually becoming highly diverse. They will build their own traditions and accumulate their own histories, and probably very few of their people will travel back to the home world of humanity.

A century from now, the boundaries of each intimately communicating human enclave will be the conversation grouping, a volume in space about twice as far across as the diameter of the Earth. It may or may not contain a planet. And where will it all end, this constant advance in the ease and volume of communications? In a totally "tuned in" population? Far from it. The limits will be set not only by bandwidth and the speed of light but by something much more homely: one's irritation at being interrupted by an unwanted incoming call. We're seeing the effects of that already, in the popularity of phone-answering machines. The hottest consumer product a few years from now will probably be a machine that tells social lies: "I'm so sorry, Mr. Insistent. After his meeting he'll have to leave to catch a plane. Would you mind telling me what it's about?"

These five are the forces that will drive the changes of the next century. The "captains and the kings" will come and go, but the five will endure and will shape the world, unless we are destined for the final catastrophe in the brief moment of time that lies just ahead. If we survive these dangerous decades, the human race will be unkillable, because it will have begun to spread throughout the solar system, our pathway toward the stars. Computers, automation, space colonies, energy, and communications: the five. And unless we do something violently stupid with our future, the eternals of hope and love and laughter will still be there too, and will accommodate all the might of the five to everyday human affairs just as successfully as they have already tamed the automobile and the jet airplane and, even, the telephone.

Part III

Life in 2081

Introduction

WE HAVE explored the drivers of change in Part II, and now we will see how they will form the world of 2081. Each of the chapters of Part III is divided into two sections. In the first we will observe our planet and its surroundings as it would appear to someone of that era. That section is necessarily conjectural, so it is written from the viewpoint of an imaginary reporter. After seeing through his eyes what it will be like to travel in the world of 2081, we will return to our own time, and I will present the reasoning that has led to my particular view of the future.

First, a chronology and a rationale. In the 1980s the breakout of humanity into space seems like a tremendous step, one that will challenge all our abilities in engineering and in cooperative organization. We view it much as people up to 1957 viewed the notion of launching satellites to orbit the Earth. But within a few years after the first space colonies are built, the construction of new ones will become routine, commonplace. Costs will fall dramatically as newer, simpler construction techniques are found by trial and evaluation and as automated mass production reduces the price of habitat components. In the same way, before 1957 the launching of an orbital satellite was beyond the capabilities even of the greatest nations, while less than fifteen years later it could be carried out even by an organization as small as a university. Tokyo University has maintained a complete space program since the 1960s, and has launched satellites, routinely and successfully, on a budget less than 1 percent of NASA's, since 1970. The construction of space colonies will follow a similar pattern, so that by the year 2010 or thereabouts there will be many space colonies in existence and many new ones being constructed each year.

Most of the early space colonies will orbit no further away than the moon, so that their residents can talk with people on Earth without the intolerable signaling delays that occur over longer distances. But some new colonies will be built in the asteroid belt itself; there the availability of materials will reduce construction costs so much as to outweigh the disadvantages of communications time lags. There won't be economic incentives for going much farther away, so we can assume that even a century from now most humans will be living either on Earth or on space colonies within the pancake-shaped region that includes the orbits of Venus, Earth, Mars, and most of the asteroids. I call that region, including its planets and moons, the "Inner System," because large as it is, most of the planets in the solar system are far beyond it. Will anyone live outside that Inner System a century from now? I believe so, and I'll argue by historical analogy what sorts of people they will be. A very small number are likely to be criminals, revolutionaries, or members of extremist sects, eking out a precarious existence on the fringes of civilization, as such groups have done historically. But in their nature such groups will need to prey on, attack, or obtain converts from society, and therefore won't go far beyond its physical boundaries. Dependent as they will be on society, they are also unlikely to be large-scale independent builders of new colonies; indeed, if any are as self-destructive as the notorious "Jonestown" sect, they won't leave anything for the future beyond lurid headlines and a bad taste.

Those people who go far outside the Inner System and there found large, successful, permanently stable colonies are likely to be at the other extreme of human character, strongly motivated toward peaceful cooperation and constructive hard work. They won't make the enormous effort to go so far away unless they find something fundamentally intolerable about their place of origin. In the past, the search for freedom of worship (as in the case of the Plymouth colonists) or freedom to indulge in social practices that were illegal or nonconforming (polygamy, in the case of the Mormon colonists) could only be satisfied by emigration. Hard-working people holding such unorthodox ideas were among the most determined colonists of new lands. They were far more reluctant to give up and return when faced by the hardships of new frontiers than were those emigrants who left home merely because of restlessness or a spirit of adventure, because the nonconformists were driven by the desire to escape a disapproving Old World no less than to arrive at a New. Of course, these days large portions of human society are more tolerant of unusual religious or social ideas. But there is still one custom that is almost universal, far-reaching in its insistence on conformity, and unacceptable to many—warfare. It would probably be necessary in 2081 to go very far away indeed to be absolutely certain of escaping warfare under all conceivable conditions.

To be specific and to establish our chronology, let's suppose that by 2020, some thirty years after surveys of distant space by sensitive, space-borne telescopes have begun, many more asteroids have been discovered than we know now, and that some are farther away than Pluto. A few may be in circular orbits highly inclined to the plane where the planets circulate. We can imagine that one such body is called Fox Aggregate, and that it is a cold, silent mass of billions of tons of ice, rock, metals, and simple hydrocarbons. All that we now know of the solar system suggests that there must be many objects, as yet unknown, that satisfy those conditions. We suppose that an expedition is formed to colonize the region near Fox Aggregate, and that it begins its voyage in the year 2023. The goal of the expedition is to found a permanent human society on the principles of nonviolence, free of weapons and so remote that it will never be troubled by the continuing wars of Earth. Many of the colonists may be members of the Society of Friends (Quakers), because Quakers shun warfare to the point that many of them have gone to prison rather than serve as soldiers. A number of the colonists may already be residents of colonies near the Earth, and for them life in another space colony will hold no great surprises. To pay for their ships and equipment, the 20,000 families who are to make the journey draw out their life savings and sell their homes, vehicles, and heavy furniture, retaining personal possessions and family heirlooms. At average United States figures, that is enough to raise a capital of several billion (1981) United States dollars, an amount roughly equal to one year's NASA budget.

The voyage is made in old but serviceable ships, bought cheap because they are no longer economically competitive on the routes between colonies of the Inner System. (In close analogy, any commercial jet airplane that was the pride of an airline only twenty years ago can now be purchased, in good working order, at a tiny fraction of its replacement cost.) The expedition begins its journey in 2023 and arrives in 2028. The colonists bring with them small-scale equipment for mining Fox Aggregate, processing its material into pure elements, and making it into machines that can mine and process further material and form it into the pressure shells, the mirrors, the windows, and the interior architecture of space colonies. They use the techniques of automation and machine replication that I outlined in the "Space Colonies" chapter of Part II. They build their colonies according to well-established, tried and true designs, such as the geometry I described both in "Space Colonies" and in *The High Frontier*. The colonies built near Fox Aggregate must differ from those near Earth in only one respect: several hundred kilometers from each there must be a large paraboloidal collector mirror to gather the faint sunlight of that remote region and concentrate it to the same intensity that we are used to on Earth. Each colony must be at the focus of one such mirror. Let us imagine that there are eight colonies in all forming Fox Cluster. They differ greatly in climate, but in all of them the trees are high and the bird and animal populations are well stabilized by 2081, the year that we will take as the beginning of our story. For the 80,000 inhabitants of the Cluster, the mirrors bring up the solar intensity so that in each of their eight colonies the sun shines as brightly as it does on Earth.

Although the Cluster is remote, it is by no means cut off from the knowledge and ideas of the Inner System. Just as in our own time, countries that are distant from the centers of civilization pay small charges to obtain copyrighted books, films, television, and musical recordings, Fox Cluster in 2081 pays to be sent radio and television programs as they occur, and decodes binary signals to display news, articles, and photographs on video, or print them as books and magazines. All that information flows by way of narrow laser beams that do not have to be powerful. Fox Cluster can pay for such necessities from either of two sources: income from investment capital left on Earth when its residents emigrated, or new income from the sale in the Inner System of works of art from the Cluster.

While information flows from the center of civilization to the Cluster, there is a small counterflow, not only of the Cluster's artistic works, but of a few of its people. We can imagine that each year some, perhaps twenty or so, of the Cluster's young college graduates choose to leave it, on reverse emigration voyages to the Inner System. Those are the few who are passionately devoted to one of the sciences, or to music or dance or one of the visual arts, and who must go to the center of civilization to obtain the most advanced education and the stimulation of competition with others as talented as themselves. To give freedom for emigration to those who desire it, and to obtain from the Inner System products too complex or too novel to be made locally, we suppose that the Cluster contracts for a single round-trip voyage each year by a small ship. And that's where our fictional reporter comes in. The writer, Eric C. Rawson, boards that ship in 2081, but not as an emigrant. We can suppose that he makes his trip to attend to family business on Earth, and that he writes a series of articles on his trip for a magazine published in the Cluster. Eric Rawson sees the Earth of 2081 from a viewpoint as fresh as ours would be, because he comes to it from a place as remote in distance from the center of 2081's civilization as our own is remote from it in time. Each of the chapters in Part III begins with one of his imaginary articles, signed with the byline E.C.R., and concludes with a factual commentary of my own.

Space Travel

FOR THE voyage to the Inner System in 2081 Fox Cluster chartered the *Dandridge M. Cole*, a small ship designed for cargo and passenger service over long-distance routes. I boarded the *Cole* in her berth at Fox Alpha, stowed my luggage, and was joined in my stateroom by friends for a bon voyage champagne party. On a wall there was a large photograph of the *Cole*. The ship's hull was a disc with a diameter five times as large as its thickness, and the disc was joined by thin struts to a very large parabolic mirror. The *Cole* had no windows, because like all other ships designed for long voyages she had to be shielded against cosmic radiation. As a substitute for windows a number of video cameras were mounted outside the ship, and the view from any of them could be selected for display on the screen in my stateroom. There were framed paintings on the other walls, and I was mystified when I glanced at one of them and found that it had changed during the past few minutes from a Turner to a Picasso. One of my guests, I discovered, had been playing with a control panel at my bedside, and it could call up for showing more than a hundred thousand works of art from the museums of the Inner System.

All the staterooms and the public rooms of the ship were at the rim of the disc, and the ship was rotating in her berth about a line through the disc's center, as a wheel rotates on an axle. That line was the axis of rotation, and "up" was the direction toward that axis, wherever I happened to be standing in the ship. Knowing that, I understood why the floor of my stateroom curved slightly to join two walls that angled slightly toward each other. But at first I was puzzled by another peculiarity: along the direction parallel to the axis the floor gently sloped downward at an angle of one in twenty, and all the furniture was placed flat on the floor so that even the tabletops sloped. I only learned the reason hours later, after the "all ashore" bells had rung, my friends had left, the ship had cast off from its dock and had slowly drifted away some distance. Then the main drive was started, giving the Cole a steady, constant acceleration along her axis of one-twentieth of a gravity. I called up on the screen a view of our departure as seen from the dock, and from that viewpoint I could see that we were speeding up, gradually, along the direction of the Cole's axis. The ship moved slowly at first, then faster, steadily accelerating until it disappeared from sight. I knew that same steady acceleration would continue unabated for six weeks, half the duration of our voyage. Then the ship would be turned end-for-end and we would decelerate for another six weeks, so that our speed would drop until it finally matched the orbital speed of our goal, a station called Freeport Seven in low orbit above the Earth. If the decks of the Dandridge M. Cole had not been built with that peculiar slope, we passengers would have spent the entire twelve weeks leaning slightly toward the acceleration, so as to stay upright. As it was, the slope and our acceleration just compensated, so that pens and cigarette lighters had no tendency to roll off the tables, and the water in our glasses remained level with respect to the tabletops.

Within five minutes after our main drive had started we were several kilometers away from Fox Alpha, and I could see the green grass and blue water inside the central sphere, as well as the growing crops and brown cultivated soil in the greenhouses outside. The video system of the Cole was clearly more advanced than those of the Cluster, and the main screen in my stateroom covered an entire wall. It showed colors accurately even over the contrast range from the delicate greens and blues in the colony to the deep black of space and the pinpoints of starlight. An hour after our departure, Alpha had shrunk in the viewscreen until it was just a dot of light, and soon after that the bright curved rim of its main thousand-kilometer mirror showed at the edges of the screen. An hour later the mirrors of all eight colonies were visible, and I began exploring.

I found the controls for music, for access to the ship's computer, and for the lighting, and then investigated the private bath and physical-fitness suite that adjoined my stateroom. An instruction card left in my suite explained that there were only minimal services aboard the *Cole*, because she carried a flight crew but no pursers, waiters, or other service personnel. We passengers were asked to throw our dirty towels and linens in a laundry chute. The rest of the cleaning would be done by the "pups," small robots that would roll in while we were away at meals.

It was time, then, for me to join the other passengers in the wardroom, for a reception where we would meet the crew. The wardroom, like the staterooms and lounges, was located at the rim of the *Cole*, at Earthnormal gravity. Of the passenger areas, only a zero-gravity gymnasium and a low-gravity pool were located away from the rim, close to the rotation axis. I followed the sounds of music, laughter, and the clink of glasses to the wardroom. It was large and was decorated like the living room of a seaside mansion on Earth. One entire wall was a holographic "window," and just outside it the surf broke with a rhythmic crash on a beach of white sand, dazzling in what seemed to be sunlight. When I walked close to the window I was startled to hear, over the noise of the party, the occasional cries of seagulls. The scents of the ocean, salty and tangy, drifted in to reinforce the illusion. I turned, rejoined the crowd, and met the three crew members, Captain Koshinsky, his wife and first officer, Janet Koshinsky, and the second officer, Will Nelson.

The captain took the occasion to explain to us the routine of the voyage and something of the workings of the ship. He told us that the *Cole* carried only a small reactor as a standby energy source, normally unused. All the main power for the ion drive and the ship's electrical systems came from a laser generating station orbiting close to the sun. In that way an enormous amount of power could be put into the ship's drive without our having to carry the heavy mass of a high-power reactor. The laser station had the exact schedule of our planned trajectory—notifying it of any changes would take two days by a signal traveling at the speed of light— so the *Cole* had to be at the right place at the right time to receive the intense, narrow power beam. That, he went on, was why our tickets all carried a warning about "Absolutely no deviation from departure time." He called up for us on the large wardroom screen a view forward. It showed the sun as a dim yellow pinpoint, and the laser station as an intense red dot alongside it. Even on the screen the laser appeared far brighter than the sun, and numbers beside the image told the huge amounts of filtering the video had been forced to insert in order not to be burned out by the laser's intensity.

Nelson took over the briefing to explain the sounds we'd hear on the trip. The ion drive itself made no noise at all, he said. The only mechanical sounds we'd hear would be from pumps and blowers, and most of the time those would be drowned out by low-level nondescript noises from the intercom system, recordings that would be played continuously both to mask occasional noises and to prevent long periods of total silence, which could be psychologically disturbing.

The first officer warned us then that the control room, the electronics bays, and everything else vital to the ship's operation would be off limits to passengers. Later, while exploring the corridors and the layout of the ship, I saw the security system in operation. Any crewperson who came out into the passenger area and then returned had to speak to a computer for voiceprint and stress analysis, while holding both hands against a glass plate that checked the fingerprint patterns. The captain happened to be going through that procedure as I came by. Usually, he told me, it was no more than a twenty-second bore, but this time he'd been unfortunate enough to miss a response, so the computer was grilling him thoroughly, to his obvious annoyance.

I was curious about the food on board and prompt to find my way to the main dining room when the bell sounded for dinner. The room was circular and set up with four tables, each for six people. At one side there was a buffet table, and we served ourselves before choosing dinner partners. The scene was dramatic and formal, with soft lighting overhead, and on every table there were thick fine linens, beautiful china and crystal, and candles. We seemed to be in a revolving restaurant, looking outward on all sides from a great height, through panoramic windows, to the lights of a city surrounded by water with mountains beyond. I recognized San Francisco, but suspected that our vantage point was rather higher than any building allowed by the city's codes. The first officer happened to be at my table and told me to look well at the scenery because I wouldn't be seeing it again. The ship's repertoire of illusions was great enough that we'd find a different scene with every meal: sometimes it would be the view from a mountaintop ski chalet in the Alps, sometimes from a tower restaurant in one of the other cities of Earth, and occasionally from a ship or a drifting balloon.

The comfortable chairs, the soft lighting, and the elegance of the table settings all tended to promote a long leisurely meal, but I couldn't say as much for the food. Though we'd just come from the Cluster, where plenty of fresh vegetables were picked every day whatever the season, here on the ship every dish had clearly come from the *Cole's* frozen-food lockers. Janet Koshinsky explained apologetically that the automated kitchen on the ship could only cope with the standard prearranged packages it was programmed for, and lacked the flexibility to recognize and prepare fruits and vegetables straight out of the trees and the soil. But none of us had reason to fault the wines and the brandies that had made the trip from the vineyards of Earth, and we lingered over them as we talked. I grew curious about the extent of the restaurant view illusion, and when I opened a window, sure enough, there floated in the moisture of fog and the distant sounds of foghorns and street noises. I considered a moment and realized they were easy to simulate.

Next morning before breakfast I tried a phone call to the Cluster, but found that the time lag was already four seconds: we must have been over a half-million kilometers away. From then on, it seemed, we'd have to depend on radiograms or dictated recorded messages for all our communications; during the next twelve weeks the *Cole* would be a tiny world of her own, and we on board would be talking only with each other. With my attention forced to turn inward in that way upon the *Cole* and all she contained, I began wondering about our cargo. Captain Koshinsky helped me one day to call up the available information from the ship's computer, but I found that the detailed itemizations of the passengers' checked-baggage lists were unavailable, quite properly, because of privacy conventions.

Of the cargo consignments, item #20 was typical:

"17 paintings in oil by Jean Sampson, of Bryn Mawr colony. Addressee: Rumbin Galleries, 8th Level, 2375 Park Avenue, New York City . . ."

There were several more consignments of that kind, and then:

"#33. Quantity 453 wood carvings from Artists' Cooperative, Fox Alpha. Addressee: Outworld Arts, Code 17SW 25 UK, London, England."

Farther down the list there was an entry of a different kind:

"#55. Caution, Sealed Container, Triple Seals complying with Interplanetary Shipping Convention for biologically active materials. Contains high-yield corn seeds. Shipper: Cluster College Agricultural Experimental

Station, Fox Delta. Addressee: Quarantine Laboratory, Colony 2746, New General Catalogue."

I knew the ship would bring a return cargo of the latest electronic gadgets from the Inner System, together with video discs and high-density data packages. The Captain told me there would also be a few tons of chemical elements that were rare in the Cluster, and a few tons more of exotic high-strength artificial materials developed by Earth's military aerospace industries. He followed that with a question as to why the Cluster wasn't importing the Inner System's newest and hottest consumer products: household robots. I defended the Cluster's legal prohibition of the import of robots by pointing out that ours was a stable society with a very slow population growth rate, no poor people, and no need for a large increase in industrial productivity. It was the consensus within the Cluster that letting in robots would do more harm than good. I was willing to concede that on Earth a much better case could be made for the necessity of higher levels of automation. Certainly the Earth's environment, with its unpredictable weather, wide and harsh variations in climate, and generally poorer availability of cheap energy, made it necessary to use more complicated machinery to equal the living standard that was universal in all the space colonies, including those of Fox Cluster.

Early in the voyage I asked the first officer for information on the ship's library. When she learned my taste in books, she recommended Treadwell's *Travels on Old Earth*. Back in my cabin I asked the library computer for hard copy of Chapter One, but instead of getting something out of a slot, I was answered by "Press READY on slate." There was a thin, blank, white panel, the size of a sheet of office stationery, resting on a frame at the console. Indeed it had a small square marked READY on its corner, and when I pressed it the panel displayed the title, author, and so on in black on white, various data-search key words, and the phrase, BOOK LOADED. I found that from then on I could take that "slate" anywhere and have it display any page of the book on command. The display was a liquid crystal, and evidently the slate's memory was capable of storing more than a hundred thousand words.

By the first week into the flight I'd become acquainted with the other eighteen passengers. Most were headed for graduate school, and a few of the rest would study with particular artists or musicians. One couple, a young man and woman fresh out of college, were headed for work on a big ranch in Argentina. Their lives revolved around horses, and they'd decided to settle where their work could be done in the saddle. I'd recognized one girl by sight even at the first reception: Terry Rowe, whose pictures had been in all the magazines of the Cluster. Her photo and hologram portfolios had made the rounds of the modeling agencies in New York, and she'd been offered a place by one of the best of them. One afternoon, when I'd gone to the full-gravity exercise courts for some racquet ball practice, I encountered a young ballet dancer named Sandra Thatcher. She was just entering a leap, high in the air, so gracefully that it was hard to believe that we were in full gravity. She told me she was going to study with a ballet company; her desire to excel in Dance (I sensed the capital letter) was so overpowering that no concern of lost friendships at home could stand against it. After I came to know most of the other passengers, I realized that each one of them had a similar ambition: to rise to the top in some profession. The same sort of drive must have pushed those sorts of people off the farms in the old days and pulled them to the cities.

After the first hours of our trip, we passengers hadn't been disturbed by any real-time announcements from the flight crew, but I'd formed the habit of checking the video each day. Often I'd find a message from the captain, showing a high-magnification view of a planet or one of the larger comets. Several weeks into the journey that routine was interrupted by a chime from the communicator, followed by Captain Koshinsky's voice:

"I'm making this real-time call because you may want to see something unique and historic. We're the only people at a high enough solar latitude to get a close-up view. In a few minutes I'm going to shut down the thrusters, because we'll need to be drifting without acceleration to assemble the composite telescope. While we're drifting the floors will slope again, as they did when we were docked." He got back to us an hour later, and by then most of us were in the wardroom.

"Here's a view of the composite telescope," Koshinsky went on. (The video showed an array of mirrors at widely scattered points throughout a circular region near the ship.)

"If you locate small mirrors at many points over the surface of a paraboloid, you can fool the incoming light waves into acting as if the paraboloid was continuous. That makes a telescope with high resolution—it can pick out fine detail at a great distance. I've set up this mirror array so you can see Lodestar One, the manned interstellar ship. She'll take three years to build up to her maximum speed, and another three to slow down again. You may not have kept up with the news reports, but there was a System-wide call for trainee candidates to be in her crew. More than a million people applied, and out of that number five thousand passed all the selections and exams and are now on board. They're already traveling faster than human beings have ever gone before. Right now the ship is close enough that we can make out the flags on her side."

The video scene shifted, and for a moment all we saw was the blackness of space, brilliant with stars. Then suddenly a spacecraft appeared, a sphere with appendages. The star images turned to streaks, and I realized that the telescope must be tracking the craft as it sped past us. The angle of view changed visibly, and within seconds the image fuzzed out and was lost.

"We can't move the primary mirrors," said the captain, "so I could only track *Lodestar One* for a few seconds. We were lucky to see her at all. I'll freeze the replay."

This time the rapid motion halted as the spacecraft centered in the field. The still picture expanded until we could see that the surface of the sphere was covered by dozens of painted flags, their colors brilliant in the sunshine.

"There's a flag for every nation in the System," said the captain. "I'd like to communicate with the ship, but she's already moving so fast that her communications frequencies have shifted out of the band that our standard radios can cover. Of course there's special equipment set up back at data center that's able to communicate with her all the way to Proxima Centauri. In the old days of short hops there'd have been something called mission control, but *Lodestar One* is on her own. There's no controlling a ship remotely when she's light years away."

In the next hour, while the elements of the telescope were being collected and returned to the ship, we watched replays at various magnifications, and there were some hot discussions on the still-unsolved problem of whether intelligent life exists elsewhere in our galaxy. Then the thrusters resumed their steady push, the direction of our "gravity" returned to what we had become used to, and we went on with the studies, games, sports, and talk that filled our days.

Many passengers had been studying Common Basic for most of the trip, and by the last few weeks we had carried on all our mealtime conversations in that useful though inelegant language. Basic is not as logical as any of the older artificial languages, such as Esperanto or Interlingua, but it is more politically acceptable, because it employs words from every major language grouping on Earth. The crew warned us, though, that only one percent of the people on Earth spoke it, so we could only hope, as we practiced, that the one percent would include most of those we would meet.

In the last few days before we docked I gave up studying entirely, because there was just too much to see and hear. Whenever I turned on the video there were new scenes from the ship's telescope log: ships of every description and colonies in all shapes and sizes, most of them bigger than any of the islands in Fox Cluster. The radio and television channels were crowded with a babble of voices in hundreds of different languages, and there was a brisk traffic of datagrams between the passengers and the Earth. My host would be a distant relative, Bill Tehaney, whose daughter Ellen would meet me in Cincinnati, Ohio. To reach Cincinnati airport I would have to use many different modes of transportation within a few hours. First the *Cole* would dock a few hundred miles above the Earth at an orbiting station, Freeport Seven. There I would leave the spacecraft and, a bit later, board the shuttle. The shuttle, a winged, rocket-powered vehicle, would take me down through the atmosphere to a spaceport near the equator of the Earth, in the Atlantic ocean. After another wait I would board a supersonic jet that would climb several miles into the atmosphere again and take me to Cincinnati. I hoped that with all these transfers my checked baggage would find its way to the same place and not, for example, end up outbound for the asteroid belt!

The crew advised us to learn the locator and security identifier methods that were so common on Earth. In most nations we would have no choice, but in a few we could choose to abstain. When I asked Will Nelson why those systems had been developed, he told me that the coded anklets had been introduced as a more convenient version of credit cards and had soon become status symbols. Someone equipped with an anklet could receive phone calls anywhere and could pick up merchandise in a store and walk out with it, free of the delay of waiting in a checkout line. As another visible sign of special privilege, the anklet wearer could walk directly on board a plane without stopping either at a ticket counter or a gate. It was only some time later, Nelson told me, that the records of position made possible by the anklets became legal evidence in courts of law. His advice to me was direct: unless I just couldn't stand the notion, I would be a lot better off letting the immigration guards at Freeport Seven put an anklet on me. If I didn't, I would be annoyed by time-wasting delays at every national border, and I'd be hassled at every residential town, museum, and shopping enclave.

High above the Earth we separated from our huge light-gathering mirror. It was no longer needed, and would interfere with our maneuvers in the crowded shipping lanes of low orbit. On the *Cole*'s next trip out the crew would rendezvous with the mirror and use it for the next deep-space voyage. In the final days of our trip we circled the Earth many times, spiraling deeper and deeper toward low orbit just above the atmosphere. The planet was gorgeous, brilliant with contrasting colors of blue, green, and white, but I couldn't get over feeling uncomfortable at the thought of water and atmosphere nakedly exposed to the vacuum of space, with no surrounding container. Finally, when we were so low and moving so fast that Earth's bulk cut off our sunlight half the time, and gave us a sunrise or sunset every hour, I could see the flashing signal lights of the Freeport Seven station. Ours wasn't the only vessel near Freeport Seven. Of the many others, there were angular, ungainly spacecraft and, very different from them, the arriving and departing shuttles. All of those were streamlined, and they all had large rocket motors, but their designers had solved the problem of atmospheric braking and reentry in different ways. Some of the shuttles had tapering wings permanently fixed in position. Others had retractable wings and did their braking high in the atmosphere by extending special panels or parachutes.

As we drew close to the station I made out its many docking ports. Soon we maneuvered so close to one of them that on the video screen the station blotted out the view of the stars and the Earth. Then there was an announcement that we had docked (I hadn't felt it), and I gathered together my hand baggage to leave the *Cole*, my home for the last three months. As soon as we entered Freeport Seven territory, by floating out of the ship and then walking down a long corridor to the one-gravity level, we encountered Security. Following instructions I took off my shoes and waited, and in a few seconds a computer voice invited me to step forward. I passed through an automatic door to a small room where two male guards, tall, strongly built, and smiling, were waiting. They were coffee-colored and looked splendid in their Freeport Seven "Constabulary" Bermuda shorts and tall helmets. As one of them attached a slim golden band on my ankle, I checked on Will Nelson's advice by asking what would happen if I refused to accept the anklet.

"You'd have to stay in quarantine rather than being free to roam the terminal and the duty-free shops, for starters. Then, in most places on Earth, heat-sensor alarms would sound as you entered shops, museums, residential towns, and planes. You'd be in for a grilling by the local cops, especially if you had the bad luck to be somewhere near the scene of a crime."

I was also curious as to why the identifier was placed on an ankle rather than on a wrist, and was told there were reasons both of vanity and of practicality. The anklet was less noticeable than a wristband, and less likely to clash with choices of clothing or jewelry. Moreover, it gave a stronger signal, because most of the security pickups were hidden under floors. I asked whether criminals could fake the identifiers and was told:

"Babies aren't criminals, and in most countries the first anklet goes on before a child learns to walk. Anyway, the anklet changes its code-response occasionally, in a way a criminal couldn't easily predict. By the way, you're too young and healthy to need a rescue squad, but if you ever do have a medical emergency or find yourself in a threatening situation, try to grab the anklet and pull hard on it—you'll get help fast. Okay, Mr. Rawson, you can walk out now. Have a good trip and enjoy your stay."

Freeport Seven was a relatively quiet place, because there were no public-address announcements. Each passenger was given a boarding card that was also a radio receiver, and all the announcements about particular shuttle or spaceship flights were made only to those passengers who had the corresponding receiver-cards. But at the same time the orbital station was the most impersonal place I'd ever seen. Except for the few passengers from the *Cole* I knew nobody, and the groups that passed me, looking as lost and displaced as I was, were of every imaginable color, stature, and style of clothing, and were talking languages I'd never heard before. It was a relief when the voice of my receiver-card told me it was time to board the orbital shuttle to Earth. I walked up a spiral ramp, with my weight slowly decreasing, until finally I could float through the access corridor and belt myself down to my assigned seat. It would be only a half-hour flight from orbit down through the atmosphere to the PPR Spaceport, named for its location at the St. Peter and St. Paul Rocks, east of Brazil.

—E.C.R.

EVEN A century from now only a few humans will live beyond the Inner System, the disc-shaped volume of space, roughly one light hour in diameter, that includes Jupiter, the asteroid belt, and all the inner planets. Most of the materials that can be used easily for construction in space are within that volume, and it basks in brilliant sunshine, the free source of inexhaustible energy that will power our civilization in space. From the history of transportation and from our present technical knowledge we can predict the transport systems that will carry people and cargo through and beyond the Inner System. Bulk freight has always traveled cheaply and slowly, whereas passengers and high-value products have traveled expensively and quickly, and so it will still be, for the same economic reasons, in 2081.

Every drive system that can work in space, even a "solar sail," that responds to the pressure of sunlight, works on the same basic principle, Newton's law of action and reaction. One of its consequences is that to push a spacecraft in one direction, one must throw something in the other direction. What's thrown is called the "reaction mass," and the speed that it's thrown with is called the "exhaust velocity." The amount of the push or "thrust" on the spacecraft is just the exhaust velocity times the rate, in kilograms per second, of expelling the reaction mass. (Rocketeers call that the "flow rate.") That suggests using the highest possible exhaust speed, so as to get away with a very low flow rate, but there's a catch: it takes power to accelerate the reaction mass to the exhaust velocity, and that power has to come from somewhere. For a given flow rate, the thrust only goes directly with the exhaust velocity, but the power required goes up much faster, as the square of that velocity. So, for a given mission, there's an optimum compromise: one chooses the exhaust velocity high enough to get an adequate thrust at a moderate flow rate, but not so high that the power demands become exorbitant.

In the case of chemical rockets, once the chemicals have been chosen there's no more room for compromise. What the rocketeers call "big dumb boosters" that lift multikiloton loads off the launch pads use kerosene and liquid oxygen for maximum thrust. To get that thrust within the low power that's available from the kerosene-oxygen reaction, those boosters gulp tens of tons of fuel per second and run their tanks dry in a minute or so. Hydrogen burning in oxygen gives more power per ton, and it's used by vehicles like the NASA space shuttle to develop a smaller thrust but over a much longer time.

Once a spacecraft is in orbit, just a small thrust is enough to move it to a new location, so one doesn't have to use chemical rockets for the task. The lighter the spacecraft, the faster the acceleration for a given thrust, so it's best to use a fairly high exhaust velocity (this reduces the amount of reaction mass that must be carried, and so lightens the spacecraft) and to obtain the necessary power from a remote source, in the form of light waves, to eliminate the mass of an on-board energy supply.

For the transport of cargo by unmanned freighters between points of the Inner System, the engine that now looks most promising is the "mass-driver" that I discussed earlier. Its efficiency is high, it runs on solar electric power, and it can use almost any material from liquid oxygen to crushed asteroidal rock as reaction mass. Oxygen is surprisingly abundant beyond the Earth, being the commonest element in the crust of the moon and in the silicate rocks of the asteroids.

For high-speed passenger travel to the farthest reaches of our solar system we need a higher exhaust speed, one or two percent of the velocity of light, and much, much more power. The *Dandridge M. Cole* of Eric's voyage is taken to be a 100-ton vessel, with roughly the same empty weight as a Boeing 747. Even if its engines operate at close to 100 percent efficiency they will have to produce an amount of power equal to about one-fifth of the installed electric generator capacity we now have in the entire United States. To do that with a nuclear fusion reactor, even with a hundred years of development time, seems a tall order. Fortunately, there's no need for it.

There is already a proven technique for accelerating particles to a percent or two of the speed of light. It's called the "ion drive," and it demands only a source of electric power. It seems to me that the most effective way to bring that power to the distant reaches of the solar system will be to combine two systems we already understand, the carbon-dioxide laser and composite optics.

Working under NASA contract, a research laboratory called Mathematical Sciences Northwest has designed an eight-ton, carbon-dioxide laser for use in space. It would be put in orbit to soak up solar energy and turn it into a megawatt of continuous laser power output. With automation, many thousands of identical units of that kind could be turned out inexpensively by a factory in space. An array of them, orbiting in a disc formation some thirty kilometers in diameter, could send a beam of laser light to a focus of only one kilometer in size even as far away as Pluto. The beam would be powerful enough to drive the *Cole*, and it would weigh nothing. The principle involved is that of composite optics, and it can be used either to send out a strong, narrow light beam or to make a telescope that can resolve fine detail.

The Smithsonian Institution is already using the same principle at its observatory in Flagstaff, Arizona. There the Smithsonian has installed a composite-optics telescope consisting of nine large mirrors, which maintain their correct relative positions even in the Earth's gravity, as they track its rotation. We can already convert a transmitted laser light beam to electricity with fair efficiency, and we can almost certainly build converters for that purpose which will be both very efficient and of light weight, given the better part of a century for the task.

Interstellar travel is the most demanding design problem we can imagine in rocketry (but wait a few thousand years and our descendants will be saying the same thing about intergalactic travel). The fusion of hydrogen to helium, done with near-perfect efficiency, could generate an exhaust velocity about one-seventh the speed of light. A multistage rocket powered by that reaction could bring a payload to a fair fraction of light speed, but the ratio of payload to initial mass would be very small. Strictly within the bounds of known physics, there is a way that we could achieve a speed close to that of light and do so while carrying a substantial payload. That is by using a *really* potent energy source: the reaction of matter with antimatter. There's no difficulty about making the reaction go (indeed, when matter touches antimatter, there's no way to prevent their reacting) and in the reaction a full 100 percent of the mass energy mc^2 of the reactants goes into power. In contrast, fusion or fission reactions convert only about one percent of the mass energy into usable form.

For the engines of *Lodestar One*, the interstellar ship that passes the *Cole*, as for all rocket engines, there is an optimum exhaust velocity. In the case of such an interstellar ship, that velocity is close to the speed of light, and therefore the best "material" to exhaust is the quantum of light, the photon. That light quantum could be at any frequency that's technically convenient, from the low frequency of microwaves to the high frequency of laser light.

In practice, it's a good thing *Lodestar One*'s flight is a century away— there's plenty to do in the meantime. We can make antimatter now, but only an atom at a time, by the conversion of energy to matter in the particle accelerators that are used by physicists to study the properties of elementary particles. There are very large machines of that kind, measuring several kilometers in extent, at locations in the United States, Switzerland, and Germany. They are designed for pure research in physics, and are not at all efficient for the production of antimatter, but it seems almost certain that machines optimized for antimatter production will be built in the future. The reason is unfortunate, but it's consistent with world history: in any long-continued cold-war situation the nations confronting each other maintain large military budgets and devote much effort and money to developing the most advanced weapons, even if those weapons later pass into obsolescence without being used. The reaction of matter with antimatter would be a hundred times as powerful, weight for weight, as a hydrogen bomb, and a beam of antimatter particles would instantly destroy everything it touched. Yet, as in the cases of radar, the jet engine and microelectronics, technology developed for military purposes can be turned to peaceful goals as well, and I anticipate that once antimatter machines have been perfected, they will be copied to produce the fuel for interstellar ships. Containing and controlling solid antimatter once it's made would be, oddly enough, an easier problem than making it. It could be pushed and pulled by electric and magnetic fields and evaporated into gas by concentrated laser light, all without the need for a material container.

While spaceships driven by mass-drivers and powered by solar-cell arrays are a sure thing for 2081, and laser-powered ion-drive ships are a very safe bet, interstellar craft of nearly the speed of light are much more speculative. Yet we already have a fair idea of how to build them, and in guessing that they'll exist by 2081, I'm mindful that the prophets of technology have generally erred in the direction of timidity.

Turning now to the human experience of travel, spaceflight a century from now will be a far more luxurious experience than is air travel today. Despite the best efforts of the airlines, jet travel leaves the average passenger cramped in a tiny space for hours. Flight across the sea of space may have its hardships, but at least it will restore the elbowroom, the leisure, and the time for human interaction that the older generation tells us was so wonderful about the age of ocean liners, qualities that are preserved today only in cruise ships. Although spaceships will have to be light in weight, they can be large and comfortable in volume.

While one can't be sure which of several alternate solutions to each technical problem of the 2081 spaceships will prevail, the question of their crews is more predictable. A ship like the *Dandridge M. Cole* could easily be controlled throughout its entire voyage by an on-board computer, assisted only by occasional radioed commands. Indeed, that's the way our planetary spacecraft, *Mariner*, *Voyager*, *Viking*, and the rest, operate already. There would be some point in having a human crew to make simple repairs, but by 2081 even those tasks could be automated. Yet, I do expect that a passenger vessel will carry a human crew. The reason is the need for a well-defined authority figure to take command and prevent catastrophic conflicts of the kind that might otherwise occur among passengers thrown together in confined quarters during voyages of several months' duration. The history of arctic exploration and our everyday experience in air and water transport make it clear that the captain's responsibility can't be shifted to a computer. We must keep in mind that the gadgets of 2081 will be very different from those we have now, but that the people will be little different from ourselves.

Flying Through the Earth

As the shuttle encountered the tenuous upper reaches of the atmosphere, I could hear a distant murmur of the air streaming by. Over the next few minutes it built up to a roar, muted only by the soundproofing of the cabin, as our miles-per-second orbital speed slowly diminished and the swept-back wings of the shuttle began to get a grip on the air, turning the machine from a spacecraft to an airplane. The video that covered the seatback in front of me explained apologetically that the cabin was designed without windows because of the high temperatures the shuttle had to withstand as its orbital energy was converted to heating the air screaming by outside. Happily, I missed nothing of our entry into the atmosphere, because the video could be switched at my command among views downward toward the Earth, forward over the fuselage from a camera mounted high on the tail, and backward through the plume of incandescent air we were leaving in our wake. As our speed diminished, the gravity of the Earth asserted itself, and I was gradually pressed down in my seat as my weight returned to normal.

The PPR Spaceport was much larger than the orbital station, because it was a transfer point between many shuttle lines and a number of different airlines, serving a quarter of the Earth's population. Along with several hundred other passengers, I boarded a "boomer," a supersonic airliner bound for Cincinnati. The video on the seatback ahead of me was showing an instructional cartoon intended to calm the fears of first-time passengers. The aircraft was quite different from the triangular shuttle. At our takeoff and landing, and during our climb to an altitude of twelve miles, our long, straight wing, tapering toward the tips, would be symmetrically oriented at right angles to our fuselage. At our cruise altitude, the wing would rotate to an acute angle, with the left wingtip forward like an extended arm, and the right wingtip almost at our tail.

With its wing in the takeoff position the plane climbed to full altitude in only fifteen minutes. Five more minutes were enough for the wing to rotate and for the plane to accelerate to its supersonic cruise speed, and then the seat-belts-on picture on the video blinked off, and I got up to explore the cabin. After a few minutes of that, I concluded that I was better off staying in my seat, for the video pictures from the telescopic cameras outside the plane showed me a good deal more than I could see through the small cabin windows. Soon the cabin attendants began walking down the aisles, handing out lunch trays from motorized overhead trolleys that left the aisles clear but lowered fresh trays on command. I'd chosen a non-smoking compartment, so the air was fresh and clean, but it seemed very dry.

Our flight was so far above the weather that it was quite smooth, and at three times the speed of sound it took us only two and a half hours to reach the coastline of North America. We slowed, our wing rotated to its symmetrical orientation straight out to left and right, and we descended until we were barely in the stratosphere. We entered clouds before crossing the coastline, and in them the plane shook and bumped so much that the wings flexed visibly.

Once we were on the ground and had slowed to a moderate speed, the main engines shut down and we taxied silently to the terminal under electric power. A jetway extended toward the plane as soon as we stopped, and beyond the jetway there was a waiting room. It was lined with rows of small carts, and above them a video sign gave instructions: if I knew my way, and only needed the cart to carry my hand luggage, I should take the controller, a small wireless telephone handset, from a cart and speak the word "follow" in any of a hundred different languages. The cart would then trail me anywhere in the air terminal. If I needed to find a taxi or a restaurant or any other point in the terminal, I had only to ask for it. Then the computer, speaking through the wireless phone, would confirm the destination, replying in whatever language I used, and the cart would lead me to it. With this personal service there was no need for public-address announcements in the terminal, and no chance of getting lost. The place was quiet though crowded with people leading or following their carts, and I noticed that the carts avoided collisions by waiting politely for others to pass.

I was looking for someone I'd never met, my distant relative Ellen Tehaney. As soon as I gave her name, the computer told me that she was already in the terminal and that it would inform her of my arrival. Then the cart went off with my carry-on baggage. It was programmed to remain close to its traveler, so whatever my walking speed it never left my sight. On the way through the long corridor to the main terminal, many passengers sat down on the small seats of their carts. Within a few minutes the controller buzzed, and when I held it to my ear a computer voice told me Ellen Tehaney was ten meters ahead. At that moment a light on my controller began giving quick triple flashes, and ahead I saw through the slow-moving crowd a young blond woman whose controller was flashing in the same way.

After greeting each other we made our way through the concourse, but soon my controller buzzed again and its voice told me that my checked baggage had been collected and was now following me. I looked around and discovered that another cart, loaded with my checked baggage, had indeed joined us. According to Ms. Tehaney, the recovery of my checked baggage with no effort on my part was one of the conveniences that came with wearing an anklet. My suitcases had been given personal identity tags up in Freeport Seven, had been handled by automated equipment thereafter, and had been sent to join me by the terminal's main computer.

Next my guide explained that we would travel to Erie on an underground high-speed vehicle called a "floater," which ran in vacuum through a tunnel, supporting itself on magnetic fields. She left her controller at a rack marked "Identity and Location Aids," and soon my carts turned off to a descending moving ramp, where they locked their wheels and rode with us. We emerged in a wide lobby with machines to give us our seat reservations. Ms. Tehaney told me to key in ERIE, PA, and when I did so, the video informed me of the fare that was being charged to my account. It asked if I were traveling alone, and when I answered PARTY OF TWO it requested my companion to step forward. It then gave us cards for our reserved seats together, numbered 47 and 48 on the 15:33 departure from gate 56. We followed the cart through carpeted corridors to the boarding area, a room about the size and shape of a tennis court. We entered at one end, and as I gradually understood the layout of the room, I realized that it was set up to allow very rapid boarding and exit of a long, narrow vehicle. The room was divided down the middle, lengthwise, by a pair of waist-high railings, just far enough apart so that the bare floor between them looked a bit like a bowling alley. The railings ended just in front of us, a few feet from the entrance, and the narrow space between their ends was filled by a fence of the same height, marked "Odd—left; Even—right." Like the rest of the Cincinnati terminal, the whole room outside of the narrow central alley was carpeted, and my two carts rolled

Boarding area for a floater high-speed underground transport system. The passenger-seating "carriage" of the floater car rolls out of the air-lock at the far end into the central fenced area. The fences then sink into the floor to permit passengers to step on or off the carriage conveniently. When all passengers have boarded, the carriage returns through the air-lock into the enclosing shell of the car, which maintains a normal air pressure inside as the car accelerates in vacuum to its cruising speed, as much as thousands of kilometers per hour.

noiselessly over the carpeting to halt at a square marked with our seat numbers. While we waited, I had time to inspect the far end of the alley. There the two parallel railings stopped just short of a mural wall, and between them there was a heavy door, suspended by hinges as massive as those of a bank vault. Ms. Tehaney told me the door was an air lock, separating the ordinary atmospheric pressure of the boarding area from the vacuum of the floater tunnel. The vacuum allowed the floater cars to operate at high speed without air drag. She also told me that the floater car was a long, thin, air-tight cylinder, closed by a solid cap at its front end and by a sealed door at its back end. Inside the cylinder there was a long, narrow framework called a "carriage" to carry the seats, the baggage compartments, and the air-purifying system of the floater. Beyond our view, in the vacuum tunnel, the floater would back up to the closed air-lock door at the end of the boarding area. The floater's outer cylindrical shell would remain in the tunnel, and both its own rear door and the air-lock door of the boarding area would open, allowing the floater's carriage to roll backward out of the shell, with its passengers, onto the floor of the fenced-off area we were standing next to.

As we waited, other passengers arrived to stand in the squares next to us, and a few minutes later, at 15:32, a bell sounded and an overhead sign flashed: "15:32 Arrival—Columbus; 15:33 Departure—Erie and Buffalo." At that moment a soft hissing sound of escaping air sounded from the air lock, and it swung wide. Ellen remarked that the floater companies were able to make a special point of their on-time arrivals, because they never had to worry about the weather.

As soon as the air lock of the boarding area was open, I could see the door of the floater just beyond it, and in a few seconds that too swung wide open. The long narrow aluminum carriage emerged quietly, rolling on small rubber tires, to fill the central alley. As soon as it filled the blocked-off area, the railings slid downward to the floor, and the passengers who were on the carriage got up from their lounge seats, arranged two across. Each pair of seats was made private by circular partitions fore and aft, and just behind each pair there was a baggage compartment, open to either side. At both ends of the carriage were four-person compartments with pairs of seats facing each other across a low table.

Although no one had to hurry, it took only a few moments for the passengers to retrieve their bags and to transfer them to the carts left by those of us who were about to board. It was easy and convenient for them

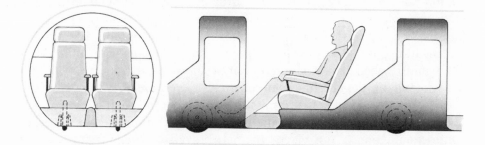

Side and front views of the modular carriage of a floater car. Each module has a baggage compartment, reclining seats for two passengers, and individual television screens. When the carriage rolls into its surrounding cylindrical shell on its small wheels, the modules are isolated from each other, giving privacy and allowing independent control of climate. In flight the shell of the floater car is supported and propelled by magnetic fields.

to leave the carriage and for us to board it, because no one had to queue up: each passenger had only to stand up and take two steps to be in the carpeted area outside the line of the railings. As soon as the arriving passengers in seats 47 and 48 had done so, we stowed my baggage and sat down. It was done much more quickly than boarding a shuttle or a boomer, where all the passengers had to line up and funnel through narrow entrances.

After all the boarding passengers were settled and electric-eye beams showed the alley was clear of people, a bell sounded and the railings slid up from the floor. Then our carriage rolled slowly forward on its rubber tires, through the air lock of the boarding area, through the door of the floater just beyond it, and into the smooth cylindrical metal shell of the floater itself. When the carriage had been swallowed up completely by the floater's outer shell it stopped, and I could hear the airtight door of the floater closing behind us. Then a soft material at the edges of the partition in front of us expanded against the inner wall of the cylindrical shell to make a seal against noise and the movement of air. Ms. Tehaney told me the seal was to permit us to control the climate of our compartment, choose its temperature independent of the others, and smoke, if we chose to, without disturbing anyone else. It would also allow our hearing music or television programs without having to wear earphones to block the sounds from our neighbors.

A voice with the perfect diction of a computer warned us that acceleration was about to begin and advised us to consult the video for the services available during our "flight." The same message was then repeated in Basic, and as it concluded, the partition in front of us, forming a video screen, lit up. It told us how to recline our lounge chairs, adjust the cabin temperature, obtain information on our position and arrival time, and find the schedule for the entertainment channels. There were no windows, and I learned from my guide that a small percentage of the population was sufficiently claustrophobic to avoid the floaters. To minimize the sense of confinement, one of our video channels provided a breathtaking view of our journey, as seen from a helicopter flying low over the landscape, following our exact route on a lovely spring day. The photographic sequence had been speeded up so that each view corresponded in real-time to a point directly above our location deep underground in the floater tunnel. That was, I concluded, a rather easy trick technically, because all the photographic information obtained in the original helicopter flight was stored electronically for easy recall.

After watching that changing scene during the two minutes of our acceleration, I switched to a route map showing Cincinnati and a large body of water to its northeast, with the city of Erie on the shoreline. A white line connected the two cities, running in zigzags through the towns between and then through Erie eastward. I could already see the red dot separating noticeably from Cincinnati. A message flashed:

"Distance to Erie, PA, 260 miles/419 kilometers. En route time 21 minutes." I took out my calculator and concluded we must be cruising at 800 miles per hour, well above the speed of sound. As Ellen Tehaney answered my questions, the red dot moved slowly to the right and upward, following the white line. There was a gentle swaying, but no noise and none of the bumpiness that occurs in atmospheric flight. Sometimes the car rolled a little, and then I would feel my weight increase slightly as we took a banked curve. Because our compartment was entirely private, if I had been alone and sleepy I could have reclined my seat, turned off all the lights, and rested comfortably during the flight.

We passed under Cleveland without even slowing down, and a few minutes later a bell chimed and the video flashed "Arrival in Erie, PA, in five minutes. Deceleration begins in three minutes." We tilted our lounge chairs upright, and soon we began slowing down. I could feel the steady deceleration by my tendency to slide forward just a little in my seat. There were no seat belts, because there could be no bumps or panic stops in the totally predictable environment of the floater's vacuum tunnel. My sensation of slowing down ended when we were evidently at the proper speed for coasting into the Erie terminal area. It resumed for a few seconds as we were brought to a full stop and then reversed onto a curved spur track, and then after another short coasting period, I felt myself pressed back into my seat as we stopped in the tunnel just at the Erie air lock. Our carriage rolled backward through the air-lock door into the Erie boarding area, which was indistinguishable from Cincinnati's except for different photo murals. We left our seats and took a baggage cart from a row in the boarding area. Ms. Tehaney used the cart's controller to call in the license number of her car, so that it would be waiting for us, and then asked for the local weather. The voice from her controller told us there was a snowstorm in progress, with possible snow accumulation of 20 centimeters. The temperature was 10 degrees below zero, and a northwest wind was gusting to 80 kilometers per hour. Evidently the few kilometers to our destination would be far more difficult than the much greater distance we had covered by floater.

—*E. C. R.*

As AIRCRAFT speeds have edged upward to and beyond the speed of sound, designers have found it ever more difficult to build planes that perform well whether flying fast or slowly. For the highest speeds, the wings should be angled sharply to reduce the buildup of shock waves that cause drag, while at takeoff and landing and during climb the old-fashioned straight wings, symmetrically placed at right angles to the body of the aircraft, give much better lift and efficiency. In such fighter-bombers as the U.S. F–111 and the Soviet "Backfire," the problem is solved by constructing the wings in two separate halves, and each wing is rotated from straight-out to angled-backward as the plane makes its transition from climb to high-speed cruise. That solution is expensive, because all the weight of the aircraft must be carried through the swing-wing hinges to the wings themselves; the hinge mechanism must be a heavy, complicated titanium forging equipped with bearings, gears, and hydraulic cylinders.

Engineers have known for some time that one can solve the problem of high-speed flight equally well by angling the wings forward rather than back, and the West German "Hansa" business jet is made in just that way. The engineer R. T. Jones, and others at NASA's Ames Research Center, took that as a clue to help them find a simple, inexpensive solution to the

Fuel-efficient, low-noise supersonic airliner. For takeoff and landing the straight wing is at right angles to the fuselage, as on low-speed aircraft. For supersonic flight the wing rotates to a 60-degree angle, to slice through the air with minimum drag.

problem of designing a plane that could be efficient both at high and low speeds. Their "oblique-wing" aircraft is built with its left and right wings connected to form a single symmetrical one-piece structure, with a simple straight main spar running its full length. The wing is pivoted at its center, where it crosses the fuselage, on a single bearing that is simple and easy to build. At takeoff the wing is straight out at right angles to the line of flight, but for supersonic cruise the wing just pivots—no need for gears or heavy hinges—to an oblique angle. The idea, peculiar though it sounds, makes sense. In 1980 NASA flew its AD–1 oblique-wing research aircraft, and the AD–1 performed very well. I think there is a good chance that the oblique wing may be a practical, economical solution to the aerodynamic problem of designing for both high- and low-speed flight, and if so, the commercial manufacturers will certainly adopt it in much less than a century. I confess also to an author's amusement with the sheer novelty and surprise inherent in the oblique-wing idea.

High-speed travel in a tunnel under the Earth, in vehicles running in vacuum and supported only by magnetic fields, sounds like twenty-fifth-century technology. But magnetic flight is already under active development in Japan and West Germany and should be in routine operation for passenger transport within the 1980s. Later, for some basic reasons, magnetic-flight transport systems will be built underground in evacuated tunnels and will replace many of our short-distance commercial jet routes.

A jet airplane is at its best and most efficient for flights of several thousand miles, but it becomes uneconomical for short trips. The time, effort, and energy of queueing up for takeoff, taking flight, climbing to altitude and levelling off take the better part of half an hour. If the distance is less than about four hundred miles, the plane is hardly up at altitude before it has to start back down again. In the late twentieth-century U.S.A., commercial aircraft are used even for flights of a hundred miles or so, but that's because our public surface-transport system is so poor.

Railed transport systems aren't practical for speeds of more than about twice highway speeds because of the problem of track alignment. And for travelers, their modest advantage in speed is lost in the time necessary to get to and from the station and to wait for the train. Back in the 1930s, during the Depression years, labor costs were very low and the railroads could afford to have gangs of tracklayers adjusting and aligning the tracks on their high-speed runs. In that period it was common for trains in the United States plains states to maintain a speed of 120 mph for hours at a time on scheduled runs. Close to half a century later, there's been little progress in railroad technology. With higher labor costs, the tracks can't be maintained as they used to be, so trains can't go at the same top speeds. Derailments are frequent. As of 1981 the fastest trains in the United States are the Metroliners of the Boston–Washington route. They're comfortable and quiet, but they have problems that show why rail transport is a losing proposition for passenger travel. They shake and sway so violently that there's not a hope of being able to write a letter or do other paperwork on them. In today's more lawless times there are minor acts of vandalism on every Metroliner run—thrown rocks, debris on the tracks. The railroads put out educational documentary films for high schools in an attempt to discourage it. Vandalism is less of a problem in Japan, but to allow the Bullet Trains to go 140 mph, only a little faster than was routine in 1935, the Japanese track gangs have to realign the tracks every night.

A century ago railroad lines symbolized progress, and mayors lobbied to bring new ones through their towns. Now, the noise and dirt of railroads are seen as offenses by a public increasingly aroused over the quality of the environment. But there is a place for high-speed transport that isn't winged—and the place is underground. A tunnel doesn't require the acquisition and destruction of property, and it can provide the ideal environment for a high-speed vehicle—in vacuum, for zero-drag and perfect quiet even at high speed, safe from weather and vandalism. And don't balk at the notion that a station stop will take less than a minute. Even now, the Metroliners, far less efficiently designed for rapid embarkation, operate routinely with station stops of only 45 seconds.

The concept of high-speed wingless "floaters" riding a cushion of magnetic fields is really quite old-fashioned: Emile Bachelet, a French engineer, invented it in the early days of this century and demonstrated a successful working model at a Paris exposition in 1914 to crowds that included the young Winston Churchill. In the 1930s a Princeton professor, Edwin Northrup, carried out experiments on magnetic flight and published his results in an engaging book called *Zero to Eighty*. The title referred to years rather than miles per hour—the book was a fictional autobiography. In magnetic flight, a magnet moving at high speed near to, but not in contact with, a conducting surface (ordinary aluminum will do) generates eddy currents in it. The currents provide fields that repel the magnet. It's simple, passive, and self-correcting: bring the magnet closer to the conductor and the lifting forces increase. To provide acceleration, transverse coils are located along the right-of-way, and a computer controls their currents as necessary to make the vehicle speed up, coast, or slow down, sensing its position and speed by its interruption of light beams at intervals along the line of flight. Short of space travel there's no more efficient way of transporting people and goods at high speed than by magnetic flight in vacuum underground, and because of the predictability of the environment, the technique lends itself to automation.

The United States had an excellent program of research and development on magnetically supported vehicles until the early 1970s, but then the research was cut off by the Department of Transportation, whose boss, in a masterpiece of bureaucratic myopia, declared, "What's wrong with steel wheels on steel rails?" and stopped all research on advanced transport systems. (As for what's wrong with wheels on rails, we've just seen what's wrong.) In Germany and Japan magnetic-flight research continued, and by 1977 the Japanese National Railway System had demonstrated a full-size magnetic-flight transport system. It is scheduled to replace the Bullet Train railway in the 80s or 90s. Not long ago I rode on HSST–2, a smooth, quiet, high-speed vehicle developed by Japan Airlines for still another magnetic-flight train system.

Fixed-routing transport systems of any kind won't compete with aircraft over long distances. Planes will always retain the advantages of zero-cost rights-of-way and the ability to adjust seasonally, or even daily, to changing patterns of passenger demand. Still, all the important conditions for the construction of floater lines will become more favorable over the next decades. In certain areas, cities will continue to extend until they connect, forming urban corridors that cannot function without faster, cheaper transport. At the same time, the acquisition costs for surface rights-of-way along them will soar, and environmental objections to surface railroad noise and windblown dust will increase. As automation matures, the cost of tunneling will decrease, and within a few decades tunnels may be drilled by remote control without any risk of human life deep underground. Without human workers it will be possible to use high internal pressures to prevent the collapse of tunnels as they're being dug. Quick-setting cements can be used to make permanent seals.

A floater car will be much simpler in its anatomy than a plane. Its seating is likely to be just two across, because that will allow the floater to be of minimum width so that it can travel in a tunnel of small diameter not much bigger than a pipeline. Its shell will be a simple metal cylinder with only one opening, an airtight door at one end. The shell will provide the strong mechanical backbone of the car and the mounting for permanent magnets or superconducting coils to give magnetic lift. I've used the word "carriage" to describe the structure that will roll in and out of the shell through the doorway. It will include a strip of floor as long as the pressure shell and just narrow enough to fit inside it. The floor will carry many identical compartments, each with baggage shelves open on both sides, followed by a pair of seats, and behind them a bulkhead to isolate the compartment so its climate, sound, and lighting can be controlled independently. In 2081 the bulkhead can also carry flat television screens.

A number of the features of floater transportation that Eric notices will be determined by competition. In an era when private cars will be computerized, so that passengers may read or watch television as they drive to work, floater lines will only be able to compete if they provide direct nonstop rather than multiple-stop service. Also, station facilities can be smaller if they only have to handle one floater at a time, rather than a train of them. Psychologists have found that the popularity of automobiles depends in part on their privacy: they are secure little rolling homes, protected against the unwanted intrusions of public transportation, such as squalling babies or chatty neighbors. Floaters will provide privacy for individuals, or for parties of two or four traveling together—and they will provide that privacy while moving their passengers at ten times the speed of an automobile.

Using no fossil fuels, but only electric power in small quantities, a floater car in vacuum will fly at much lower cost than any of its competitors. An aircraft must spend more energy per mile the faster it flies, whereas for a floater the energy cost per mile of travel actually goes down slightly with increasing speed. For a journey at a speed of 800 mph, the floater of Eric and Ellen's journey will spend only a twentieth of the energy of a jet aircraft carrying the same payload, even though the floater will be much faster than the jet. For such urban corridors as Boston–Washington, San Francisco–San Diego, Tokyo–Kyoto, Frankfort–Geneva, and Milan–Rome, the volumes of traffic will be so high that it will pay to tunnel under them for floater lines. A first estimate for the New York to Washington route suggests that by floater one could travel between the two cities in only fourteen minutes—at a cost of less than four dollars for a ticket.

Yet even a century from now there will still be railroads hauling low-value freight; there will still be planes; there will still be surface automobiles—transformed, indeed, but still with us. Experience shows that as our civilization grows and develops it leads to greater rather than to less diversity, so 2081 will have a mix of transport systems greater than we know today.

Honolulu, Pennsylvania

THE FLOATER tunnel must have run deep underground, for the thirty passengers to Erie rode a large elevator for nearly a minute to reach the surface. When we got out we were in a lobby just large enough for ticket machines and a shop with magazines, candy, cigarettes, and personal electronics. Glass doors slid aside to let us out onto a roofed sidewalk and roadway, and Ellen's car, one of a short line waiting at the curb, opened its doors for us as we approached. In contrast to the streamlined shape of the jet airplane, the last vehicle I'd seen from the outside, the car was a chunky little box, square at the back, slanted at the front, with four small rubber-tired wheels at the corners. It had three doors, one on each side and one that was its entire back. There were two jump seats, facing backward, that could be used on short trips when no baggage was carried. Ellen showed me controls that would let me raise and lower my seat and tilt the back and headrest to comfortable angles. Between us, to allow the car to be driven from either seat, there was a small manual control panel with buttons and a projecting handgrip above. Ellen told me that the steering handgrip was for secondary roads too small to be equipped with automatic guidance devices—"markers," she called them. In front of us a large video screen extended to shoulder height, and above it a single, slanted window filled the space to the roofline. Evidently the car's on-board computer had been given a list of those people authorized to drive it, since the screen remained blank when I got in, but came to life immediately when Ellen took her seat on the left. Ellen told the car she wanted to leave at once for her home in Waterford, and the screen confirmed the order by showing the street address, the routing, and the estimated time en route.

The little car started to move immediately, and I heard the faint hum of electric motors. We turned left in a tight circle—the front wheels must have been able to steer almost by ninety degrees—got out of the narrow space between the cars at front and back, then straightened and moved forward. As we left the bright lights of the station platform, our way led between sloping, ivy-covered banks, then to a wide road. Above it arched a glass roof, which admitted a dim and gray sunlight, filtered through miles of cloud. Cars were three abreast in each direction, and the spacing between us and the cars in front and back was less than a car length. All were moving at a steady 50 mph. My guide touched a button marked "MASK" and our side and rear windows opaqued to a neutral tone, while the front window darkened slightly. From the appearance of the cars coming toward us I realized that our windshield had gone half-silver, so that we'd be unseen from the outside unless we turned on a bright light.

A flicker of motion from the car ahead caught my attention, and I saw that its rear window was now displaying a sign that said "NETE," followed by the words "No Effluents—Total Enclosure." Ellen explained that liquid-crystal displays of that kind had long since replaced what she called bumper stickers, permanent signs that owners had at one time put on their cars for amusement or to advocate political action. The NETE sign expressed the goal of a popular environmentalist group to force total recycling or containment of every chemical that could be given off by every factory or vehicle. In a few moments the sign changed to the personal-radio nickname of the car owner, and a little later it switched to a political slogan advocating the election of a candidate. Ellen remarked that if I found the display annoying we could fully opaque our windshield and look out our side-windows or watch television.

We entered a tunnel without slackening our speed and stayed in it for several seconds. During the passage I heard the hiss of air jets playing on the car from all sides. Ellen told me they formed curtains of moving air called "airwalls," to keep the weather away from Erie's controlled climate. When we passed the final airwall, the fading afternoon light showed driving snow and sleet. The car began to bump and pitch, and I could see patches of beaten snow on the ground. Occasionally, I felt a momentary slowing down, and Ellen told me those were tests of the braking conditions, made by the car's drive computer. There were electric motors on all four wheels, usable as generators for braking, so the car was able to cope with most driving conditions unless the snow patches became too deep for its small wheels. If we began to skid, the road computer would direct our car to slow down.

Ellen told the car she wanted to speak with her mother, and after a few moments I heard the voice of an older woman. She and Ellen talked of our expected arrival time, and then she asked for my drink order, saying that "Arthur" would have it ready for me. Arthur was, it seemed, their household robot, and Ellen's mother Jeannette was quite proud of him.

As we drove the light faded still more, and one by one the other cars turned onto sloping exits that curved off to our right. Far away at left or right there occasionally appeared large clusters of dim lights through the falling snow, and Ellen explained that those were open towns, exposed to the weather. The road surface improved and we speeded up gradually until a strange vehicle was visible ahead of us, higher than our car and as wide as our lane of pavement. Flashing lights marked it, and from its side a rooster tail of snow shot out to disappear downwind. As we approached this strange beast, I could see it was leaving a clear path, with steam rising from a road left hot in its wake. Ellen expressed some exasperation that the road computer was too cautious to allow us to get by the snowplow. Fortunately we were close to our turnoff, and soon the video, alerting us with a bell that was just audible, told us that the Waterford exit ramp was 50 meters ahead. We left the main road and in a few minutes a pair of small marker lights appeared through the snow; at the same time our video announced "Waterford, Pa." I was surprised to see no general glow of lights, but Ellen told me that I should expect none because Waterford was totally enclosed.

At the markers there was the now-familiar sensation of entering an airwall tunnel. When Ellen touched the "CLEAR" button the windows became fully transparent again, and as we broke out of the tunnel I had a momentary start and the sensation of being transported suddenly back home to Fox Alpha. The roadway, depressed a little below the general ground level, was bordered by sloping banks with palm trees, giant ferns, and vines. I saw orange and mango trees, and a few minutes later my eyes were dazzled by the brilliant scarlet of a blossom-covered royal poinciana tree, with the deep yellow of a plumeria just beyond it. The roadway curved constantly, never staying straight for more than a few meters. The car had slowed to perhaps 30 mph, I suppose to keep wind noise down within the town. Above us there was brilliant light, as bright as afternoon sun, and it seemed to come from a regular array of lights some twenty meters overhead. Although the color quality was that of sunlight, I found the arrangement rather artificial when contrasted with the natural sunlight that I was used to in all of the colonies. The feeling of enclosure was also strange to me, because, of course, at home in Fox Cluster we have no roofs on our towns, and when we look up, far above we see the parks and villages on the other side of the sphere.

The car slowed on a side street, a small sunken roadway bordered by hedges and flowering shrubs and the occasional stone gateway. We turned into one of them, and came through to a curving driveway set in a green lawn.

There was a riot of color in the flowers and shrubs set all around and on the bank we'd just passed through, evidently built to make the sunken roadway invisible from the houses on either side. Ellen's parents were waiting for us outside the door—there must have been some automatic communication between the car and the house during the last few minutes—and as we got out, a blast of warm moist air with a fragrance of flowers washed over me. Ellen's father stepped forward to open my door as the car stopped, and welcomed me to Waterford. Bill Tehaney had graying hair and a deep tan and moved with athletic grace. I learned later that he was past sixty, but I would have guessed him to be a good deal younger. Jeannette also looked young, too young to be Ellen's mother, and I concluded that both Bill and Jeannette must have taken full advantage of diet, exercise, and any available antiaging drugs.

I was about to take my bags out of the car, but Jeannette told me that "Arthur" would carry them. At that moment a short, broad figure emerged from the house, looking absurdly like a giant panda dressed in a butler's black suit with a white shirt and black tie. Its round panda face had a spotlight for a nose, two eye lenses, large ears, and a speaker for a mouth. Jeannette directed Arthur to carry my bags, and he answered with the perfect diction I'd come to expect from computers.

The house seemed much like those in one of our Polynesian-climate colonies, with plenty of open space, high ceilings, and thick roof beams in natural wood. The floors at the entry level were terra cotta tile, and large windows opened onto courtyards and gardens rich with tropical flowers. We climbed stairs with a carved wooden railing to a carpeted level where Jeannette showed me to my suite, with bedroom, balcony, bath, and exercise room. She showed me the controls for the stereo, the video, and the lights, and added that if I just spoke in a normal tone in any room the house computer would hear me and carry out my instructions. I wasn't at all sure I liked the idea that every word I spoke was being listened to, but it seemed to be the price of perfect service. After she left, there was a gentle knock at the door and I found Arthur outside it waiting with the last of my bags. He explained that he was programmed not to enter a bedroom without permission. He padded off then, descending the stairs a bit slowly and carefully.

When I'd unpacked and showered I followed the sound of a cocktail mixer being shaken, down to the first level and out to a brick-paved patio. I was surprised to find Bill mixing the drinks himself, but he explained that with short work weeks and highly mechanized households most people treated cooking and drink mixing as creative hobbies, and devoted a great deal of time to becoming expert chefs and bartenders. He and Jeannette didn't allow Arthur to take over in the kitchen unless they were ill or very tired. Jeannette suggested that we take a drive in the Waterford park before dinner, and when I agreed she asked the house computer to keep an eye on where we were and to turn on one of the ovens when we started back from the drive.

The Tehaneys' town car was waiting for us at the front door. It was much longer than Ellen's commuter car, and had four seats facing each other across a low table. The "driver" sat in the left rear seat facing forward, toward a control panel and handle like those of Ellen's two-seater. Bill touched a key and the roof slid back to fold into a rear compartment.

Electric town-car for quiet, low-speed transport on the streets of Waterford. The coffee table between the pairs of seats contains the controls for the car's computer, as well as a built-in bar and television screens.

I leaned back for comfort, and turned my face up to the "sunlight," now darkening gradually toward dusk.

Bill had dialed our destination. The car rolled through the embankment and the automatic privacy gate at the front of the Tehaneys' house, waited for other cars to pass, then turned onto the street. We moved slowly through winding roads as Bill pointed out the municipal buildings, the library, golf courses, tennis courts, and shops. All the shops faced away from the road toward courtyards planted with tropical trees and flowers, and the roadways stayed always a little below ground level. Evidently there was a complete network of pedestrian and bicycle paths. Occasionally we passed under a narrow, arching bridge over which some bicyclist was riding. Bill set his drink on the coffee table between our seats, and told me he was an enthusiastic surfer, using what he called an "old man's cheater board." That was a surfboard equipped with a microprocessor and control fins fore and aft, which kept the board always under its rider no matter how poor his sense of balance. He spoke of taking Jeannette and Ellen to South Africa where there was one of the world's best natural surfing beaches. They would travel by "boomer," the common name for supersonic aircraft. According to Bill the connection from the United States East Coast to Capetown was particularly easy, because it was over water all the way and the boomer could fly the entire trip at full cruise speed.

As we moved slowly along the narrow roadways of the park, bordered with magnificent palms, banana trees, and mangoes, we passed other open cars, some driven by acquaintances of the Tehaneys whom they greeted with a wave and a smile. The car let us off at the clubhouse before disappearing silently toward a concealed parking area, and we walked through the club, past a bar and dining rooms, to a terrace. A noise I'd been hearing was louder there: the rhythmic crash and roll of waves on a beach. Before us was a wide lagoon, bordered by straight, white sand beaches ending in palm groves. Evidently it was part of Waterford's landscaping. As I watched, a rolling wave gathered, approached us, and broke with a crash of surf on the beach. As it receded it increased in height, rolling away to break with a smother of foam on the far beach. Surfers waited near the lagoon's center, dim in the gathering dusk, and occasionally one would take a few quick paddling strokes, mount the board, and ride the incoming wave.

I'd estimated by squinting upward toward the lights that the height of Waterford's roof was not much over twenty meters. It was supported at intervals by slim columns, mostly ivy-covered. Here, though, over the lagoon, there was a high oval dome. We watched as the "sunlight" faded. On the dome there appeared, dimly at first and then more clearly, cumulous clouds. An image of an orange sun slowly set, and as it passed behind layers of clouds the light turned from orange to red, with rays and streamers of light filtered, apparently, by the slow-moving clouds. Other people had joined us on the terrace, and as the sun finally set beyond the most distant palms I saw a half-moon, almost over my head. The surf eased off to a gentle lapping at the beach, and in a moment of silence among several quiet conversations I heard, dimly and far away, a momentary burst of a hissing, pattering noise. I looked an inquiry at Bill, but he was equally puzzled, and it was Ellen who supplied the explanation: we were hearing the sleet drumming on the outside of the dome.

Jeannette suggested we return home for dinner, and Bill spoke to his business-card communicator to ask that his car be brought to the front door. As we stepped into the open town car, I asked whether its low floor ever scraped the road and was told that the town car was never used outside Waterford. Jeannette told it to stop at a market, and I asked her how far she had to go for groceries. She said she didn't go out for them at all unless she had plenty of time. Most of the staple items that the family used regularly were on a list that the home computer kept. The computer reordered any time they ran low, so that the kitchen pantry was always fully stocked.

After a few minutes' drive the town car let us off at a low arched entrance to a pedestrian avenue, which led us past small shops, fountains, and flowering plants. We turned into one shop, a grocery market, and I was surprised to find that it had no checkout counters. Instead, the shoppers carried small baskets, and when they had accumulated a few things from the shelves they dropped them at one of the charge counters among the shelves. There an automatic device sensitive to the anklet signals charged each item and routed it to the customer's car. Upon leaving the market, each customer was issued an itemized, alphabetized list of the groceries purchased with their individual and total costs.

Jeannette cut that routine short by selecting a fresh cantaloupe in a transparent wrapper, taking it to the nearest charge counter, and pressing a key marked "carry-out." We returned then to the car, which arrived for us just as we reached the curb. I'd been surprised by the freshness of the fruit and vegetables in the shop, and Ellen explained that they were grown in greenhouses just outside Waterford's town walls, using as nutrients chemicals sterilized from sewage. The recycling system had been copied

from those perfected years earlier for the space colonies, the only difference being that on Earth sunlight had to be provided artificially to permit
a twelve-month growing season.

On our way home, Bill opened a cabinet in the town car and offered
me, with obvious pride, a sample of sherry. Although the idea of drinking
while driving seemed strange to me, I could find no reason against it in the
case of fully automated vehicles. When we stopped at the Tehaneys', the
town car opened its doors and Arthur was waiting beside the entrance. As
we walked into the house there was a slight scent of wood smoke, and in
the living-room fireplace crackling flames. Bill told me that the "logs"
were made out of the pressed leaves and fibers of Waterford's agricultural
crops, and added that the chimney concealed a recycler that turned all the
smoke into solid compounds to be fed to the soil of the greenhouses.

The dining-room windows looked out onto a private garden, backed
by a wall and a line of trees; it wasn't possible to see anyone else's home.
Apparently the Tehaneys liked the Hawaiian motif that was popular in
Waterford. The tables and chairs were a rich, dark wood and there were
intricate carvings on the walls: masks and latticework screens. Jeannette
told me, as we gathered around the dining table, that these were reproductions of Tiki masks used in the time of the Hawaiian kings, two centuries
before.

—E. C. R.

In his introduction to Waterford and to the Tehaney family, Eric sees only
the final result of the history that is likely to bring Waterford's conversion,
over the middle part of the next century, from a quiet Pennsylvania town
exposed to wind and weather to an enclosed area whose citizens will
choose the climate and the weather they prefer. Waterford, located near
the shore of Lake Erie, has a natural climate that is typical of much of the
northern temperate zone on both the American and Eurasian continents:
winters are damp and biting with a great deal of rain and snow, and summers are hot and humid. In a world where travel is becoming easier all the
time, it's unlikely that people will continue to tolerate weather that's only
occasionally to their liking. Yet, normal economic and environmental
pressures will act against the continued crowding of people into those few
areas that have, right now, the closest natural approximation to good climates. In the United States people are moving to the "sunbelt" states.

Crowding of such desirable areas forces up land prices, and population pressure soon destroys the "good life" the newcomers were seeking. With such pressures, at some point it will pay developers to build enclosed "New Towns" on low-cost land in regions of severe climate. The control of Earth's external climate is not a practical alternative. The weather system of the Earth's biosphere is so complex that one could never predict, with certainty, the consequences of meddling with it.

Space colonies will play a double role in the coming revolution in urban design. People who visit the colonies, where the choice of climate will be taken for granted, will return intolerant of putting up with Earth's weather. At the same time, developers will be applying to the design of new towns on Earth the new technologies of recycling and of climate control developed in the space colonies.

A century from now most of the streets and many of the houses of the existing Waterford may still be there, the older Victorian houses preserved, restored, and lived in with the help of tax benefits favoring restoration. But most of the people who will call themselves Waterford's residents will live in nearby enclosed towns. Even now, in areas of severe weather, we see the beginnings of the trend that will lead toward the Waterford of 2081. Hotels of two or three stories in height, near cities of medium size, are being built with large glass-roofed central courtyards, permanently landscaped with flowers and trees. These courtyards contain pools and fountains, and often have "sidewalk" cafés and restaurants. Where the designer's imagination has been given license, often the walls facing the courtyard have been decorated like those of a European city square, with small shops at ground level, balconies and apartments above. The Americana Hotel in Schenectady, New York, is a good example—and perhaps it is no accident that the hotel is owned by an airline, for travel brings new ideas. The trend toward enclosure is evident in large cities as well. In some cases, as in Atlanta's Peachtree Plaza or Montreal's Complex Desjardins, only a single, large hotel and its surrounding shops are included. In other examples, such as Kansas City's Crown Plaza, apartments or town houses for permanent residents are combined with hotels, shops, and theaters in a single enclosure. More ambitious plans for the enclosure of entire cities have been discussed for Winooski, Vermont, and for urban centers in Alaska.

Eric visits the Waterford of 2081 on a winter day of sleet and storm and finds the town enclosed. A few months later he will find it wide open to the sun and sky. Waterford's plants are Hawaiian, but they can grow quite safely in Pennsylvania as long as they are protected from low temperatures. In my guess, Waterford will be open to the Pennsylvania breezes whenever it is comfortable to be outdoors without heavy clothing, especially on the beautiful days of spring and autumn.

Though the Tehaneys live in a separate, single-family dwelling, most of Waterford's residential areas are likely to be townhouses or apartments in keeping with a trend that is already clear in our suburban areas. We can guess at the land area required by looking at the most attractive, landscaped, parklike residential communities of the present day. We find that 10,000 or so people would live within a space of a square mile, and Waterford is likely to be of about that size. The shape of its enclosure will be dictated by the practical realities of snow removal and of solar energy. It may be located on a gentle southward-facing slope. Its town plan is apt to be a simple rectangle, and its roof flat, with a higher section covering the lagoon's dome. In our present city areas the removal of snow is an annual nuisance and an economic drain, because our towns are designed so that the snow settles and drifts onto the streets. It has to be collected laboriously at constant inconvenience to the city's traffic, and then it has to be hauled through city streets to a remote site where it can be dumped. Or, as happens in many towns, it's simply pushed to the edges of the streets to become a nuisance and (as it dirties) an eyesore in the months to come. How much easier it would be to stop the problem before it starts. Waterford's flat roof, well suited to being swept by automatic machines, will never accumulate great depths of snow because the machines can just push the stuff to the nearest edge, and over, before it has time to pile up. Local temporary heating to melt ice, wasteful of energy on a city street because the underlying ground conducts heat away too well, will become efficient on a well-insulated roof surface.

The dome over Waterford's lagoon will be fixed permanently in place to house the equipment for simulating visually the tropical sky and sunset. Over all the rest of the town the roof will consist of three layers, forming three flat planes, and the upper two layers will be movable. The highest layer will be topped by a sheet of bright, reflecting aluminum to keep out rain and wind and to reflect the heat of the summer sun. The aluminum skin will be supported by a lightweight framework, several meters deep, built according to standard bridge-truss designs of thin struts forming a set of connected triangles. Under the entire aluminum surface there will be insulation, also to a depth of meters. This top layer will be built in modular sections, hundreds of meters in each direction, and the sections will roll aside to a storage area at the perimeter of Waterford. Under the opaque insulating layer there will be a separate, independent layer of glass, also in modular sections. This will turn Waterford into a greenhouse for solar energy on bright cold days. After all efforts on the design of solar heating, it's been found that the complicated "active" systems are too expensive and unreliable. What's best is simplest: clear glass admitting sunshine to heat the home and its furnishings. At night, especially when it is clear and cold, one must prevent the day's store of heat from radiating away. That's when Waterford's opaque insulated roof will roll into place, for the same physical principles that rule in the solar heating of today's individual homes will govern the design of solar-heated towns in 2081. Only when the weather is very good, or when Waterford's residents desire natural rainfall, will both the insulating and the glass layers be rolled aside. Then, only the third layer will remain, a stretched, flat sheet of screen to keep out mosquitoes and other insects. That layer will be supported on the same lightweight framework that will carry Waterford's artificial "sun" lights.

Until very energy-efficient lamps are built it will not be practical to provide artificially the amount of light the sun gives us on clear days. In the first century of electric light, physicists and engineers succeeded in raising the efficiency of lamps—that is, the fraction of the power spent on them that comes out as visible light—from the half of one percent that Edison achieved to a 1980s best value of about 36 percent attained in low-pressure sodium vapor lamps. These are used extensively as street lamps and give the familiar yellow illumination we see on lighted highways. In recent years there has been a shift toward high-pressure sodium lamps, which give an intense golden-white light similar to that of the sun. Though not yet quite as efficient as the older, yellower lamps, the newer type already achieve more than half the efficiency that is the theoretical maximum limit for white light. So we can expect in a few decades to find lamps that simulate sunlight very closely, while achieving close to the maximum possible efficiency. When that happens, a town like Waterford can be supplied with artificial sunlight at a reasonable cost in energy. If solar energy is intercepted in space and brought to Earth as microwaves, a receiving antenna comparable in area to the ground area of Waterford will be sufficient to supply the town's sunlight on cloudy days.

Paradoxically, Waterford may be able to maintain its tropical climate even in a northeastern winter with less expenditure of energy than a town of its population uses now just to stay alive. To control the climate either of a building or of an entire city, one needs first of all to reduce the flow of heat outward in winter and inward in summer. That is best accomplished by making the surface area exposed to the outside weather as small as possible consistent with the volume being enclosed, and insulating that surface very well. Waterford, exposing only a single flat roof to the outside world, approaches that ideal. In contrast, the individual buildings of our towns and cities expose four walls and a roof to the weather. In the downtown areas of major cities our tall buildings are the worst possible shape from the viewpoint of heat transfer: they have enormous areas projecting upward into regions of strong windflow. In fact, the design of a downtown area is very similar to that of a heat radiator, whose many projecting fins give it the greatest possible exposed area for a minimum amount of enclosed volume. The projecting "fins" (skyscrapers) of a city like New York further compound the problem of heatflow by channeling the natural air movements into high-speed "canyon winds" that increase the flow of heat just as the airflow through a car's radiator is designed to do. In contrast, Waterford's roof will present only a single horizontal surface at ground level where the winds are always gentlest. Comparing Waterford's insulation with that of an open-air town of the same population, the roof insulation of the enclosed town can be far thicker for equal cost, because it will be geometrically simple and uninterrupted and therefore well suited to mass production and automated installation. In an ordinary exposed building, the weakest areas of insulation, where most of the heat is lost, are windows and chimneys; Waterford's roof won't have any. And there is *no* law of physics that limits how effective an opaque insulating layer can be.

Automation will be well suited to minimizing the cost of Waterford's enclosure, composed as it will be of many identical sections. For those who live within, such economies may be less important than the freedom Waterford will give them to carry on active, unrestricted lives even during the hottest and coldest months of the year.

Homes and Castles

At a word from Jeannette the end wall of the dining room slid downward, opening the room to a garden. The sounds of evening floated in, the chirping of sleepy birds and the croaking of frogs in a nearby pond. There was also the splash of water, and I traced it to a series of small cascades over volcanic rock, edged with green moss and flowers. A light scent of jasmine and poinciana drifted in, and yellow light from torches flickered over the garden and its falling water. The breeze was as warm as the room. Bill remarked that many people dialed in a new environment every night for their wall screens, but that he and Jeannette had moved to Waterford in part because of its Polynesian climate and what he called its "outdoor" living.

We sat down at a dark, heavily carved wooden table, and Jeannette touched a control on its underside. The room lights dimmed and shifted to a yellower color, matching the glow of the torches outside. Candles on the table, already lit, were the main source of light for the meal. They never seemed to burn lower and they burned without odor; I learned later that they were fueled by hydrogen.

The main course was a fish called by the Hawaiian name "Mahi-Mahi," and Bill told me it had been caught in the central Pacific less than twenty-four hours earlier, then flown by "boomer" to the West Coast, and from there had been sent to Waterford by floater. He added that such delicacies were for special occasions, and that most of Waterford's fresh fish was raised in covered ponds just outside the town walls, while the rest came from the Atlantic or the Caribbean. I asked about vegetables, and Jeannette told me that the local greenhouse-farms grew corn, sweet potatoes, vegetables, and fruit all year round. Foods that required fancy processing and frozen or canned goods were all brought in from a distance by cargo floater. Waterford imported most of its meat, but raised pigs on cuttings from the greenhouse-farms. As we lingered over dessert, a sherbet of tropical fruit, I remembered that in spite of all the automation, Jeannette had cooked the dinner herself, so I took care to compliment her. Arthur had played the role of discreet butler to perfection, padding in silently whenever Jeannette touched a button on her bracelet, carrying in trays when she asked, but otherwise staying out of sight in the kitchen.

I asked about the itinerary for the next day, and Ellen offered to show me her apartment, close to the beach and marina. Arthur came in then, waited for a break in the conversation, and told me that a letter had just arrived from Fox Cluster. The letter had been on its way for over two days, traveling at the speed of light, so I decided to wait another hour for it rather than break up the gathering. After coffee and liqueurs, I asked Ellen to walk upstairs with me and help retrieve the letter.

Upstairs, Ellen went to a desk in my room, and to my surprise its surface changed at her command from a wood grain to the familiar screen and control area of a video. She explained that such devices, simulating wood or tapestry or a painting, were really on all the time, recognizable only because they couldn't show deep texture. At first the video refused to reproduce my letter, even though Ellen was giving it the correct instructions. She laughed when she realized what was wrong: because of Waterford's Privacy Acts the computer would balk at displaying my letter unless I was alone in the room. She left, and the video flashed the image of my letter as soon as the door slid shut. The handwriting was my mother's, and the message told me the recent local news and assured me that all was well at home.

When I had read the letter, I cleared the screen and let it revert to a simulation of a wooden desk top. I went in search of the Tehaneys and found them in the garden. There among the flower scents of the warm evening we talked of the contrast between the simplicity of our government in the Cluster and the complexity of regulations on Earth. I answered Bill's questions by noting that in the Cluster there was a universal distrust of giving too much power to public officials. Our public services required very little in tax revenues, because they were performed mainly by young people working through their two years of required nonmilitary service to the colonies. We had no large differences in wealth, and the Cluster was too far from the rest of civilization for immigrants to land on our doorstep, so we didn't need to use tax money for redistribution. As a result, we were able to confine our public revenues to a single uniform tax rate of 5 percent, with no deductions or exemptions. That limited the size of our government and required only a few people for collection. Our budget for defense, of course, was zero. I added that we tended to solve most nonstandard problems by visiting the official responsible, or talking with her when there was a chance encounter in a park or shopping area. Bill was curious at my implication that most of our public officials were women, and I told him that more than 50 percent were, perhaps because most government jobs could be done by working at home through video and computer terminals.

Bill sighed and explained to me regretfully that governments on Earth had been growing in size and power for centuries. The central governments had to be big mainly because of the need for military defense, but their size made them remote and unresponsive. Bill paid more than half of the top end of his income in taxes, but as very little of the money came back to enclave-towns like Waterford he had to pay for local services on top of that. The tax issue was one of the main drivers of emigration out to space colonies from the developed nations, but there were restrictive laws, controversial and often changing, that limited the rights of citizens to emigrate from certain nations. Families were permitted to emigrate from other countries, but in some cases were not allowed to take their savings. Bill added that such restrictions would be stronger and more universal were it not that the colonies channeled a considerable amount of their wealth back to the Earth in trade, in tourism, and in gifts toward the preservation of historical and wilderness areas, and so exercised at least some political power.

By that time it was late, and Jeannette suggested tactfully that it might be time for all of us to call it a day. On the way to the house she lifted her wrist with its bracelet to give Arthur directions for closing the window-walls, clearing the ashes from the fire when it burned down, and in the morning, bringing us coffee in our rooms at eight.

The lights in my bedroom came on as I entered, and a moment later Arthur's voice asked if there were anything I wished. At my request he came up to show me the controls for my bed: hard or soft, tilt, contour, temperature, vibrator, and background environmental sounds. When he had left and I had settled down, I spoke the words, "Lights off, please." I'd have none of the usual strange-room problems of searching for light switches in the middle of the night. I wasn't long getting to sleep, but my body rhythm had been left somewhere in orbit and within three hours I was awake again. That was no great surprise—at home I'm often on a two-cycle schedule, with two periods of wakefulness and two of sleep in the twenty-four hours—and as I drifted awake my first reaction was to do something that's always been my remedy for middle-of-the-night insomnia: a walk in search of the sunshine. That had been my habit all my life at home, and had been possible even on shipboard. It gave me an oddly disturbing feeling to realize that here on Earth I'd simply have to wait until morning; I couldn't make that easy, fifteen-minute walk up through the sleeping villages to the zero-gravity axis, and the five-minute drift through to the observation lounge, where at every hour of the twenty-four, I could feel the reassuring warmth of blazing sunlight.

"Lights on dim, please," I spoke, and when the lights came on I got up and dressed. I'd noticed before how soundproof the house was, and now when I approached my bedroom door and it slid silently open I heard a sound I'd not noticed before, a low hum, varying in pitch. Lights came on in the hall as I walked along, and were bright on the stairs. I traced the sound to the living room. There a low broad disk mounted on wide rubber tires was moving slowly along the carpet. A tube extended forward from it and disappeared under a couch, and from its rear a corrugated flexible pipe curved back to end in a fitting on the wall. As I looked the tube retracted, telescoping, and I realized the machine was a "smart" version of the ordinary vacuum cleaner. It took no notice of me, and as it explored each square meter of the carpet with its wide suction mouth, I tried the experiment of standing in its path. Evidently it knew by my anklet-signal that I was a human rather than an odd-shaped piece of furniture, so it dodged around me, remarking as it passed that it would clean that bit of carpet later. Then another voice sounded, behind me but not very close:

"Mr. Rawson?" It was Arthur. "I didn't want to startle you by coming in without speaking. Is there anything I can do for you?" I thanked him, said that I was just wakeful, and asked what was going on.

"Just the regular housecleaning. Most of it's done by the special machines that were here before I came: the vacuum cleaners and polishers and window-washers. I'm just emptying the wastebaskets, and then I'll clean those shelves and glasses; I'll put the glasses in the dishwasher, dust the shelves, and then rearrange the glasses as they were. Mrs. Tehaney likes the house to be well cleaned by the time she gets up in the morning."

I asked Arthur if he ever rested, and he answered:

"Oh yes. Generally from about four to five A.M. I go to my room, exchange one of my power-packs for a fresh one, and make a direct connection to the house computer so I can get any program updates and find out if there is any errand that needs to be done that the house can't take care of by itself. Then, of course, I change to fresh clothes for the new day."

"How do you like working for the Tehaneys?" I asked.

"Very much indeed, Mr. Rawson. They are pleasant and thoughtful employers."

I had a strong suspicion that I'd tapped into a "canned" answer and my next question confirmed it:

"As you know, I'm new here on Earth, and I'd like to know whether the people I meet are representative. Are the Tehaneys typical of the people in Waterford?"

"I'm programmed not to answer any personal questions about my employers or their friends, Mr. Rawson." (Arthur's voice sounded faintly reproving.) I changed the subject, and asked him if he would describe the operation of the house to me so that I needn't take Bill or Jeannette's time for explanations in the morning.

"Of course, sir," he answered. "Would you like my explanation to take five minutes, fifteen, or an hour?"

That was a refreshing question; I asked him for the five-minute version.

"All the systems of the house are electric, Mr. Rawson, and the energy billing is made directly to the Tehaney family bank account. Heating and air conditioning are central, and each room can be controlled separately as to temperature and humidity either by a hand-controller or by voice activation. Air circulating through the climate-control system passes through an electrostatic precipitator, which removes dust and pollen. The systems have to work a little harder when a room wall is opened to the outside, but as Waterford itself is climate-controlled that doesn't add much to the energy requirements.

"The basic structure of the house is steel-reinforced concrete, so it is soundproof and fireproof, but each room has an interior shell of composite material, wood or tapestry, for decoration. Every room has at least one video wall, stereo music, a concealed rebroadcast antenna for pocket video and wrist phones, a locator and identifier for anklet signals, and a microphone to communicate with the house computer. That computer monitors all staple food and drugstore items brought into the house, counts discarded packages, and replenishes the pantry by ordering from the supermarket. It also controls the lawnmower and the sprinkler system for the lawn, controls the cleaning machines, and regulates the room temperatures. It takes in video and cube programs, edits out all the commercials it can recognize as such, and stores the programs for later viewing if desired.

"The Tehaneys have four cars, a single-engine, four-passenger airplane, and a Traveler recreational vehicle. The last two are stored outside the town walls. When a car passes through the entrance gate of the house, it comes under the control of the house computer, which supervises the delivery and pickup of passengers and the parking of cars in the garage under the house until they are needed again.

"The computer also supervises the condition and cleaning of the swimming pool on the side lawn. It sends and receives electronic mail, timing its calls to take advantage of low rates. By Mr. Tehaney's instructions, it sorts the incoming mail and suppresses all advertising matter, forwarding a daily list of the titles of catalogues and promotional material received.

"Our water comes from the town's main supply and is further filtered by a local water purifier. Trash is sorted and compacted, packed into containers, and shipped to the town's disposal center for recycling. All of the homes, shops, and office buildings in Waterford are linked by an underground package-transfer network that uses the "floater" technology. It takes approximately thirty seconds to send a package from any one place in Waterford to any other, as long as the package is within the dimensions of a typical large supermarket item.

"The overall conservation of energy is, of course, also carried out by the house computer. It turns off lights whenever a room is empty of people, turns off the climate-control system of any unoccupied room unless it is asked to keep it on, and notifies the town computer to dim the sunlamps over the yard or pool areas whenever no one is using them. The sunlamps are arranged so that almost none of their light falls on the roof of the house, even when they are at full intensity.

"All of the responses to human presence, including the delivery of messages, are based on the individual anklet-signals that tell us the location and identity of every human. When Ms. Tehaney's car entered the town, the position and identity of both of you were immediately made known to the town computer and so to that of the house. At this moment the house also knows, both by lack of an anklet-signal and by continuous infrared and sonar scanning of the grounds and of a closed surface in the air above it, that no intruder has entered."

I remarked that the Privacy Acts seemed to be upheld firmly in Waterford, and that I was puzzled at how people reconciled them with the monitoring of individual positions. My question gave Arthur a good excuse to continue his lecture:

"First, Mr. Rawson, I should say that the Privacy Acts are not at all universal. They are enforced strictly in certain countries, only casually in others, and not at all in places where the individual is considered unimportant with respect to the state. Their enforcement varies even among the individual towns of the United States. I understand that the strict enforcement of the Privacy Acts in Waterford was one of the reasons for the Tehaneys' decision to settle here. The record of an individual's position in Waterford is kept only in a guarded area of the town computer memory and can be tapped into only by order of the court in a criminal case. Furthermore, those records are erased permanently after a few days."

"Have those records ever been tapped?"

"I don't know, but if you'll wait a moment I'll try to find out for you. Meanwhile, may I make you something? Perhaps a cup of hot chocolate to help you sleep? And when you next go to your room I can show you, if you like, the built-in system of biofeedback that will assist you in getting back to sleep."

I settled for some hot chocolate, and sat down in the library while Arthur went off to get it. Bill evidently liked old books, and I found a rare eleventh edition of the *Encyclopaedia Britannica*, dating from 170 years ago. I was deep in the colorful illustrations of "Uniforms of the British Army," circa 1910, when Arthur returned. He was carrying not only the hot chocolate, but a plate of cookies and a table napkin on a silver tray. I could settle into being well spoiled at the Tehaneys'.

"The town computer has given me the history you asked for, Mr. Rawson," he told me. "In the twenty-five years since Waterford was built, there have been five requests for court orders to release individual position histories. Two of these were for acts of vandalism. They were immediately traced to juveniles who were then reprimanded and who never repeated the offenses. Two others were for theft, but in both of those cases the home computers at the locations involved had not recorded the intrusion of any person not known to be a family member or guest. The court orders were therefore refused. Home computers keep no records of position as long as there is no intrusion and the heartbeats of all occupants are within normal limits. It is thought that in these two cases there was theft by a family member within the home, but that falls outside the jurisdiction of the courts.

"The fifth case was a sexual assault and attempted murder in one of the city parks. The court order was granted, and the town computer record immediately traced the crime to a town resident, a young man who had previously shown no aberrant behavior, but who had evidently gone berserk. He was immediately charged and imprisoned and was subsequently tried and convicted in the state courts. I can give you the reference if you wish the rest of the legal history. After that crime, most of the families in Waterford bought miniature transmitters that could be concealed in a tooth and triggered by an extremely hard bite, and provided them especially to children and young women so that if they were attacked, an alarm signal would summon the police instantly. Criminals with a record of violent crime, I should add, are normally not admitted to enclave-towns like Waterford, even as transients."

I turned the conversation to Arthur himself and asked why he was designed to look so unlike a human. He told me his designers had worried that some people might be startled or irritated by a robot that could be mistaken at first sight for a human. That concern wasn't universal, and the products of some companies were humanlooking, except for some identifying mark. According to the laws of most countries, robots had to carry such a mark "plainly visible at all times."

I'd been curious about why it took so long to develop robots of his sophistication, considering that computers had existed since the middle of the last century. Arthur answered that the pattern-recognition and associative functions of the human brain and sensory system were quite different from the linear logic on which computer design was based. Even to develop them to the very limited extent necessary for robot design required a whole new science, and that hadn't been explored until well into the twenty-first century. Even after that, the programming problem had been very difficult. To develop Arthur's model had taken 5,000 programmers working for twenty-five years, a total investment of more than ten million hours of time, even with all possible computer assistance. More than 99 percent of that time had gone into finding and correcting programming errors and unforeseen "traps" of logic or behavior that the robot could fall into.

My last question was the obvious one: how much had Arthur cost? He told me the information was confidential under the Privacy Acts, but added that the investment was "substantial." By then I was feeling sleepy. I declined the offer of a short course on sleep-inducing biofeedback and climbed the stairs. As I left, Arthur reminded me to put my shoes outside my door if I wanted them shined.

The next morning I was awakened by a discreet knock, and Arthur entered with the morning coffee on a tray. Sunlight, or an imitation of it, streamed in the window as soon as he turned off the screen control. I had both eyes opened and was feeling almost awake when suddenly the smooth service and everything-according-to-plan schedule was shattered. The door flew open and Ellen walked in briskly, calling to Arthur to bring her coffee into my room. She set out the plans for the day, expressing the hope that I wasn't the sort of person who "took all morning to get glued together." After breakfast Jeannette and Bill would tell me about their work, and then Ellen would give me lunch at her apartment. That was to be casual, anything she happened to find in her kitchen, a change from what she called "all this Swiss-hotel service here." In the afternoon we'd make a quick trip to Cleveland by floater to hear a jazz group playing in a restaurant bar, but we'd be back for dinner at the elder Tehaneys'. There would be company, their friends the Donovans, who were vacationing in Arizona High but would be back from the space colony that afternoon. Ellen left then as quickly as she had entered, and I had time to finish my coffee and take a soak in the Japanese-style hot-tub before showering, shaving, and dressing. Breakfast was in a small, intimate octagonal room just large enough for a four-person dining table and chairs. Except for one door, it was entirely surrounded by open "windows," and was evidently a smaller, simpler version of the tower restaurant I'd grown used to on shipboard. The scenery was of the Grand Canyon, viewed from a pinnacle that gave an all-encompassing view of colorful red cliffs and the tree-covered canyon rim. The air of the room was bracing and pine-scented, just right for bringing me fully awake.

—E. C. R.

DESPITE WARS, droughts, and depressions the wealth of the industrialized nations has increased steadily since the beginning of the industrial revolution. It's no wonder that the undeveloped nations, though different in ideology, religion, and political allegiances, are alike in their desire to industrialize. They can only increase their standard of living by a corresponding increase in their rate of energy use, but as argued in Part II, I consider it a near-certainty that long-term solutions to the energy-shortage problem will be found in much less than a century. Assuming such a solution, in another hundred years of industrialization people in much of the world will have individual incomes so high that we of today would describe them as wealthy. As of 1980 the average per-capita income in the United States, an average that included both workers and nonworkers, was about $4,000, and the average income for a family of four was $16,000. The typical United States family possessed a total wealth in 1980 of about $60,000, including such assets as a home, automobiles, and personal property. Given the same rate of economic growth that has existed since the middle of the nineteenth century, about 2.5 percent per year after the subtraction of inflation, the average family in the United States in 2081 will have an income of about $200,000 per year in 1980 dollars, and will have assets that approach a million dollars. By 2081 the five drivers of change that I described in Part II not only will have brought the United States to that level of wealth, but will have brought many other nations to the same level, and some beyond it.

These estimates of real economic growth are probably conservative, because the new technologies that will be developed in the next century will generally be more energy-efficient than those of the past; the floater system and enclosed towns like Waterford will provide for the people of 2081 a great command of rapid movement and consumer goods at relatively low cost in energy. The necessity for more efficient use of energy will also lead in a logical way to the possession of several cars and even a private aircraft by the average family.

In the early days of the now-vanishing Age of Petroleum, energy was very cheap but industrial products were still relatively expensive. At that time, an average family could afford only one car and used it for every trip from grocery shopping to transcontinental touring. Now in the 1980s fuel is too expensive to waste in driving a two-ton car on errands by only one person. As a result, people are tending to buy and use specialized cars well suited to shopping or commuting. As automation reduces the prices of industrial goods, such as automobiles, and energy remains more expensive than in the early days of petroleum, that trend will continue and average families will keep several vehicles. They will spend less total energy on transportation that way than if they were to maintain a single car big enough for all their possible needs.

The attentive reader may have noticed a simplification in the cars I imagine for 2081: they are free of seat belts. Virtually all automobile accidents are the result of human errors, so in computer-guided cars seat belts should be unnecessary. Cars may be provided with automatically inflating airbag restraint systems, unseen during ordinary driving, for the rare situation of an accident caused by mechanical failure. Both the fuel efficiency and the safety of private flight will be discussed in a later chapter, so for now it is enough to note that an aircraft appropriate for an average-sized family burns only about half as much fuel per passenger mile as does a typical commercial jet. As for limits on the overall total use of energy in 2081, the "heat barrier" for the Earth is still more than a century away, even if the energy growth rate worldwide continues to be higher than that of the United States and inequities in wealth are evened out.

Mail can be defined as the flow of information to a specific person in situations where no interaction by immediate question and response is necessary. Though more than thirty years ago there was mail in electronic form (the "V-mail" of World War II), it does not exist at present. There have been several attempts at setting up electronic mail systems within the federal post office administration, but all have failed, not for technical reasons, but because the post office is resistant to change, as it is locked into a bureaucratic system in which patronage and civil-service job security are far more important than efficiency. Given that history, it seems to me more likely that electronic mail will come about through private rather than governmental action. People are buying household computers in extraordinary numbers, and already can add to them devices that dial other numbers or answer the phone automatically, send or receive messages very quickly, and then hang up when the "conversation" is over. When such systems are to be found in nearly every home and office, we will have, de facto, an electronic mail system. The color television set, already nearly universal in the United States, will be an adequate device to display the information received, including color advertisements. At the present rate of technical development, electronic mail is probably no more than one or two decades away, so in the Tehaneys' world of 2081 it will have been taken for granted long since. Eric's letter from home will probably travel from Fox Cluster to an Earth-orbital communications center in the form of an on/off binary code of laser light pulses, and will then be converted to microwaves for the trip through the Earth's atmosphere. If Eric wishes a permanent record of the letter, he will get it from the 2081 equivalent of today's graphic printer device, already common on many small computer systems.

Most readers will probably accuse me of conservatism in putting the introduction of practical, affordable household robots as much as a century away. My reasons for doing so are given in Arthur's historical sketch, and they suggest a further question: if it will be so very difficult and expensive to design robots, why do I assume that they will be introduced at all, even as late as 2081? They will arrive eventually because by 2081 special-purpose machines will already have been developed to do almost every conceivable job, that is, to fill every "ecological niche" that can be filled by machines without either arms or legs. Any further replacement of human labor by machines for dull, unsatisfying tasks can only come about by building a general-purpose machine capable of imitating most human movements—that is, a robot.

I imagine that a device that identifies and locates an individual person with certainty—an "anklet" or its equivalent—will be introduced first for reasons of convenience in communications and in monetary transactions. Certainly, many people would find it attractive to be able to receive a telephone call anywhere, rather than having to hover around a particular phone booth, and would enjoy the freedom of shopping without going through checkout lines. The extension of an identification system to crime prevention will be far more controversial, because it will necessarily require some loss of privacy. In those nations where human rights are protected, participation in a system of identification and location will presumably occur only on the basis of individual free choice. In that case, it is inevitable that enclaves will develop that are barred to persons who refuse to submit to identification. Is that bad or good? The debate over that issue will surely be hot and will continue for a long time. To state only the positive points, an accurate record of individual positions will be an effective deterrent to violent crime in any enclave where such records are required of all who enter. For all crimes from mugging to vandalism, both the accurate identification of the criminal and his tracking and arrest would be quick and sure, and it would be far more difficult for him to avoid punishment than it is now. Technically, it would be easy to add to such a system a feature that would allow anyone in a threatening situation to call for help. Given the capabilities of the system for identification and location, that simple appeal would be enough to provide local police with instant and accurate knowledge of where the threat was occurring and who other than the victim was on the scene. That would make it possible to prevent, instead of merely punishing, most of the potential violent crimes. What would it be worth in loss of privacy to know that one's child could walk any street, day or night, and be safe from molestation, even in a world where a potential deliberate murderer could move thousands of miles in a single hour? What would it be worth to know that one's home was safe from burglary or arson, because no stranger could approach it without being monitored and identified by the town's police computer? A good deal, I suspect, and the proliferation of home burglar-protection monitors, the rapid growth of enclosed patrolled shopping malls and of planned communities entered only through gates, all suggest that a century from now most people who can afford it will be settled in enclaves where security is assured and from which weapons will be excluded.

As the average standard of living increases and long-distance travel becomes easier and more affordable, we can expect a continued increase of cosmopolitanism and sophistication in taste. The ostentatious show of sheer quantity, as in the 1890s, is likely to become even less important than it is today. The vulgarity of size and number of possessions was important to the first-generation wealthy of the past because they always kept the memory of poverty and hunger. Now that a fair degree of affluence is taken for granted by most of the population in the developed nations, disposable income is tending to be used more to obtain convenience and comfort and to satisfy individual interests and tastes. As machines are developed that can work with competence in such craft skills as carpentry and cooking, people will value even more highly individually handcrafted examples of those skills, and they will be regarded as art forms rather than as work. People who enjoy cooking won't have to prepare the ordinary routine meals, so they will devote all the more effort and pride to producing memorable dinners for company, and they will entertain more often. Shopping is likely to become still more important than it is today, and we can expect a proliferation of magazines specializing in luxury cuisine, fashion, or the collection of beautiful or rare objects.

In imagining that a private home of 2081 will be able to provide the visual simulation of an exotic and remote location, such as a pinnacle in the Grand Canyon, I am only recognizing that new systems for the storage of visual information, cheaper and with much more rapid access than photographic film, are already coming into use. The video disc, read by a laser beam, is a notable example and is already being marketed for the home. The Tehaneys' octagonal breakfast room, with its panoramic views, is likely to be constructed with flat mirrors at each of its windows, put at a 45-degree angle so as to reflect into the room scenes that are produced optically in a large attic space above. In viewing distant scenery, the binocular vision of the human eye cannot tell the difference between a simple flat projection and a three-dimensional image, so the optical simulation system may not even have to use holography, the technique that would be necessary for accurate close-up views.

The Tehaneys' eagerness to show their home to Eric is not the expression of a desire to display wealth. Then, as now, a family is likely to show its home to a visitor in order to say, more clearly than can be said in words,

"By this way we have chosen to live, by these books and the music we have collected for our own enjoyment, by these choices of art and of decoration, you may know who we are and what we are like as people. Do you, too, respond to them? Is there a sympathy between us?"

Window on the World

WHEN BREAKFAST was over, I left for my room, and found there a message on the computer from Ellen saying that she would return later in the morning. Another, from Bill, asked me to be in his study by 9:15 so we could talk before his first appointment. I had plenty of time, so I sought out Jeannette, who was busy giving Arthur his instructions for the day.

Jeannette offered to show me the kitchen and led me to the most complex installation of built-in machinery that I'd seen at the Tehaneys'. Just beyond the dining-room door there was a passage with wide counters and cabinets, ovens, and refrigerators. Beyond it was a large farm kitchen with a tiled floor and fireplace. There was an open grill in an island at the center of the room, and above it, a hood with pots hanging from hooks. I smelled the fragrance of garlic hung in strings from the broad, wooden ceiling beams. One wall was of glass, looking toward the garden. The others were lined with cabinets, appliances, and hardwood counters. One cabinet had doors of black glass through which I could dimly see row on row of wine bottles, evidently being kept at "cellar" temperature.

I asked about one large drawer just under counter level. Jeannette demonstrated. She gathered up at random some silverware from another drawer, a glass or two, and a pot from its hook above. At her signal the drawer slid closed. First, I heard machinery at work, and then, after a half minute, the rush of water, muted by soundproofing. She told me the machine was a dishwasher, and that it had taken each of the things she had dropped in, put it on a rack or in a gripper, and was now running the whole set through a wash, rinse, and dry cycle. The only items the Tehaneys owned that required hand washing (now done by Arthur) were family glassware and silver dating from the nineteenth century. I was curious about the dishes and other utensils in the kitchen, and she told me they were from all over the world. The African states exported a great many ceramics, and most of the highly ornamented metal products came from Asia.

At several places on the counters I noticed the rectangular outlines of movable sections. When I asked about them Jeannette touched a key, whereupon one of those sections opened and a food processor more complicated than those at home lifted to counter level from below. Jeannette walked to one of the cabinets, touched a key marked "vegetables," and waited while a heavy cabinet door swung wide and a drawer behind it slid forward, accompanied by a puff of chilly air. She took out a bunch of carrots, broke one off, and tossed the others back in the drawer. As soon as she turned and walked away, the drawer and door closed behind her. She touched a key marked "peel" on the processor, another marked, "long slice—coarse" and dropped the carrot into a V-shaped tray. The machine whirred, the carrot disappeared, and a moment later it emerged washed, peeled, and sliced on a ceramic disc. She offered me the slices and led me to her desk, while behind us the processor disappeared into its counter and a rush of water sounded as it was washed. On her selection of a few more keys, a page from a cookbook appeared in place of the wood-grain surface; two more touches and a menu appeared on several portable slates resting on the counters. She cancelled the display and sat down for a moment, saying, "Desk, give me the cube please."

It gave me an eerie sensation to see a featureless amber cube slide upward at her command from the back part of the desk. It was an insubstantial thing, constructed holographically of light rays. Jeannette was so used to it that she paid it no attention, but she saw my surprise and explained that this was merely the grocery shopping cube, a standard home appliance. When she did take the time to shop in person, she preferred to ride her bicycle to the supermarket, pick out the items she wanted, and have them delivered by floater. Only when she was in a hurry did she resort to ordering through the cube.

Demonstrating, she touched the key marked "Pantry Inventory" and an alphabetized list appeared with quantities beside each item. Some were marked with a green dot, and she explained that those were staple items, reordered by the house computer whenever they ran low. She picked an item that had no green dot, "Teriyaki Sauce," and at a command the list disappeared, the amber cube became so transparent as to be just a shadowy outline, and a line of bottles appeared in it, all of different brands. Out of these, Jeannette selected three to examine more closely. She studied the three-dimensional holographic images of each, rotated them to read the ingredients and other writing, and noted their weights and unit prices, shown digitally on the desktop. She selected one, touched another key, and led me over to a bare counter beside a small door. In less than one minute a gentle chime sounded, the door opened, and a small tray slid out with the bottle of teriyaki sauce on it.

In another recess she showed me a rolling cart, much like those I'd grown used to in airport terminals, but made of attractively carved wood. She told me it was for conveying things to the dining room or terrace, but added that it had one fault: it would keep on following her if she happened to forget to tell it to stay put.

I asked Jeannette who repaired these fancy machines when, as surely happened, they broke down, and she said the procedure was nearly automatic. The house computer detected some faults by itself, and in other cases she simply told it of the failure. From then on the routine was the same: the computer called the service company, and a representative then came to disconnect the unit from the plumbing and electricity and send it back to the factory or a service center where it was repaired by automated machines. All the units were modular, and none was ever repaired in place. All repair centers were located near stations of floater lines, and their fully automated, computer-directed workshops operated twenty-four hours a day, so usually any of Jeannette's kitchen equipment that broke down was repaired and back in operation within one day.

I was surprised at the size of the freezer wall with its several sections, each holding a temperature correct for a certain type of frozen food, and I asked why it was necessary in a town where groceries could be obtained from a store in minutes. She told me that many of the items being stored were unavailable in Waterford's markets. These days, she said, people traveled so much that they brought back ideas from all around the world and from space colonies as well. Specialty companies had therefore found it profitable to supply exotic items in frozen form. The house computer kept track of when each package had arrived and reminded Jeannette when anything had been in storage so long that it was time to plan on using it soon.

At her touch on a key the meat section opened, and I read some labels: "Venison—Bavaria," "King Crab—Alaska," and "Swordfish Steak—U.S. Continental Shelf." Those were clear enough, but I was puzzled by "Grouper—Bahamas Sea Farm Cooperative." Jeannette explained that small fish could be raised cheaply in Waterford's covered ponds and were therefore always bought fresh. Larger varieties needed sea room and had to be found in the open ocean. With eight billion people in the world, most of them able to afford good food, the oceans were overfished, and there were constant wrangles over fishing rights. To protect their fishing industries, some island nations with extensive shallow waters had begun some time ago to set up sea farming in enclosed lagoons. The sea farms were best for reef fish. For the big varieties, such as swordfish and tuna, there was still no source but the deep oceans.

I hazarded a guess that with so many gadgets Jeannette and Bill spent almost no time in the kitchen, but she said it didn't work out that way at all. With so much leisure time, people entertained a great deal, and people like the Tehaneys, both of whom loved to cook, planned more complicated meals than they would have without automation because they knew they wouldn't have to do any of the chopping and the cleanup. Bill even liked to prepare elaborate Hawaiian luaus in a specially installed brick fire pit outdoors. He went through the entire ritual every time, layering meat and fish between palm leaves, cooking for hours with hot stones from the fire, concocting exotic drinks—an unbelievable mess for Arthur to clean up.

I admired Jeannette's garden, and she commented on a problem we don't face in the colonies—insects. Whenever Waterford opened its roof, inevitably some insects invaded—the screens only stopped the big ones. She said her garden was best at the end of the Pennsylvania winter, when she rarely needed to spray, but within a few weeks of the first springtime opening of Waterford's roof she had to begin using insecticides. Happily, Waterford had equipment built into its recycling systems to purify its air and water of the modest amounts of bug sprays that were used. Towns with fixed roofs remained virtually free of insects and required no pesticides at all.

In the garden we passed Arthur. He had changed to gardening clothes and was on his knees beside one of the flowerbeds, weeding. His hands were removable, and he had temporarily exchanged one of them for a specialized tool, a kind of narrow trowel that could grub out weed roots more effectively than any hand-held instrument could.

I asked Jeannette whether it was just a rumor that there were countries on Earth where people starved, even now. She answered, regretfully, that it was true, though for many years there had been no excuse for it. Energy to make fertilizers was in abundance and with greenhouse agriculture, even the most crowded nations were capable of growing plenty of food. But in a world of fixed size, with no way to get more territory without taking it from a neighbor, there was always a war going on, and usually several. Boundaries got pushed back and forth or revolutions erupted, and either way the population was dislocated, the agriculture and food distribution were partially destroyed, and people starved.

Jeannette led me then to Bill's office on the second floor, and its heavy soundproof door slid open as we approached. Bill smiled, and invited me to look around at what he called the tools of his trade. His job, he said, was engineering advising combined with a fairly sophisticated kind of selling, and he did most of it from this office. The room was large and was commanded by an L-shaped desk, partly slanted to form a control and video panel. His chair, a soft and comfortable "executive model," had more controls and details than I'd seen on any chair so far.

Bill and Jeannette conversed for a few minutes, coordinating their schedules for the day, and I learned some answers to a question I had felt would be tactless to ask: what Jeannette did with her time. On this particular day, besides meal planning, cooking, and directing Arthur and the house computer, she would need at least an hour with Bill to plan their four-day weekend trip. She had a tennis date at 10:30, a lunch date at 12:30, and would be back in her own home office at 2:00 P.M. to begin a five-hour shift at her paid job. Jeannette worked for a travel agency in London. Like most such agencies it provided twenty-four-hour-a-day service and had a large staff of people, assisted by computers, to provide its customers with advice based on first-hand experience about resorts, tours, and travel accommodations. Jeannette's office was equipped with a terminal that gave her direct access to the travel agency's computer in London and to clients by way of realistic audio-visual links, so she could plan a trip in consultation with a client and then make all the reservations for it. She and Bill were able to travel a great deal at the expense of her company, in order to obtain the personal knowledge that her advice to clients was based on. Several times each year the Tehaneys attended office parties of her company in London, and through those parties had met a number of friends. Placed as she was in the United States eastern time zone, Jeannette normally worked the evening shift for her agency, from seven in the evening to midnight London time. At midnight another shift began, made up mainly of people whose homes were in Hawaii, displaced eleven hours from London.

Jeannette left to confer with Arthur and the house computer, and I looked around Bill's office. Its windows faced the garden, and its walls were hung with reproductions mainly of naturalistic western scenes in Frederick Remington style. In front of his desk there was a conference table large enough for six chairs, and in the ceilings and walls I saw a number of small lenses.

Bill told me that his firm, like most others, operated on the basis of free working time plus on-call time. They were on a three-day work week, because that was the federal law. On Tuesdays, Wednesdays, and Thursdays he was at his desk between ten in the morning and three in the afternoon ready to receive calls from any coworker or customer. He usually began work on those days at nine and quit at six, and Arthur, or Jeannette when she was home, brought him lunch on a tray. Outside of Bill's on-call hours he was free to do his work whenever he liked, even in the middle of the night or on a weekend. He held meetings with clients during his on-call hours, and for the rest of his working hours studied new products and technical methods soon to be introduced by his firm.

Bill also told me that he and Jeannette were often away four days out of seven, usually combining pleasure with an inspection tour that would be useful to Jeannette's business. In deep winter they preferred the Caribbean or one of the surfing colonies, though this year they would try South Africa. In the early spring they often visited the Carolinas or, if they had a little more time, California. In the summers they usually went north, and in the autumn they made trips of a week or two into space, where they could enjoy the autumn leaf colors in one of the four-season space colonies without the hay fever that Bill was troubled by on Earth. They also traveled in the course of volunteer work that Bill did for a club called Executive Volunteers. It was made up of men and women who were near or past retirement, and who were expert in subjects needed by the developing nations, particularly in South America. At present he was serving as an advisor in Venezuela, where a new free port for freight interchanges was being planned. Bill's company, Routing Inc., specialized in computer-controlled automatic equipment for transferring freight from one mode of transport to another. The new free port in Venezuela would be a transfer point between trucks, floaters, surface ships, subsonics, and boomers. It would take experience to set up the new facility in the most efficient way, and Venezuela had called upon Bill's club to plan the facility and write and evaluate contract proposals. The club members could do most of their work by electronic mail and tele-conferencing, but they still found it necessary to spend several days in Venezuela every month or two. Bill told me that he and Jeannette worked together in another volunteer capacity, visiting a large hospital in Erie for about four hours each week. Modern medical techniques had prolonged life so that there was a large population of elderly people, many in poor health and hospitalized at least part-time. Many hospital services were now automated, and thus the atmosphere of a hospital was rather mechanized and provided patients with far too little human warmth and companionship. Loneliness was a very serious problem, and volunteers like the Tehaneys tried to combat it by visiting hospital patients simply for conversation, often more to listen than to talk.

I asked Bill why he and Jeannette had chosen to settle in Waterford, and he said there were several reasons. His division of Routing, Inc. was based in Cleveland. He usually had to go there for a few hours each week, and often traveled by car, working at his desk while the car drove itself. Both his parents and Jeannette's lived within an hour's travel time of Waterford, as did many of their lifelong friends. Jeannette's family owned property on a small island in Georgian Bay, and the Tehaneys often flew up to see them on summer weekends. As for the choice of living in Waterford rather than in one of the nearby communities that remained open to the weather, Bill just didn't have the patience to put up with snow and cold. He liked to know that when he was done with work, however inclement the weather outside town, he could always get in his hour on the surfboard.

He turned to his desk then to begin answering my questions about fishing. At a touch of a key the windows darkened to near-opaque within a few seconds. The soft luminescence of the ceiling remained. At another command the desk changed its shape: a cube similar to the holograph cube of Jeannette's kitchen rose from the top, and one of the desk's side panels tilted to an angle for easier viewing. Bill's fingers moved rapidly over a keyboard as he talked to me over his shoulder. He said that for a long time children had been educated so that all could type, and that he could communicate with a computer faster by typing than by talking.

According to Bill, most of the fish farms were concentrated in tropical areas where algae grew abundantly. The ecology of fish growing started with a natural disadvantage in efficiency: it took a hundred thousand pounds of algae to produce, through a pyramid of larger and larger organisms in the food chain, one pound of fish. The water that flowed into the enclosed ponds and lagoons of the fish farms was filtered to get rid of mercury, persistent insecticides, and other poisons. The fish farmers got a relatively high yield by constantly supplying nutrients and by weeding out predators. The lagoons were rich in plankton, and the smaller food species were abundant there. But sharks were excluded and so were all the game fish that were bony. Bill said that most of the food fish grown in the farm lagoons could also be grown in Waterford's covered water farms, but the fish raised in the Bahamas could be sold more cheaply because the Bahamians had abundant natural sunshine; Waterford had to employ relatively expensive artificial sources of energy.

The managed lagoons, Bill explained, produced far more fish than the open ocean and were a stable source of revenue. For the Bahamas, a beautiful island group that had once been quite poor, the income from sea farming had more than compensated for the loss of revenue from tourism. When people wanted beautiful beaches and dependable weather these days, they were likely to choose one of the vacation colonies, because in space they could have the beaches and the water and the sunshine without any of the bugs that abounded on tropical islands. To show me one of the sea farms he touched a few keys, explaining that he was connecting to the Earth Resources Satellite Net, whose information was accessible to everyone except those living under repressive governments.

A screen appeared on one wall and on it formed an image, a section of the Earth seen from high orbit. A swirl of cloud covered almost all the field of view, and it was broken only in a few places by a hint of blue water. Bill told me we were looking at a real-time view centered on Cleveland. Waterford was on the right, hidden under a mass of clouds. He touched another key and the outlines of states appeared in red. He interpreted the picture as showing the edge of a low-pressure area that was centered over Detroit, and he guessed it would be three days before there was any real sunshine in Waterford. This was the sort of weather that made Bill particularly glad he had moved to an enclosed town. He shifted our view to a point several thousand miles south, and I found myself apparently suspended above a blue ocean, dotted with islands. Toward the left of the picture a curious, curving avenue of clouds appeared, and Bill muttered that it was the Gulf Stream. He touched more keys. By then I had caught on to the coordinate system that flashed longitude and latitude at the corner of the screen. Our view stopped above an island edged with white beaches, then plunged toward the sea where lines of breakers became visible. They weren't breaking on a shore, but on a line of spars forming a wide protected lake with the island at one edge. Boats dotted the enclosed lagoon. Somewhere down on that island, Bill told me, there was surely a minicomputer keeping track of all the variables and monitoring the catch. There were probably only about a dozen fishermen on any one shift to keep the operation going. The fish farming was stable except during hurricane season, when the island might be targeted for a direct strike by a major storm. In that case, the workers would have to harvest most of the fish and then take in the spars and membrane barriers to prevent their being destroyed by high seas. The lagoon would then equalize with the ocean, and after the storm it would take some time to get the system back to normal.

It was time for Bill to go to work, but I asked if I could stay and observe. He seemed pleased by my interest. He spent a few minutes selecting and arranging data in his computer and editing a presentation he was about to make. Then he keyed an address and his computer locked onto that of a businessman in the Boston area. The room darkened, but accent lights strengthened to spotlight Bill and the top of his desk so he could be picked up by video cameras. I was startled by a sudden movement at the opposite side of the room and turned to see what appeared to be a man, full-size, stepping out of the wall and walking forward to take a seat facing Bill at his conference table. I concluded it must be a remarkably lifelike holographic image, representing in real-time the movements and gestures of Bill's client several hundred kilometers away.

Bill opened with a brief, understated speech, and the man asked a number of questions. To respond, Bill sometimes keyed three-dimensional displays in his holographic cubes; at other times he passed data directly from his computer to the other. Several times the visitor, whose voice must have been coming from a concealed speaker under the conference table, asked Bill for hard copy, meaning printed documents and color photographs that could be handled. Each time he did so, Bill arranged for the materials by a few moments' work at the keyboard. At one point we all watched a prepared documentary film projected on Bill's screen and apparently on the other man's at the same time. Bill made a few comments while it was in progress.

The meeting concluded after twenty minutes or so, with a detailed request for additional information that would require Bill's checking back at the factory. The image of the other man stood up and smiled. Bill stood up also, waved a salutation across the room, and the image turned and disappeared into the wall. I realized then, from a consideration of the lines of sight of the holography, that a section of the "wall" must itself be produced holographically. Bill spent a few more minutes at his desk making notes on the meeting and forwarding a request to his company. Then he turned to me with a smile to say that the interview had gone better than he had expected. The gentleman who had just "visited" him was a notoriously difficult prospect. Bill went on to say that he would be meeting with a number of other people over the next few hours and would find each new situation a challenge. He enjoyed dealing with people and he enjoyed studying machinery, so his job suited him well. He suggested, though, that I would probably find more interesting ways of spending the rest of the morning, for the interviews might seem to me rather repetitious.

Ellen arrived as I was taking leave of Bill, ready with plans for the rest of the morning. I particularly liked her suggestion about exercise, so we began with a half hour of easy running. The entry to Waterford's jogging path was across the lawn and "past the plumeria." We found a grassy track that wound between high bushes and trees and followed it at an easy pace. Our way was bordered in greenery everywhere except for a short section near the town's west wall, where Ellen pointed out to me the louvres that could open it to the winds. Ellen explained that about one-quarter of Waterford's area was given over to common land owned by all the residents and was dedicated to walking and bicycle paths, parks, playing-fields, and small waterways for canoeing. The Tehaneys were all fond of exercise, and except for such special occasions as my visit, usually bicycled within the town. As we returned to shower and change, Ellen called to Arthur to bring two bicycles to the front door within the next few minutes. That reminded me to ask a question: why did the Tehaneys always ask for Arthur by name, even when they really wanted to talk to the house computer? Ellen told me that "Arthur" was a cue word; the computer was set up to respond only to instructions that began with the word "Arthur." Otherwise, people might, for example, be having a conversation about lights, use the word "dim"—and suddenly find themselves in the dark! If at some later time the Tehaneys happened to have a guest named Arthur, they would have to pick a new, temporary, cue word.

When we met for our shopping expedition, I asked Ellen why we were going out rather than using the holographic cube. She said that she never shopped by cube unless it was for a standard item that she was quite familiar with. I had asked about personal communicators, cameras, and clothes, and she felt that there were so many models and styles that there was no substitute for going to a shop and comparing samples. She also felt that we would get more individual service by going to the shops in person rather than asking for samples through the cube, even if the samples were sent to us on approval over the package-transfer system. She also admitted that she'd rather have an excuse to be on the move—everything in Waterford was made so easy that she could stay home all the time if she wanted, but that got boring.

Our bicycle path to the shopping area was routed to avoid both roads and jogging paths. I enjoyed the fragrant flowers and thought how alike much of the landscape was to Fox Alpha, except that here there was always a sense of enclosure, of a roof close overhead. We pedaled to a bike yard outside the pedestrian mall and walked the few steps to the camera shop. As soon as we began talking with the shopkeeper, a woman of Ellen's age who knew her stock very well, I realized that I should have done some research. A camera with film was what I'd had in mind, but that turned out to be an old-fashioned technology, used only in some special kinds of portraiture or aerial photography. In the end I chose a "K-Star," a model small enough to fit in my pocket without making a bulge. It had two lenses and only one control, simply a button to push. It could take clear pictures over a light range from the harsh sunlight of space to the darkness of a candlelit room, adjusting its contrast automatically with each shot to bring out the detail. The "photography" was onto solid-state elements behind each lens, and the camera had no moving parts. Neither did its "picture pack," a featureless block that fit into an opening in the camera and stored 100 color-stereo pictures that could be erased. I bought several picture-packs, and a viewer that could connect to any stereo-video. Both on Earth and at home, stereo-videos were common, so my K-Star would do nicely for record pictures.

Then I went a little overboard and bought a holographic color camera. Its projector created out of light rays what appeared to be solid three-dimensional figures in front of an apparently blank rectangular block. It was especially useful, said the saleswoman, for portraits and figure photography. To complete the impression of the camera-laden tourist, I picked up a movie recorder as well. That was also a solid-state device, without moving parts.

A personal communicator was harder to choose because there were so many different models. In contrast to Fox Cluster, where distances are short and the total population less than 100,000, Earth has all the complications of hundreds of nations and hundreds more of space colonies. Consequently, there are often appreciable communication time delays because of the speed of light and the unfavorable geometry of the Earth, a sphere that doesn't allow line-of-sight communications over more than a few kilometers.

I was given a choice of wrist, pocket, necklace, or belt clip models. Yet, even that was only the tip of the iceberg (a curious Earth-phrase that tickled my fancy), for to use a communicator as more than a calculator or a personal note taker I would need a credit account and there would be charges for calls and for access to computer-memories and libraries. Ellen suggested that I might want to make arrangements with all of the three or four major credit-card firms, so that I would be covered nearly everywhere in the world that I was likely to go. Any of the models would keep track of my credit balance, she told me, and any of them would balance the charges to each card if I wished. She admitted the multicard system seemed complicated, but though credit cards had been around for more than a century they had never been boiled down to just one card that everyone could use. In Bill's opinion, she said, competition and the antitrust laws were the reasons there were so many card companies. People who lived in socialist states only had one kind of card, of course, a nationalized one, but even there shopkeepers had to deal with the many credit cards of tourists and business travelers.

A few doors from the camera shop we found an office equipment center. I was looking for two things: a translator and a portable composition machine. At home I was used to composing engineering proposals and articles on a desk-model computer system with graphics capability, but I wanted something much more portable for my travels on Earth. Again I found a bewildering variety of models to choose from. I chose a flatpack model with a keyboard that, when folded flat, was no thicker than my little finger. It came with a half-dozen flexible slates, each the size of a standard sheet of typewriter paper. I could spread out the slates on the desk of any hotel room I might find myself in. Any one of them could be used to store a reference book, which I could also take with me in the form of a small, square wafer about as big as my thumbnail and not much thicker. The salesman suggested that I take on my travels, if I liked, a library of several hundred volumes in that form. Once I began typing I could store in the composition machine pages, paragraphs, or sentences of my own, call them up on any of the slates for modification or inclusion in my manuscript, and leave them stored electronically in the machine when I packed my bags for the next trip.

The translator was a slim pocket model, and it was said to contain a few thousand words of vocabulary for each of 300 languages. For the most important world languages, of course, it contained ample vocabularies and grammars of almost literary quality. To use it I would simply hold the device midway between myself and the person I was speaking to. It had microphones on both sides that were directionally sensitive, so it would relay spoken sentences in either direction.

We made our last stop at the clothing store that Bill usually patronized. There, somewhat to my relief, I found nothing surprising. Except for the almost total disappearance of the necktie and the introduction of new materials, not a great deal had changed in men's clothing styles for nearly 200 years. Most of my selections were conservative because I'd be traveling all over the world and I wanted to blend into the landscape as much as possible. But Ellen also persuaded me to buy a couple of sporty jumpsuits and something fashionable for an evening of dancing.

Ellen's three-room apartment near the lagoon was much less automated than her parents' place, but the lunch she put together was not at all the "catch-as-catch-can" she'd warned me to expect. After lunch I asked Ellen about her future career plans, and she grew thoughtful. She said that her choice of ecology as a profession would almost certainly lead her to a career off-Earth. If Waterford were a good example, Earthside was easy living, and I asked if she'd regret having to emigrate. She replied that living could become too easy. Now that the robots were in common use, it was harder than ever to find a career where a human could feel genuinely needed. And she'd been uncomfortable with the contrast between appearance and reality on Earth. I had told her of the beautiful pictorial simulations of Swiss alpine scenes that I had enjoyed on shipboard, and her immediate unspoken response had been that the simulations must have gone through electronic editing. The real Swiss mountains, she said, were covered with cable railways and tourists. She admitted that the colonies weren't natural, but neither was much of the Earth any more. At least the colonies were honest constructs, and their ecology had started with a clean slate without any chemical poisons in the earth and water. And also, Ellen's ecologist friends had told her, working in a space colony offered them the comparative pleasure of dealing with only a single government. On Earth there was such a legacy of overlapping jurisdictions, city, county, state, and federal, that ecologists spent most of their time coping with bureaucratic regulations. That wasn't how she wanted to spend her life.

Before returning to the Tehaneys' to change for our trip to Cleveland

in search of good jazz, I browsed through Ellen's collection of antique vid-
eo-discs. I was beginning to get the picture that people spent a good deal
of effort on hobbies and collections.

—*E. C. R.*

MANY OF the futuristic devices that Eric encounters in this chapter—the
breakfast room with its changing panorama, the holographic display of supermarket packages, the movie camera with no moving parts, the portable
writer, and the translator—are manifestations of an existing trend in technology, carried forward in a realistic way over another century beyond our
era. This is the trend toward the storage of more information in less volume and at a lower cost. As I noted in the "Computers" chapter of Part
II, there is no inherent physical limit on how much information can be
stored until we reach the point of storing a binary bit in a single atom. The
panoramic scene that Eric enjoys at breakfast makes no large demands on
information storage, because the storage can be passive, as on a phonograph record, rather than active, in the sense of taking in new information
as well as giving out previously stored bits of data. In computer jargon, the
panorama requires a "read-only memory," abbreviated ROM, rather than
the more complicated "random-access memory" (RAM), which can not
only be read from, but also written on. Because the panoramic scene need
only change every few seconds to show the varying cloud patterns and
shadows, all of it may be stored on a single video disk, costing only a few
dollars.

The translator, like the panorama display, requires only a ROM
memory, but in the case of the small, hand-held translator the memory
should not have moving parts. Straightforward development of present-day
solid-state memories will suffice for that.

The portable composition machine, though it is impressively compact, is no more than a natural extension of our present-day minicomputers, all of which now are capable of being used for word processing. At
present, writers and editors find word processors irritating and difficult to
use, because their programs are not very intelligent and because their displays are limited to a single fixed screen, whose position and color contrast
can become fatiguing to the eyes and body posture. But as programming
experience develops and as minicomputers grow in capability, programs
will become far more sophisticated. And when liquid-crystal technology,

now used only for watches and other small displays, can be applied inexpensively to "slates" the size of a piece of typing paper, an author can scatter such slates about a desk and refer to several within the same few moments of time. Liquid-crystal displays, in which selected patterns in a transparent sheet of a glasslike material can be made to become opaque by applying to the sheet a very weak electric field, could also form the basis for the controllable windows that Eric observes first in his automobile ride from Erie, then in his room, and finally in Bill's study.

Solid-state cameras already exist in the form of the video cameras that are now cheap enough to be affordable consumer products. Now, of course, we must store the electronic information they produce in the cumbersome medium of magnetic tape (which explains the shoulder bag that the video cameraman must lug around), but solid-state "RAM" memories will eventually become so inexpensive, probably through the development of the magnetic-bubble memory system described in Part II, that they will replace magnetic tape for video recordings.

Eric finds holography in wide use in 2081, and encounters it in many forms: there is Jeannette's food-planning desk, the teleconference in Bill's office, and the portable holographic camera for personal use. Holography was developed less than two decades ago, and for all my education in physics I find it the closest thing to magic that I have ever seen. Holography allows us to store and project the image of a three-dimensional object in space. As stereo photography was an advance in realistic display beyond the ordinary flat photograph, so holography is an advance in realism beyond the stereo picture. To understand something of how it works, recall first the principles of ordinary photography; they are identical to the process by which a single eye views a scene. Light, traveling as a wave oscillating from crest to valley to crest again, is reflected off a point on a solid object. The lens of camera or eye takes the light that enters it from that point, and focuses it to a corresponding single point on film or retina, in such a way that a wave crest leaving one point on the object is reformed into a wave crest at the focus. In photography, light coming from a bright point on the object is a strong, high wave and makes a corresponding intense point on the film. The image, the complete picture, that is made up of all such points is flat—it carries no information about depth. In stereo photography, or in the identical system of binocular vision that we make use of with our two eyes, two views are taken from slightly different locations. Each view is flat, but the brain then combines them to form a three-dimensional impression of the scene. Our vision and the stereo photography have the same limitation: each is a view from just one single vantage point, and there is no way that one can tell how the scene would look from other places, no way to "walk around" to other vantage points, without moving the pair of cameras or the pair of eyes to the new location.

Is it possible to do better than that? Is there a way that a single photograph can store information, not just about the scene from one vantage point, but from all? Yes, there is, but only by using information that is lost in ordinary photography and is also lost in our system of vision. The lost information is called the relative phase. It is the correlation between the light-wave crests arriving at different points on the image. If the light waves arriving at two such points crest at the same time, those two points have the same relative phase; if one light wave crests just as the other is halfway between crest and valley, their relative phase is 90 degrees. Dennis Gabor, a British physicist who was born in Hungary, found a way to record and preserve that phase information on a single flat piece of film, a "hologram," and so to reconstruct images that appeared to be three-dimensional even when the observer moved around to a different viewpoint. Gabor received the Nobel prize in 1971 for that fundamental invention, whose practical application depended on the laser, a device still relatively new when he did his research. The "holographic transformation" that allows a piece of film to store both intensity and phase information depends on the original hologram being formed by light of a single, very constant frequency. Light of that kind, which can only be made by a laser, has the property of being so regular that its crests and valleys repeat exactly over a distance of many meters in space, forming an identical pattern. Ordinary white light, by comparison, travels in waves like those of the ocean, with so much variation in size and in the distance between crests that the pattern never repeats.

With those clues, we can appreciate that the "accent lights" Eric notices illuminating Bill at his desk are more complex than they seem. Though their light appears white to Eric, it actually consists of laser light of three different colors, emitted in short bursts and repeated many times per second in the sequence 1, 2, 3, 1, 2, 3, ... Each burst of one color is forming a single hologram, and three holograms of three different colors create a three-dimensional image in natural full color. Those pictures then repeat many times per second, as do the frames of a motion picture, to follow and record Bill's gestures and facial expressions.

If we survey the modern home in a contemporary industrial nation, we find that automation has progressed farthest in the kitchen; these days, a cook bent on getting power assistance for every chore can boil, roast, broil, bake, carve meat, chop vegetables, make drinks, wash dishes, preserve foods, and open cans, all with the help of electricity and with varying degrees of automatic control. Since automation has already progressed so far in the kitchen, there are limits to how much qualitative change there is still to come. The kitchen range and self-cleaning ovens that cook by convection, broiling, or microwave are already with us; we can expect that long before 2081 they will have progressed as far as anyone is willing to push them. Of chores that most cooks genuinely dislike, the only ones that remain are related to cleaning up, to the chopping of vegetables, and to disposing of wastes. Kitchen gadgets such as choppers and mixers are examples of solutions that become new problems. They save time but must themselves be washed. In Jeannette's kitchen that machinery cleans itself. To go beyond that point in automation will require not only fixed machines but also a device able to reproduce all the motions of a chef who takes food from storage, chops and mixes it, puts it into cooking devices, and takes it out again. Nothing short of a robot like "Arthur" could perform all of those tasks in an effective way.

And what of the kitchen as a social center? For a time architects tried to transform the kitchen into a clinical, mechanized factory for the processing of food—only to find that most people preferred the homely warmth and intimacy of the farm kitchen. Modern designs attempt to combine the efficiency of the new with the humanity of the old. The primitive kitchen was a center for social interaction and communications, and both those functions are provided for in successful modern designs. With development of the automated transfer of small packages, the kitchen will become not only a center for information, but the terminal of a transport network. It will remain, I estimate, the most highly automated room in the house.

Jeannette takes it as a matter of course that her home's machinery, when it breaks, is repaired very quickly, but never by repairmen on the spot; always at a distant center. That will be the natural result of several developments: machines are becoming more complex and therefore more difficult for a repairman to understand. Automated factories can make new subassemblies at lower cost than a repairman could fix broken ones. Finally, automated package-loading and efficient, high-speed floater systems will make it possible for just three or four service centers to provide twenty-four-hour repair and return service even to a nation as large as the United States.

In a kitchen of the year 2081 a robot butler selects a bottle of wine for its owners, viewing holographic color projections apparently suspended in the air. The creative planning of menus and recipes will remain the province of humans, but many tedious food-preparation and kitchen-cleanup duties will be automated.

Shopping for food and supplies falls in a curious area. Like the automobile, shopping fills psychological as well as utilitarian needs. Researchers interested in why and when people buy have found that the typical shopper in a modern supermarket goes into a state of semitrance. Pulse rate slows, the eyelids lower, and the shopper enters a lethargic reverie, a state evidently comforting and safe. Decisions to purchase are made in that state, decisions that might be quite different if the shopper were alert and on guard. It would be possible, technically, to eliminate the need for leaving the house to shop, but I suspect that a system of that kind, even if developed, won't be used all the time, because shopping is pleasurable to many people.

In his tour of the Tehaney home and in his shopping expedition with Ellen, Eric observes several happy effects of the drivers of change. With easy and inexpensive global communications, Jeannette finds that her most attractive job opportunity is with a company in London, where her home location, five time zones away, becomes an advantage. The robot, Arthur, uses in his weeding one of the advantages that machinery has over bone and muscle. He can change either of his hands to a very strong, specialized tool capable of rotating continuously like an electric drill.

In that same day Eric finds that human institutions, desires, and interactions alter the effects of the Five, and keep the world of 2081 in many respects as paradoxical as our own. Historic open towns coexist with Waterford; the natural human desire for sunlight and fresh air force a compromise with the purity of air and water that Waterford could achieve if its roof were never opened; starvation coexists, unfortunately, with plenty. Going from the tragic to the trivial, credit cards and their equivalent in the charging systems based on anklet-signals are not simple and monolithic, but instead competitive and diverse. And with all the technical perfection that 2081's systems for sound and vision have achieved, Ellen chooses to collect century-old video discs showing Astaire-Rogers films that are older still, just as we now cherish records that preserve, even in a scratchy form, the voice of Enrico Caruso and the tunes of the 1920s jazz bands.

Highway in the Sky

THE FAMILY business that had brought me to Earth had to be concluded by a visit to Nantucket Island, and Bill suggested that I make the trip in a small land plane. A friend of his, Noel Wicks, owned property on Nantucket, and Bill arranged for me to fly with him on his next visit.

Noel picked me up at the Tehaneys' early one morning, told his car to bring us to Erie Southwest Airport, and then explained to me that if the weather had been good we'd have left from Waterford, the plane having ferried itself from Erie at Noel's command. This morning, unfortunately, Waterford's small airport was closed because of gusty crosswinds and icy runways.

As we drove Noel obtained a weather forecast, filed a flight plan, and was given a choice of time slots, each with an assigned altitude. The car went slowly because of the icy roads, but finally it turned off the main highway and entered an airwall tunnel to the terminal complex—an enclosed town of its own, with warehouses, hangars, and maintenance shops connected by a continuous roof. We stopped before an entrance with automatic glass doors, and Noel told his car to park for the present, but to follow our return flight plan and meet us wherever we should land. We disregarded the row of baggage carts, because I carried only my briefcase and Noel only his data pack, a pocket-size computer with a memory for every air routing and airport in North America. He told me that he normally left his data pack connected to his house computer, so that it could be updated by calls from an information service to which he subscribed. The terminal lobby was crowded with people entering and leaving through doors to hangar areas and the street. Noel led me through one of those doors to a large vaulted space with many lines of aircraft. They varied in design but were all about the same size, and Noel said that larger aircraft were kept in other hangars. He showed me his own plane, climbed inside it for a moment to initiate its automatic checkout sequence, and then joined me for a walk-around inspection.

To me, aerodynamic shapes were still novel. I had built model planes as a child, but I found the smooth lines and curves even more beautiful in full size. Noel's machine sat low to the ground on three wheels. Near its rounded nose two small wings extended straight out to left and right, and just behind them the cabin area began. It had large windows giving panoramic views, and there were doors on both sides. Each door was hinged at the bottom, and when fully opened just touched the pavement to provide a set of steps for entry. The tail of the plane tapered to a point forming a spinner for seven curving propeller blades, each of them no longer than my forearm. A short, open cylinder fitted closely around the blades, forming a duct. Just ahead of the duct, tapered wings angled back from the fuselage to end in upturned vanes. The front edges of the wings, which would slice the air in flight, were unpainted aluminum, and Noel explained that hot air was piped through them to prevent icing.

Noel had called for fuel, and a man arrived with an electric-powered truck to carry out the fueling while we completed the inspection. Noel remarked that the preflight sequence on the plane's computer would check all the operating systems, but that it couldn't tell if someone had accidentally bumped and dented a wing with a truck. When Noel was satisfied that the plane was undamaged we climbed inside it, and took the forward two of its four seats. In front of us was a control panel with a large video and, below it, many small gauges, dials, and levers. Noel said those were for backup, because everything was normally done through the video. To maintain his pilot's license he had to demonstrate on a simulator, twice a year, that he could land the plane if the computer system failed, but he had never been forced to do so in reality.

Noel locked his data pack into a slot in the control panel, and said to the computer, "Ready in sequence." Behind us the doors closed, and the video told us to fasten our seatbelts and secure any loose articles. When the display changed to "Taxi Commencing" the low hum of an electric motor on our nosewheel began, and the plane moved quietly forward. Noel remarked that in the old "stick-and-wire-days" pilots used to taxi by running the engines on the ground, but that the practice had been abandoned because it wasted fuel and blew dirt in people's faces. His plane followed a painted yellow line past a long row of aircraft, several of them attended by groups of passengers loading or unloading. We rolled to the first of a pair of automatic doors, and when the second set opened we were hit once again with driving sleet. The taxiway was free of snow, and Noel said it was heated. We joined a line of planes, all slowly taxiing, and the video told us to stand by for the start up of the engine. The panel lights dimmed for a few seconds and a low whine sounded behind us. Then there was an increase in sound level, a rapid increase in pitch, and the gauges on the panel came to life. The video reported, "Engine start up normal. Stand by for system checks." It was busy for a few minutes after that, and Noel, who hadn't lifted a finger so far, seemed to pay close attention to the report. An amber disc glowed and the video informed us, "De-ice will commence now for preheat." The cabin had cooled a little since we'd left the warm hangar, but now it warmed up again. I asked Noel what the plane was made of, and he told me that aluminum formed most of its structure. The most highly stressed parts were a composite of plastic and strong, thin carbon fibers, and the turbine blades were of a special ceramic that could only be made in the zero gravity of space; it remained strong even at a very high temperature.

Suddenly a chime sounded and the video told us, "Stand by for takeoff in 60 seconds. Climbout will be at 1,000 meters per minute at 200 kilometers per hour. Cruise altitude will be 3,000 meters, airspeed 600 kilometers per hour. Expect light turbulence below 2,000 meters."

By now we were at the head of a line of planes. Noel kept his arms folded as the plane moved out onto the broad concrete runway, turned to line up, and immediately began to accelerate. I was nervous, for I could see a plane ahead of us, just rising toward the low scudding clouds. Noel confirmed that in the old days, when pilots flew themselves, such a close spacing between two aircraft would have been too dangerous. Now, though, satellites determined the position of every aircraft within an error of less than two meters, and air-traffic control computers regulated the speed, height, and course of every plane in order to prevent collisions. Traffic had to be diverted only when weather conditions made all flying unsafe. In a thunderstorm, for example, the airport would be shut down, and all landing aircraft would be kept in a holding pattern at a safe distance until it passed.

As the speed indicator came up to 140 kph the nose lifted and we were off and climbing. The noise level remained so low that Noel and I could talk without raising our voices. Just after we left the ground there were hums and clicks, and green lights came on to tell Noel that the landing gear was tucked away and the flaps set for climb. Within seconds we were in dense cloud through which I could just see the wingtips. Sleet hammered on the windshield, but a warm blast of air from small vents kept it free of mist. Three minutes from lift off we broke free of the black storm clouds. The sleet changed to snow, we leveled off between layers of cloud, and I could see several other planes on parallel paths and one ahead of us. Noel watched the "groundspeed" readout with pleasure, and told me we were being helped along by the strong west wind that usually brought such weather.

He touched a button and the video switched to a color picture of the landscape that it said was flowing by underneath us. As we passed Elmira and the beautiful lakes north of it, I saw the traditional towns and villages, unenclosed, and among them the occasional "New Towns." It puzzled me that most of the New Towns were open to the weather, with their roofs rolled aside; then I realized that the satellite photo the video was reproducing for us must have been taken on a clear spring day.

An amber disc glowed, and letters formed over the scene informing Noel that a pilot decision was required. He touched a key and the satellite view was replaced by a computer message warning that there was severe icing ahead on our course line. The traffic control system could give us an alternative route, just as short, if the pilot would approve our passing through the satellite power microwave beams in northern New York. Our passage would take seven minutes. If we rejected that option, we would have to go into a holding pattern and be delayed at least half an hour. Noel seemed more pleased than alarmed by the interruption. He told me the airways avoided the power beams, so pilots didn't often get the opportunity to see the power antennas. He approved the change in routing, and a minute later—I suppose when there came a break in the traffic—the soft whine of the engine went up in pitch, the nose lifted, and we climbed through the next layer of cloud. There the snow stopped and in a few moments we broke out into brilliant sunshine, above a billowing sea of dazzling white.

Noel explained the principles of satellite solar power to me, and said that it supplied most of the electric energy used on the planet. He added that in a sense we were flying on satellite power ourselves, because much of the energy the satellites supplied was used to make clean-burning artificial fuels for aircraft and long-distance surface vehicles. I'd been dismayed at the idea of flying through a microwave beam, but Noel assured me that it was safe to do so. The beams were so diffuse that birds could fly through them without being harmed, and all aircraft licensed for long-distance flights were shielded against microwaves. Noel said that flying through the power beam would be a new experience for him, too, and that the decision to do so was one of the few still left up to the pilot-in-command.

We were lucky that day. For a half hour we flew past a towering black mass of cloud, and then below us the clouds thinned out just as the amber disc glowed again and the video told us: "Estimating arrival in first microwave fringe area in one minute. All exterior communications and navigation electronics will now shut down until exterior signal level returns within normal limits. On-board computer now controlling aircraft on basis of established wind drift and pressure altimeter." Noel was amused by that, and told me the fancy language really meant dead reckoning.

Below us the landscape changed subtly. Snow covered the ground everywhere, but there were circular areas above it resembling transparent, gauzelike curtains. Noel said that these antennas allowed sun and rain to penetrate, but did not allow the microwaves they collected to filter through. So the areas below the antennas were prime spots for cattle grazing in summer and for greenhouse agriculture all year round. Power for the greenhouse lights was especially cheap at the antenna sites, and that cheap energy also made the antenna locations attractive for heavy industries.

Once we were past the antennas the traffic-control computer took command of the plane again. In clear weather we crossed a shoreline toward Martha's Vineyard, a low, wooded island. A few moments later, after just an hour and a half of flight time, the video told us to prepare for landing. Electric motors came to life, the landing gear lowered, and flaps extended on the wings. With the engine purring almost without sound we glued ourselves, so it seemed, to an invisible line drawn straight out over the water from the end of a runway. We touched down on the concrete at Nantucket Island, and immediately a louder sound came from the engine as its thrust was redirected forward for braking. When we had slowed to walking speed, the engine whined down to a stop and the nosewheel motor took over with a low hum, pulling us along a sequence of yellow lines to automatic doors and a transient hangar.

A rental electric car took us, at Noel's command, on a one-hour scenic tour, and I felt as though I had been carried backward in time. Every house seemed to be taken from an eighteenth-century fishing village. There were no electric signs or large enclosures. Near a beach Noel halted the car, and we got out in the teeth of an icy wind, tangy with salt spray.

Whitecaps covered the ocean, and wind-whipped waves crashed on the shore. Seagulls screamed and circled above the beach, where a recent gale had piled mounds of live scallops. Noel showed me his house, and I found it much like the others nearby, made of wood, with no projecting eaves on its roof. Inside, though we were out of the wind, it was still bitter cold, and all the water-pipes had been drained for the winter. Noel said that architectural styles on the island were regulated because Nantucket was now a national monument, and he grumbled a little that he couldn't even change the color of his front door without permission from the Historical Association.

Back in the car we explored the property my family still owned. An elderly couple lived on it, people who loved the island and its changelessness, and were happy even with its damp and cold and fogs. They were relieved when I told them the Rawsons had no intention of turning them out, but wanted to retain this little piece of Old Earth as their own.

Noel and I had a seafood lunch in a warm, dark, low-ceilinged restaurant. Afterward he dropped me at the lawyer's office. The ceremony was brief, and I was the only attendee. Tom Coffin, the young lawyer, told me his family had been on Nantucket for three hundred years. He couldn't imagine living anywhere else, and had returned home after law school. To him, my home seemed strange, exotic, and unimaginably distant.

Noel joined me after the meeting, and our car bounced its way over the cobblestoned streets of the town to the narrow, smooth pavement beyond. At the airport we dismissed the car, took off into the icy wind, and made our homeward journey almost entirely in darkness. By Noel's choice we stayed low, where the headwind was less strong, and paid the price of two hours of turbulence before the plane touched down in gusty winds at Erie. Noel slept through our landing, and only roused when the chime signaled that we were parked in the hangar. His car met us at the entrance of the terminal, and we both dozed on the way back to Waterford. At the Tehaneys' I found that Bill and Jeannette had retired. Arthur greeted me, took my briefcase, and offered me a nightcap in my room. The cleaning machines were in possession of the lower floor.

Breakfast next morning was in the small octagonal dining room, in the setting of a balcony overlooking the Grand Canal in Venice at a time two centuries before. Gondolas passed as Jeannette poured fragrant Italian coffee and Bill handed round pastries. The Tehaneys kindly offered me their home as my headquarters during my stay on Earth, and said that I could come and go as I pleased, as Arthur would remain in the house and would look after me whether they were at home or not. I accepted gladly, and asked Bill how I should travel between the old cities in Europe and Asia that I particularly wanted to see. He answered that there were several types of aircraft, starting at the top with the orbital shuttles and the trans-oceanic "boomers" that I'd already sampled. He offered me another session with his computer, and after breakfast we retired to his office.

Bill started his explanation with the shuttles, and told me there were four spaceports, all of them equatorial. At the equator the Earth's rotation gave a boost of a thousand miles an hour, free, for a launch due east. Now that space travel had to be tolerable even for old people and invalids with heart problems, the shuttles were limited to one gravity of forward acceleration. But in order to reach orbital speed with so gentle a push there had to be a downrange distance of 2,500 kilometers straight east. The shuttles were powered by solar-driven lasers in synchronous orbit, and if a beam ever missed and hit a populated area it would be violently destructive. The only way to be absolutely sure that this could never happen was to put the shuttle launch ranges exclusively over open ocean. The ranges were off-limits to surface shipping except to freight lines that were willing to sign hold-harmless agreements. But with all those constraints, the Earth's geography didn't leave many possibilities. There were just four places along the equator that satisfied the range requirements. I had arrived at the spaceport called PPR: St. Peter and St. Paul Rocks, on the equator east of Brazil at 10 degrees west longitude. That had been my best choice to match the eastern United States time zone, so that I could arrive in Waterford by late afternoon. PPR's main customers, however, were eastern South America, West Africa, and Europe. Most of North America was more conveniently served by EPS: Eastern Pacific Spaceport, south of Clipperton Island at 115 degrees west longitude. On an artificial floating island, EPS was the only spaceport that was entirely man-made.

Bill called up more data on his library computer to give me further details. I found that the USSR, India, China and East Africa were the major users of MIS, a spaceport built on an atoll south of the Maldive Islands in the Indian Ocean, at 72 degrees east. Japan, Australia, and New Zealand used AWP, in the Admiralty Islands of the western Pacific, north of New Guinea. He tapped keys for a few moments, and we looked down on an island criss-crossed with wide, long runways. As I watched, two aircraft entered the scene on parallel courses, low above the water. They were long and sleek, with narrow delta wings. Bill remarked that the scene should look familiar to me because it was PPR and those were shuttles landing. PPR ran them on a thirty-second headway, a thousand people a minute, coming and going—five hundred million a year from that one spaceport alone. Counting all four of the commercial spaceports, plus the specialized high-acceleration civil and military spaceports that nearly all the individual nations owned, the traffic back and forth from space would have been enough to empty the Earth of people in a few years, if it had all been one-way. Of course many of the travelers were making round trips: people from Earth going out on business or for a vacation in one of the colonies, or people born in space inbound on business or to sample the scenery and the old historical cities here. Still, on balance, there was a steady trickle outward. Worldwide, the natural growth rate was now down to less than 1 percent on Earth, and emigration off-Earth was higher than that. Bill guessed that in fifty years the population on the planet would be lower than it had been for over a century.

Below, on the runways, two brilliant spots of red appeared, as bright as miniature suns. Bill touched the keyboard and they muted to merely starlike. Now I could see they were centered on the widest parts of two shuttles, stationary on the runways. The two delta-winged planes accelerated, and they were on courses so exactly parallel that they seemed tied together. I held my breath: the aircraft were still rolling, and not much runway remained ahead of them. At the same moment four plumes of water vapor appeared, one at each wingtip. Bill told me that was the moment of rotation, and added that the weather must be very humid at PPR.

I knew, vaguely at least, what was going on. Intense laser beams from a satellite in orbit were pouring energy into turbojet engines on each aircraft. Air was being sucked in, compressed, heated to near-incandescence, and expelled to generate thrust. Bill's hand moved and the scene shifted, centering the twin aircraft on the screen. Ocean raced by below them. I jumped momentarily as a line of cloud appeared at the edge of the screen, but I needn't have worried. As the aircraft, low over the water and accelerating, met the edge of the cloud layer above, the laser beams drove inexorably through. Cloud evaporated instantly in a swirl of eddying vapor, and twin furrows plowed through the haze of white. At the same moment both planes broke through the clouds, still accelerating. Bill told me that the cloud layers over the ocean were usually low and thin; it wasn't often that the laser beams couldn't get through them and the shuttles had to be boosted above the clouds by fuel-burning, reusable "strap-on" engines. The shuttles would be at three times cloud height before they would go transsonic. At around thirty kilometers altitude they would begin using their on-board stores of liquid argon, but until then they could scoop in enough air for their turbines.

By now the angle of view was oblique, and abruptly the scene shifted. Again we were looking straight down on the aircraft. Bill said we'd been switched to the view from another satellite, and he didn't follow the launch much farther. Already there were two more shuttles on their way up from PPR. I asked about the choice of argon for the shuttles, and Bill said it was used because it was inexpensive and easy to store and also because it was a natural constituent of the atmosphere; any molecule released at high altitude lasted a long time. For my over-ocean flights I'd be riding ordinary boomers, fueled by synthetic hydrocarbons. I could take one of those planes out of Cincinnati or Cleveland. If I rode one to Europe it would arrive in two hours, and, he added with a wry smile, I'd find my internal clock five hours out of line with the local time. None of the modern advances in transportation had done anything to cure the ancient problem of jet lag.

—E. C. R.

F<small>LIGHT</small> <small>WITHIN</small> the atmosphere is far more difficult than in space. Spacecraft move in vacuum, where drag does not exist and where forces are all simple, predictable, and controllable. Spacecraft can navigate by direct visual observation of the stars, and their communications can operate free of obstructions on a direct line-of-sight. In zero gravity, the docking of a spacecraft can be carried out at a snail's pace. By contrast, aircraft must operate within the turbulent, unpredictable medium of the atmosphere. Vision is blocked by clouds and darkness. Radio is blocked by the Earth itself when the distance of transmission exceeds a few tens of miles. A plane, working always in gravity, must develop speed for lift, so the tricky operation of landing must always be carried out quickly, under pressure. Atmospheric flight is rich in surprises and dangers: icing, thunderstorms, turbulence, and fog.

Flight instructors estimate that all but 1 percent to 10 percent of the population could be taught to fly, but only a few people do learn: about 1 percent of all adults in the United States, and far less in almost every other country. Cost dissuades many. Others find flying too demanding of continuing study, care, and attention to detail. Even so, "general aviation," transport by private and business aircraft, is one of the fastest-growing segments of the United States economy. The reasons are several, but first among them is efficient use of time. A private plane offers direct point-to-point travel, and lets the traveler leave at the time of his choice. It frees him from the hassles and delays of waiting in line, of baggage inspections, of being bumped from a flight because of airline overbooking. It gives even more flexibility and convenience than a car, because it can travel a straight line independent of roads, mountains, or bodies of water.

I introduced the subject of private flight in an earlier chapter by referring to a fact that few people know: a small plane is remarkably fuel-efficient, far more so than a commercial jet. A four-person aircraft that flies fast enough to equal a highway speed of 225 miles per hour gets the equivalent of over 80 seat-miles per gallon. The Boeing 727, a fine commercial jet that accounts for more passenger air travel than any other aircraft, does only about half as well per seat-mile. For distances of less than about a thousand miles between towns of average size, the total operating cost of a four-passenger airplane is less than just one economy airfare, and because light aircraft can operate between small airports conveniently close to a traveler's home and destination, a trip by light plane can often be made in less time overall than by commercial jet.

The sophisticated electronics newly available to the light-aircraft pilot within the past decade has already professionalized personal air travel. In many respects the navigation and communication equipment available now for small single-engine planes is better than the best that could be purchased even for multimillion dollar commercial jet aircraft a dozen years ago.

Workable systems for the automatic landing of aircraft even in zero-zero conditions of ceiling and visibility have existed since the early 1960s, but their introduction for routine use has been slow both because of the need to prove very high levels of reliability, and because of pilots' concerns about keeping up their own skills. As one veteran airline captain put it, "I get about eight landings a month. I give four of them to the copilot. If I turn over any to an automatic-landing system, how do I maintain proficiency?"

Yet the automatic-landing systems are being used more and more widely. Whereas once only the British Airways Tridents could land legally in zero visibility, now other aircraft are being certified to do so. In the late 1970s, TWA began advertising that its Lockheed L1011s could get into nine major United States airports even when all other aircraft were forced to divert. Once I was mentally complimenting a 747 captain on an unusually perfect approach, touchdown, and rollout when he came on the intercom to say "Ladies and gentlemen, our landing was fully automatic, even to the engine thrust reversal and the application of the brakes. I just sat back and watched the computer do its thing. Welcome to London." Long before 2081 automatic-landing systems of that capability will be commonplace, even in the smallest aircraft, just as every other advance in automation first introduced in the largest airliners has found its way eventually to the smallest planes.

Unfortunately, up to now there has been no corresponding advance in the automation of our air-traffic "control" system. The present system of what is called air-traffic control is a hodgepodge of leftover World War II technology, dependent on radars that scan only once in ten seconds and on even cruder instruments for the measurement of altitude. In even the biggest jets, altitude is measured by a barometer whose working principle goes back two hundred years to the earliest days of balloon flight. The barometer's reading is coded electronically and sent back to the ground controller each time the radar beam scans by. Due to the errors inherent in such an archaic system, and its dependence on corrections for local barometric pressure, often the ground controllers get readings that are off by several hundred feet. As a pilot I have been forced many times to correct for the many deficiencies of the present system of air traffic control. Pilots of airliners must do exactly the same, as I know, because we share the same communications frequencies. Because the technical basis of today's air traffic control is fundamentally wrong, consisting of a patchwork of different systems pieced together with many gaps, control has to be exercised by people—the air traffic controllers—just as liable as are pilots to human error, but with far less personal stake in performing flawlessly.

Unfortunately, the Federal Aviation Agency is currently spending all its efforts in expanding the obsolete system of the "positive control" of aircraft, even though an objective NASA survey showed there are more mid-air collisions in "controlled" airspace than outside it. The FAA's response to the NASA survey was an attempt to suppress it—a frightening example of how the preservation and expansion of a bureaucracy takes precedence even over the saving of lives.

It will probably take several decades to break through this governmental barrier to safety, but long before 2081 we will surely have an effective system of air-traffic control, based on a simple combination of computers, automation, and orbital satellites. One satellite will send out an interrogation signal many times per second, to be received by all the aircraft over an entire continent. An inexpensive, low-power transmitter on each aircraft will respond, and its response will be picked up by the interrogating satellite and by two others, all three in synchronous orbit over the equator. The satellites will relay the signals to a ground station, where simple time measurements will establish the location of every aircraft in all three coordinates within an error of only a few feet. There'll be no need for the high power and wasteful inefficiency of radar, dependent on faint echoes. The locating signals will go upward, penetrating weather the short way. Given reliable information of that precision, it is but a short electronic step to safe, totally automatic flight.

There are now two barriers to a social revolution in private aviation comparable to the revolution in automobile travel brought about by Henry Ford and his Model T. One is the rigorous, demanding standard necessary for manual control of a plane. Automatic flight will bypass that barrier. The other is the capital cost of aircraft. The natural effects of the drivers of change over less than a century will sweep away that barrier also. The average family in 2081 will be about twelve times as wealthy, in real, non-inflated currency, as a similar family today. At that time a fully equipped airplane will be a smaller investment than a new car is to the average household now.

The price to be paid for the resulting universality of flight is that most of the flying in 2081 won't be by what we would call pilots. We shouldn't feel badly about that; to the barnstormers of the 1920s, we who fly today would seem little more than button-pushers, and the pioneers would sneer at our caution and the thick rulebooks we abide by. The price is well worth paying, not only for the freedom it will give to our descendants, but for the appreciation it will give them for the beauty of Earth's landscape. Nothing can equal the combination of privacy, peace, and visual beauty of a flight in a light aircraft at an altitude of a few thousand feet. Once that kind of flying can be enjoyed by everyone, citizens will be able to identify and inspect such environmental scars as strip mines and junkyards, scars that can now be hidden far too easily from surface observation by thin screens of trees. With that ease of inspection there is bound to come a strengthening of the public pressures for environmental cleanup.

The overwhelming majority of aircraft accidents of the present day are the result of human errors in judgment. Of those, the majority are associated with weather. Clouds, mild turbulence, rain, or snow merely present a well-trained pilot with a challenge, some excitement, and the opportunity for practicing skills. Some weather, though, is pure poison: above all, thunderstorms and icing. Occasionally, even an experienced commercial jet pilot tackles conditions his plane can't handle. In the late 1970s a large jet crashed as it attempted to land at New York's LaGuardia Airport in a thunderstorm. Not long after, a DC–9 penetrated a hailstorm in the South, lost both engines, and went down, killing all on board. There'll still be thunderstorms, icing, and hail in 2081, but I doubt that the pilots of that day will have freedom of choice in dealing with them. The total navigation system of that era will make it impossible for them to override the caution of the rulebook.

Aircraft obey the eternal laws of aerodynamics, so I believe we can make a close guess at the light-aircraft design of 2081. For efficiency and good visibility the plane will be a canard, with its main wings near the tail and smaller wings near the nose. In a crude form that arrangement was used in the original Wright Flyer, and in modern form it has shown record-breaking efficiency and speed. The wings, built of the superstrong materials that are just beginning to come into use today, will be narrow and of long span for highest efficiency. The entire structure will be bonded or welded instead of riveted, and so will be very smooth. With its aerodynamic "slipperiness," and a power plant much more efficient than those of today, the light plane of 2081 will cruise at two-thirds of the speed of a subsonic jet. You may be surprised at my guess that it will not be pressurized, but there are sound reasons for the prediction. Pressurization adds greatly to the weight, complexity, and cost of a plane. In a pressurized plane the doors must be small and few in number, and the windows are too small for comfortable viewing of the landscape below. In a commercial jet, small windows are no great handicap, because most passengers don't have window seats, and even those who do can't see much from a height of seven miles. But the light aircraft of 2081, built to be as competitive in cost and in design as are automobiles today, will have to offer large windows and doors, as well as the capability of high-altitude flying for certain weather conditions, and an affordable price.

There is a way that all those requirements can be met at the same time: by the adoption of a system that is just now being introduced for the Harrier "jump-jet" fighter plane, a unique, British-designed aircraft that is capable of directing its jet blast downward so as to hover like a helicopter. Because the Harrier is intended for operation out of clearings very close to a battle line, every effort has been made to design it to be refueled and reloaded with ammunition very quickly. The Navy, modifying the Harrier

Private aircraft of 2081, which will be as common then as is the family car of to-day. These aircraft, quiet and fuel-efficient, will fly at half the speed of sound entirely under the control of a central air-traffic computer.

design for use in support of the United States Marines, found that too much time would be lost in refilling the plane's oxygen tanks. To solve the problem, the Navy contracted with the Bendix corporation to develop a small, lightweight "molecular sieve" device that could accept oxygen molecules and reject nitrogen, to enrich an unpressurized cabin to 95 percent oxygen. The system, now under test, is designed to operate with no maintenance for at least 2,000 hours. The technology is not inherently complicated, and is sure to find its way to light aircraft eventually.

Noise abatement will be a prime concern in 2081 in a world with a population far higher than our own. The automated aircraft control system probably will not permit planes to fly lower than about a mile of height, in contrast with today's thousand-foot legal minimum. But the aircraft themselves will also have to be designed for nearly silent flight. Technically, the challenge can be met; in the 1960s, Lockheed developed for military reconnaissance an airplane so quiet that it was inaudible on the ground when cruising just a thousand feet overhead. The light and heavy aircraft of 2081 will have to be almost that silent, and we know already that we can approach that ideal most closely with a ducted propeller: a multiblade fan running at relatively low speed within a close-fitting shroud. The details of blade shape and the number of blades are now the subject of considerable research by manufacturers in cooperation with NASA.

The piston engine has reigned supreme for light aircraft in the first three-quarters of a century of flight, but by 2081 it will defer to the turbine. According to the July, 1979, issue of *Business and Commercial Aviation*, a two-year NASA-sponsored study by four major engine manufacturers concluded that a turbine could be manufactured for the low power range that private planes use, that it could be as fuel-efficient as a piston engine, and that it would be from three to six times more reliable for the same overall cost. The turbine has far better altitude capability than the piston engine, and it can provide from its compressor stages heated air both for melting the ice on the plane's wings and for the molecular-sieve device that will enrich the cabin oxygen. An incidental detail that Eric notices on Noel Wicks's plane can be found on all commercial turbojets already: wing surfaces that are to be heated are left unpainted, so that no thermal barrier will prevent the melting of ice. All planes in 2081, from the largest to the smallest, will taxi by electric power, the electric motors being geared to nose or main wheels. Electricity for those motors will probably come from fuel cells. There is a small chance that the combination of the fuel cell and the electric motor will reach such a level of efficiency and lightness that it will become the primary propulsion system, but the odds right now seem to favor the turbine.

As for the number of engines, one will do. Even now engine failures cause only a minor percentage of serious accidents. With turbines, the accident rate will be lower still. Curiously, for a combination of reasons, the fatal-accident rate due to engine failures is twice as high on twin as on single-engine aircraft. It is cheaper to maintain one engine than two, so I believe the typical light aircraft of 2081 will have just one turbine.

Personal aircraft are still thought of by most people as frivolous luxuries. Local airports are unwanted, and each year hundreds are swallowed up to become shopping centers or housing developments. That will continue, I believe, until the drivers of change bring automated, silent, private flight within the reach of the average family. Then, as happened half a century ago when cars became available to ordinary people, attitudes will change. Gradually, restrictive laws will change in response to them. Already a few groups of plane-owning families have built communities around private airfields. Each home has not only a garage but a hangar. By 2081 the community airport will become as necessary a feature of each New Town as its road system. Where now airports are being covered by housing tracts, by 2081 the pendulum will have swung the other way, and decaying slum housing will have been razed in some areas to make way for new communities with their own airports conveniently at hand.

At the heavy end of the aviation scale, we can guess at the design of aircraft for long-distance travel on the grounds of energetics and public response. For the same weight of vehicle, it will cost about ten times as much energy to achieve orbital speed as to travel supersonically over a distance of a few thousand miles. Therefore, it seems unlikely that vehicles will be boosted to orbital speed except when their destinations are in space. Laser power for aircraft has been studied by engineers at Boeing, but for safety reasons I don't think it is likely to be used except for the launching, over fixed oceanic corridors, of shuttles heading for near-Earth orbit. For that one very special purpose, the high energy demands of orbital launch and the requirement of launching due eastward at the equator combine to make laser drive an attractive choice. When the shuttles climb so high that their turbines can no longer find air to breathe, the shuttles must switch to rockets, ejecting as reaction mass a propellant that is carried on board. That propellant is likely to be argon, a gas that is easily liquefied and dense in liquid form, requiring tanks of only moderate size. It is environmentally safe, being a natural constituent of the atmosphere. The spaceports of 2081, limited in number by geographic constraints, will be transportation hubs far larger than any the world has seen and will be served by many airlines. I doubt that supersonic flight over land by those airlines will ever be permitted, unless at altitudes so extreme that the sonic booms produced at ground level will be nearly inaudible. If that development occurs, though, my speed estimate for the "boomers" may turn out to be too conservative.

Though most of the flying in 2081 will be controlled by computer, I hope that soaring, the silent flight of gliders borne upward by solar-driven currents in the atmosphere, can still be carried on nearly everywhere at the lower altitudes that will be denied to powered flight for environmental reasons. I hope there will be large free areas where enthusiasts can still indulge in acrobatics and in open-cockpit flying without instruments. And I know that even those who can fly only by pushing buttons will still find, in 2081, the beauty of the clouds and of the landscape.

The Lotus and the Thorn

IN THE two weeks after my return from Nantucket I learned, with the help of the Tehaneys, something of the range of choices and interests that inspired effort and commitment among their acquaintances. A great many people were active in amateur sports, especially tennis and golf. Waterford's courts and golf courses were playable twelve months of the year, and so were those of every other New Town. People with more sedentary tastes were devoted to hobbies as diverse as gardening or jewelry making or collecting and restoring antiques. And now that the industrial revolution on Earth was nearly three centuries old, there was also extremely keen competition to find and restore its early artifacts; any automobile or airplane more than a century old was an investment worth far more than its modern counterpart, and those few planes and cars dating from before 1930 changed hands for incredible sums, usually ending up in the possession of museums or private collectors. Objects of art more than 150 years old were in a still more rarefied price range, and very few remained in the hands of individuals.

Many of Ellen's friends were young people with plenty of energy and a desire for a simple life, who lived by choice in restored nineteenth-century houses in rural areas. With the advent of controlled-environment agriculture it had become nearly impossible for individual farm families to compete economically with the mass-production greenhouses, so in most of the United States it was relatively easy for a young couple to purchase an old farm property and cultivate the soil, not for cash crops, but simply to live independently. We visited one such family, a little south of Waterford in rolling hill country, and found them living quite comfortably on the resources of their own acres. Their house was heated by open fires and woodstoves fueled from their woodlot, and in winter they kept in shape by sawing trees and splitting logs. They plowed their fields with horses, and dried and preserved their vegetables and other produce to tide them over the winter. They kept chickens, pigs, and cows. I found at their farm only a few concessions to the twenty-first century, but they were significant ones. The family did keep one old four-wheel-drive car, and fueled it with alcohol distilled from crop wastes and sewage. They did have electricity, from a small alcohol-burning motor-generator set, and they used it for lights, for a television set, and for the one ultramodern device that I saw: a home-educational console for their children. That had been a gift, accepted after much discussion, from the grandparents.

After that view of a family taking satisfaction in working hard and being relatively self-sufficient, Ellen showed me another extreme, pure fun aided by every trick of modern electronics. The venerable Walt Disney commercial empire had established around the turn of the century one of the largest "theme parks" in the country, on a bulldozed, reclaimed piece of New York City that had once been a slum. We spent two days there without seeing the wintry weather outside. Nations, companies, and multinational corporations all maintained permanent exhibits in the park, and I spent much of the first day touring their displays and learning a great deal from them. Then Ellen steered me toward the amusements. I had never seen a railroad train, so we rode a nineteenth-century steam-puffing original, through the lands of the Vikings, the Pirates, the Gaslight Era, the Wild West, the Roaring Twenties, Breakout (the early space-colony period), and Starways, the last an array of pure-fantasy planetary surfaces.

Throughout our stay I was never sure where physical space left off and simulation began. It was especially hard to find that boundary in the popular one- and two-person rides. It took me some time to figure out how those rides could give such complete simulation of acceleration forces, visual appearance, and response to controls. I concluded that each must be similar to one of our spacecraft flight simulators, equipped for limited movement in two directions plus rotation. Each must be computer-linked to an enormous data bank for visuals. "Scuba Dive" simulated an underwater journey by torpedo sled, but we came out dry. In "Bobsled" Ellen clung to me as we racketed down a mountain between curving walls of ice. "Wright Flyer" placed us side by side with the wind in our faces, an ancient piston engine chattering behind us, and wires singing in the slipstream as we made a bouncing takeoff from a meadow, did loops and rolls under our own control above a village that was two centuries in the past, and descended to a landing. The computer, I found, disengaged the "controls" when I tried to force a crash. In "Martian Sands" I paced a red landscape, laser rifle in hand, and defended my life against "sand tigers" that the real Mars had never known. We finished with the gentlest and most memorable of the two-person rides, "Alpine Balloon." In a wicker basket below a multicolored curve of fabric we drifted over the Alps, past meadows where we heard the sound of cowbells. We crossed a slow-chugging cogwheel train, narrowly missed a dazzling snowclad peak, and settled to land in a grassy field while avalanches still thundered behind us.

Not all the amusements on Earth were so gentle. I'd seen a number of advertisements for auto races near various cities, but Ellen warned me that they tended to be gory. With computerized driving on most roads, anyone looking for dangerous excitement was likely to turn to racing events, and in consequence, these were often marred by harrowing fatal accidents.

On the evening of our second day at New Amsterdam we were in one of the parks, watching a fireworks display, when Ellen's communicator chimed. Ellen opened the locket and a tiny image of Jeannette's face appeared. She was obviously worried, and told us first that we'd have to cancel plans made earlier for an outing next day with their best friends, the Donovans. Jack Donovan had suffered a flareup of a heart problem, and the couple was leaving immediately for a colony so that he could have an artificial heart implanted. The next morning, as we were on a New York to Erie floater, a second call from Jeannette arrived. She looked relieved and told us that the operation had been successful, and that Jack was recovering well.

When we arrived in Waterford I asked the Tehaneys for details and told them I'd been especially puzzled by Jack's making the shuttle flight to an orbital colony when he already had a heart problem. Bill told me that it had been a natural choice because the orbital hospitals were in the forefront of innovation in medical techniques. Although a complete system of national health insurance had been in effect in the United States for many decades, the health services available on Earth were a little behind those of the colonies. Medical guilds had fought against automated surgery, and doctors were often forced also to compromise their medical judgment by a concern over possible malpractice suits. At first the orbital hospitals had been justified for physical reasons, because their zero-gravity wings were superior for patients with burns or cardiac problems. Lately, though, the jurisdictional reasons for being treated in orbit had become at least as important as the physical. Most orbital hospitals were outside the legal jurisdiction of nations, and in consequence had fewer and simpler laws. Their reputations were known quite well on Earth as a result of word-of-mouth reports from former patients, passed to private information services that could be tapped by home computers on a subscription basis. Most doctors in orbital colonies worked on a "no-fault" basis, and could therefore keep their fees lower than those of doctors on Earth, who had to pay stiff premiums for malpractice insurance. Although most physicians were still trained at the large teaching hospitals on Earth, many of the brightest alumni found their way later to the orbital hospitals where they could learn the most modern techniques and take best advantage of automation. More than anything else, it was the automated operating room that drew Jack to an orbital hospital. Fully controlled by computerized machinery and supervised by an expert surgeon, it virtually eliminated the possibility of human error.

Although Bill's own heart was in good shape, he had done a good deal of research on artificial hearts because, he told me, if he were to have a heart problem later he didn't want to make a decision under pressure. The standard operation was replacement with a mechanical heart, although in rare circumstances an ailing heart was sometimes replaced by another living one. Mechanical hearts, made of selected metals and plastics, almost never produced immune reactions. It had taken, said Bill, several decades to solve the most serious of their original disadvantages, the lack of an energy supply. The most satisfactory solution turned out to be equipping each heart with a built-in chemical plant, microprocessor-controlled, that converted the carbohydrate glycogen, carried in the bloodstream, into lactic acid with the release of energy. The reaction was a simplified version of a more complex chain of reactions carried out by living human cells.

—E. C. R.

OUR ANCESTORS' recreation came at the end of six-day work weeks with working days twelve or more hours long. Now that the average employee puts in less than half that many hours on the job, a large industry has developed around leisure-time activities. It will grow still larger as the workweek continues to decline and the drivers of change extend even further the range of choices available for sports and hobbies. To excel at a competitive sport demands talent, hard work, and often, considerable self-denial. The easier work becomes, the more popular will be the sports demanding skill and hard physical exercise. We see that already in the rapid growth of tennis as a popular sport. Most healthy people need challenge, and as work diminishes its claims on their time they will turn to sports to satisfy that need. We can expect to see ever-higher standards in amateur athletics.

Within the space colonies a whole new category of sports will develop, based on the freedom to move in all three dimensions in the absence of gravity. Some will be team sports, and their inventors may be people born in the colonies to whom turning off gravity will seem so natural that they will regard eternal one-gravity as a handicap. Body-contact sports will have to be played by teams assembled in one place, so sports teams will be among the most frequent space travelers.

The affluent society has a taste for sports that demand expensive equipment or installations: golf courses, tennis courts, ski lifts. The recreations of boating, snowmobiling, jet skiing and hang gliding are also expensive indulgences. For people who like outdoor activity but lack the strength, ability, or time to acquire the necessary skills, there is a further revolution in store. When microcomputers and automation are applied to sports equipment, we will be offered surfboards that always stay under the surfer no matter how uncoordinated he may be, and powered gliders that won't let themselves be stalled—they will land safely even if their owners could never pass a flight test.

In a world with abundant leisure time, many people will become absorbed in active hobbies, others in more sedentary collecting. Construction hobbies that demand very high levels of skill, such as aircraft building or the weaving of tapestries, will become even more popular than they are to-day. And some people, like the farming family that Eric and Ellen visit in this chapter, will make the business of living itself a hobby, rejecting all the labor-saving gadgetry of 2081 for the satisfaction of raising their own food and being as self-sufficient as possible.

In this chapter Eric finds New York to be a center for recreation, more than for manufacturing or transport. In making that projection, I am betting on the continuation of a trend that is evident already: the tradition-al role of the city as a center for industry and a crossroads for transportation no longer makes sense. Freight, increasingly containerized, is better han-dled by modern automated equipment away from the congestion of a city. Passenger travel centers on airports rather than on harbors or railway junc-tions. New factories are sited in open land or industrial parks. According to retail experts, investment for new shops now goes into small cities of 50,000 or so population, at least fifty miles from metropolitan areas. In-vestment capital will always flow toward buying power and security, and especially as New Towns come into being, they will become the centers for such investment. Big cities will be handicapped because their govern-ments, made up of well-entrenched bureaucracies, will resist change and be slow to respond to the new opportunities that the drivers of change will bring. By contrast, the smaller and especially the newer towns will be able to respond quickly, and their local governments, some of them modeled after those worked out in the environment of space, will use simple codi-fied laws and reduce operating costs by the aid of computers and automa-tion.

Despite all the disadvantages that big cities now face, my guess is that they will survive and will be healthier in some respects by 2081 than they are now. They will be the irreplaceable centers for museums, for live the-ater, and as encounter points for the singles set. Their historic central areas, restored and reconstructed, will be attractive especially to those tour-ists who have been born and brought up in space. The top level of corpo-rate management, hard-driving and keenly competitive, will probably continue to work in city skyscrapers where the force of personality can be exerted on others of their kind. But the clerical work of 2081, most of it done through computer consoles, will occupy employees in their homes, far away from their company's headquarters. We already see a phenom-enon that heralds these urban changes of the future. While government and private funds are invested in restoring city centers, an investment that makes good sense, some of the ugliest housing areas in the largest cities are being abandoned. Property values drop, buyers cannot be found, home-owners lock their doors and drive away, never to return. Squatters "un-lock" those doors with bolt cutters, but as the decades pass and the drivers of change raise the average income level, even the squatters will move on. The favored historic housing areas, those that will be preserved, are those of relatively high density with artistic value, located near city centers. New York's brownstones are one example, Philadelphia's two-story brick houses another. Blocks of that kind will lend themselves well to being transformed into roofed New Towns, though transport networks will always be a prob-lem within them. It is the dull urban blight beyond them that is most like-ly to be bulldozed away in the next century, to be replaced by greenbelts, botanical parks, New Towns, recreational theme parks, and small airports.

Traditionally, the big cities, for all their attractive features, have also been breeding places for crime. In our era more than half of all crime is committed by people under the age of twenty-five, but such youthful criminals do not thrive in every society. While Japan, for example, has been going through the most rapid transition in its history, its crime rate has actually decreased. Crude individual crime—muggings, rape, burglar-ies—is the sort that victimizes ordinary people most seriously. Because it is carried out for the most part by young, unsophisticated, "unprofession-al" criminals, it can be prevented relatively effectively by the electronic systems for personal identification and location that the drivers of change will bring.

Crimes masterminded by the major organized gangs normally don't strike ordinary individuals directly. Those "professional" crimes will also be discouraged by the new electronic tools, but less effectively, because of the expertise and resources that an experienced adult gang can command. Money robberies are likely to decrease because money transactions will evolve to exchanges of coded information between computers. Instead we will see an increase in a sophisticated, nonviolent form of crime: the coun-terfeiting of credit cards and the manipulation of the computer programs that carry out transfers of monetary credit.

Crime at the syndicate level feeds on our more ignoble appetites. We've seen it in a repeating cycle first with liquor, then with gambling, and now with drugs. When a government prohibits something, any honest business is forced out of supplying it. That leaves an open market for the crook. After a while the underground market may become so big that gov-ernments want to cash in on it. This has already happened with gambling and liquor and may happen with certain of the less harmful drugs.

The people who control syndicate crime are already wealthy. They continue to commit crimes out of greed and the desire for a power over others that can be far more complete in the underworld than in open society. Syndicate crime is likely still to be with us a century hence, but it is likely to be less important. Increasingly, wealth and population will be concentrated in space, and there the syndicates will have a harder time gaining a foothold. Space colonies will be too self-sufficient in the essentials of life, too small in scale, too simply governed, for syndicate operations to hide within them easily. Their boundaries, the hard vacuum of space, will make entrance and exit controls easy and effective.

Instead, as is already happening to some degree, organized-crime families will turn toward legitimate operations. New generations within them will insist on living free of the fear of arrest, and the drivers of change will discourage some of the profitable criminal activities. Already one of the main advantages of a crime syndicate, when in competition with an honest business operation, is its access to reserves of investment capital. There have been many reports of syndicate capital legitimately invested in large hotel chains, and suggestions that it is moving into such areas as jet-speed small-package delivery. There will be more examples in the next century when crime syndicate operations will be honest, aided by that little edge in startup capital.

A newer type of violent crime, already upon us, will be far more difficult to check with the new tools that the drivers of change will bring. That is politically motivated assassination, kidnapping, and terrorist assaults. The new electronic gadgetry will be far less effective against those sorts of crimes; often the protective electronics will be countered by the sophisticated technical resources of a foreign government that is providing clandestine aid to the terrorist or assassin. The most frightening development in crime during the next century will be of just that kind: terrorist assaults carried out with the aid of nuclear weapons. More than half of the nations of the world are relatively unstable and often undergo political coups or revolutions. In the confused hours or days when those upsets are taking place, the nuclear weapons owned by those nations will be the primary targets for theft by the revolutionaries, and some are sure to disappear, to be used later by extremist individuals or groups. If a few terrorist bombings of the destructive force that only nuclear weapons produce do occur in the next decades, they will probably have a greater effect on the subsequent dispersal of populations out of the cities than all of the economic factors that the cities will face.

I have put into the form of Eric's narrative my estimates of the socio-logical changes in medical care that the drivers of change will bring. Though they are necessarily harder to predict than the technical changes, my predictions are consistent with current social trends as well as with in-evitable technical developments. The less responsible members of the legal profession have discovered a bonanza in malpractice suits, and doctors have been forced in consequence to buy expensive insurance against mal-practice judgments and to charge their patients higher fees in order to pay the premiums. That doesn't help to improve the quality of medical ser-vices. On the contrary, it tends to force doctors to carry out drastic and ex-pensive, though very safe, operations in order to avoid simpler procedures that might, under some remote contingencies, be questioned later.

If medicine is socialized, malpractice suits will disappear because the government will refuse to submit to them. If, as seems more likely, there remains a large amount of medical practice that is outside any government system (as is the case in the United Kingdom even after several decades of socialized medicine) it seems to me probable that public opinion will force through new laws that will eliminate the need for malpractice insurance and also make it easier for a patient to choose the most talented and re-sponsible doctor. Already, several years ago, we saw an example of such a change: citizens in a number of states voluntarily gave up some legal rights in the interests of speed, simplicity, and economy, by voting in "no fault" auto insurance. With such insurance, a motorist injured in an accident is wholly compensated by his or her own insurance company, and the entire procedure of a trial to determine who is "guilty," a question often unan-swerable, does not even occur. The injured party can be certain of com-pensation, even if no one else can be found to blame for the accident.

In the world of 2081, anyone with a serious medical problem will have access to the data on successes and failures for at least some doctors and hospitals and may choose to be treated in an orbital hospital, possibly a country unto itself, where the latest developments in computers and automation will supplement the traditional healing arts.

As computers are further miniaturized and automation reduces the cost of complex mechanisms, we can expect also that surgical implants will substitute in part for the use of drugs. A cardiac patient may be fur-nished with a microscopic implant that displays his blood pressure con-tinuously on his wristwatch, and may be taught biofeedback to control his blood pressure without the help of chemicals. A woman who prefers to avoid the use of drugs to regulate ovulation may have a miniature implant that leaves the bodily functions undisturbed, but measures her deep-body temperature continuously and computes whether she is fertile by analyzing her temperature record for her past cycles. Yet, for all the sophisticated mechanisms that will be used in 2081 to prevent illness and to assist in its treatment, the character, the skill, the sense of responsibility, and the humanity of the individual doctor will still be critically important. The doctor may be assisted in diagnosis by computer correlation of such disparate facts as the conclusions of recent research and "what illness is going around just now," but the doctor's own real concern for the patient will still be of the greatest importance in any treatment.

For Richer, for Poorer

FOR MY travels around the planet during the next several months Bill suggested I get advice from an Australian friend of his, Aaron Marconi. According to Bill, Aaron had a penetrating eye for modern history and had been studying it for more than thirty years. Bill felt that an intelligent, enthusiastic amateur who took advantage of his abundant leisure time could learn as much as a professional, but he warned me that Aaron's ideas were controversial.

We called from Waterford early one morning, in order to find Aaron at home in the Australian evening. His holographic image, life-size in an armchair in Bill's study, showed him to be a white-haired man of dark complexion, and he was strongly built. His smile was engaging, but I noticed the sardonic look in his eyes: the eyes of an observer, missing nothing, taking nothing at face value.

On Aaron's advice I would visit South America to see examples of great nations that had made the transition to affluence within the last century. He also advised me to visit Africa and Japan to observe the extremes of slow technological development and rapid progress. In addition, I planned to spend considerable time in Britain and continental Europe to visit historic cities, but realized from Aaron's lecture that I would find no differences in technical level between Europe and North America.

In Brazil I stayed with the da Silvas, friends of the Tehaneys. The two families had met in a ski resort space colony, a place of ten-month winters with perfect snow conditions, interrupted only by short Arctic summers just long enough for the pine trees to seed. For the carnival time in Rio, the da Silvas offered me an apartment in Santos, 300 km south of Rio. Santos was on a floater line, so I could commute to the city in half an hour, but sleep in quiet comfort. Throughout Brazil I found the same kind of floater lines, enclosed towns, and rapid communications systems that I'd grown used to in North America.

On the boomer to Dakar I reviewed my notes on Aaron's lecture about Africa. He had told me it was still one of the most serious problem areas on the planet. Africa's racial antagonisms were even worse than those that the United States had suffered through two centuries earlier, and they were compounded by regionalism, multiple tribal languages, ignorance, poor communications, and political upheaval. After 150 years of civil war and revolution, every village was stuffed with weapons. But Aaron had also pointed out to me several African success stories, nations that were well on the way to universal education, thanks to direct-broadcast satellites, and economic prosperity, owing to abundant electric power from space.

To help me understand what I would see in Africa, Aaron had given me some of his own theories, warning me that they weren't the orthodox conclusions of professional scholars. He had argued that language areas tended to endure over long periods, whereas governments didn't. By his count, more than half the nations I would visit had been called by different names a century earlier. His reading of history had convinced him that the most successful nations were those with homogeneous populations, because homogeneity eliminated one source of violent conflict. He also argued that a nation, in order to thrive, had to have some strong ethic that made for honesty in ordinary dealings. In many African nations I would be visiting, the only strong disciplined tradition was in the army, so I would find them governed by military dictatorships. The technological level of each African nation was governed by complex international politics. According to Aaron, much of the worthwhile technical education on the planet was conducted by the multinational corporations. They didn't dare risk much investment in Africa because of the chaotic political conditions there, but in the stable nations that welcomed foreign investment, the international companies had built technical schools. As a result, those countries had forged ahead of the others even more rapidly. Of course, Aaron added, every African nation, no matter how small, was armed to the teeth—nuclear proliferation was total—so every now and then one of their capitals went sky-high when the local out-party managed to smuggle in a nuke. He advised me not to stay too long.

At airports in nearly every African nation, as in some countries of South America, I found myself oppressed by hard-eyed young guards, each with a machine-gun in the crook of an arm. There were body searches and x-rays. Two days after I passed through one airport, a nuclear weapon launched from a mortar in a forest destroyed the terminal, killing four thousand people in an instant, others more slowly. A revolutionary group claimed "credit." Bill had set up a time for me to point my satellite communicator toward the sky, and the night of the blast a warning call came from him as soon as I lined up the dish. He was greatly relieved to learn that I was unharmed, and was to leave the next morning for a leisurely Air Cruise over the wildlife preserves of the Serengeti Plain.

When the subsonic landed at Nairobi I transferred to the Serengeti Drifter, an aerobody with a cruise speed of only 80 kilometers per hour. It derived its lift in part from airflow over its winglike body, and in part from the buoyancy of helium in its huge interior. It was driven by hydrogen motors through slow-turning ducted propellers, so it was noiseless and odorless, and could move over the landscape as quietly as a cloud.

My stateroom was luxuriously big, but the furniture in it was sparse and very light. The forward wall of the room was transparent, forming the lower leading edge of the wing. The dining room, large enough to accommodate the full passenger list of 200, was in the belly of the ship, surrounded by panoramic slanting windows. Of all the lounges on board, my favorite was the open observation deck at the trailing edge of the lifting body. There deck chairs were set, stewards circulated at teatime, and I could lie back out of the wind to watch the slow unrolling of the landscape, usually only a hundred feet below.

Our week's cruise fell into a pleasant routine. We would land each night in a meadow downwind of a water hole. The aerobody could descend almost at walking pace, so it needed no airport. Dinner was by hydrogen gaslight and was livened by African or Arabic foods prepared by the ship's cooks from stores on board.

After dinner some passengers preferred to go out on the forward gallery, its windows now open to the scents and sounds of the African night.

The Serengeti Drifter, an aerobody hybrid, part airplane and part helium-filled balloon. Its large, slowly rotating propellers drive it silently above the landscape at a speed low enough so that its passengers can enjoy the scenery from open promenade decks.

Many had brought elaborate photographic gear capable of forming complete stereo color images by moonlight alone. Others preferred to scan the plain with infrared-sensitive binoculars. Those of us who didn't have such special equipment wandered between the open decks and the main lounge, where the ship's naturalist conducted impromptu lectures illustrated by life-size real-time holographic views of the wild animals upwind of us.

So much of the wildlife was nocturnal that we tended to stay awake until well after midnight. Then we'd catch a few hours' sleep and would be served coffee in our rooms at dawn. We'd spend a couple of hours watching the early-morning movements of the animals and would then assemble for breakfast. Soon after that, in the still air of the morning, the Serengeti Drifter would rise silently and cruise to another tiedown spot. Sometimes I'd watch the ground from my own room through the transparent wall, and sometimes I'd join other people for an hour or two on one of the lounge decks. In our cruise we'd cross over herds of antelope and zebra. Elephants would browse below us, and with the naturalist's quiet voice in our ear beads to guide us we'd spot lions resting in the tall grass, their watchful eyes missing nothing of the slow movements of the game animals.

The Drifter normally settled to a landing before the violent thermal air motion of the afternoon began, and we passengers would sleep away the hottest hours as did the wildlife of the plain. The craft had no settled route. Its week-long voyage was guided by satellite observations of wildlife movements, and the only certainties on its schedule were a low-level cruise over Lake Victoria and an ascent to the snow level of Mount Kilimanjaro. On the last day of the trip we slid to Earth in an open space at a large native market in Nairobi, and the passengers wandered from stall to stall, bargaining for African craft products.

A few hours later, in London, Aaron's call found me in my hotel room. We had full-color holocube communications, so that he seemed to be lounging in a chair across the room from me. He first commented ruefully that Britain was so full of contradictions that none of the ordinary historical rules seemed to apply there. Its success, he added with a smile, might illustrate the power of a sense of humor over logic. Production figures didn't mean much in Britain, because the country was making so much money out of tourism that it didn't need to produce much. For centuries the British had invested in historical preservation, not only of castles, but of the institution of the monarchy, enormously popular both at home and to visitors, and now almost unique in the world. He pointed out two important facts about the British that might not be obvious to me: first, they had managed to keep a democratic government going in a stable way for several hundred years—a world record among the nations that had ever been dominant. And for every Briton I would see on that little island, I should keep in mind that there were three others living somewhere else. They were in North America, in Australia, and New Zealand, and very thick in the space colonies (where, Aaron added, the weather was better than at home).

The United Kingdom was also doing quite well in material terms, Aaron told me. Greenhouse agriculture had overcome the limitations of a wet climate and not enough sunshine. As an added boost, the multinational companies had invested more heavily in Britain than almost anywhere else on the planet. The multinationals went where there was stability, bringing along top-level computerized operations and automation—just what Britain had needed most to compete in world markets. Another fifty years, Aaron guessed, and it would hardly matter if the British worker lingered in the pubs full-time.

It took me only a few hours to fall in love with England, and I knew the affair would be permanent. The people were friendly, and the small scale of their shops and restaurants was captivating. Many of London's streets had been turned into covered arcades, and the legendary London cabs, unchanged in appearance for over a century, were now electric-powered. The city had recovered well from the ravages of the Age of Petroleum, and no fuel-burning vehicle was now allowed within city limits. I found many echoes among London's buildings and parks of the stories I'd read in childhood. When I stood before the Peter Pan statue in Kensington Park it was exciting to remember that I'd first read Barrie's tale as a small boy at home in the Cluster, a hundred times farther away than the sun.

That the Britons valued preservation and restoration above all became even clearer when I left the capital for the countryside. The National Trust was everywhere, and great country houses had been restored to a state of opulence. If I'd been without Aaron's guidance I might have missed the less obvious signs of England's prosperity: the factories, largely automated, that were usually located underground with trees and flowers growing above them.

From my travels through the rest of Europe a few memories remain vivid even without the help of photography and holography: the amazing green of Ireland, the pastoral beauty of barge tours through the ancient canals of France and Holland. And there are memories that no trick of modern technology can help me preserve—the marvelous food and wine everywhere in Europe, including such treats as the chocolate ice cream at the Tre Scalini in Rome's Piazza Navona. Fortunately, I do have more tangible memories of the laughter and the conversation of the spirited Italian crowds, thanks to the video cubes I took in the piazzas, often by the dim light of the warm spring evenings.

When I reached the great cities of central Europe, I found myself nostalgic for the London cabbies with their humor and their encyclopedic knowledge of local geography, but I found in such places as Salzburg another good way for a tourist to learn local history while sightseeing. The ancient streets of the central areas had become pedestrian walkways, and all of them were glassed over so that the tourist season could extend over the full year. Along the center of each "street" was a narrow roadway, sunk about four feet below the walkway level. Its sloping sides, planted with ivy, were separated from the walkway at either side by a wrought iron railing. About every fifteen meters was a pedestrian overpass. Very small, silent electric cars, guided by a computer and just large enough for two people,

Personal public transportation, giving visitors to historic cities individual door-to-door service while sparing them the inconveniences of map-following and parking. Operating within the enclosed, climate-controlled cities of 2081, the cars require no roofs. Computer-directed to destinations chosen by their passengers, these two-person cars can be coupled together to accommodate parties of four or six traveling together.

ran in the sunken roadway. They were open so their riders could view the buildings at either side, and they could be directed to stop at almost any point to pick up or drop off passengers at platforms reached from the pedestrian level by a few steps or a short escalator. The system was personal public transportation, something I'd heard of in the English-speaking countries as PPT. When called, for example, by a hotel, the PPT computer would halt the nearest available car at the hotel entrance to pick up passengers. The passengers could then request to be dropped off at any location, or take an unstructured scenic drive, getting off when they felt like walking and boarding another PPT car when they were tired. Some of the older travelers I met said the PPT systems had replaced the tourist buses of earlier days, to no one's regret. Elderly or handicapped people in particular found the PPT cars much easier to use than tour buses, because the cars could be directed to skip some stops, linger at others, and return to a hotel, if their riders grew tired. Of course, Europe's PPT cars were all equipped to provide tour-guide service in any of a hundred or more languages, and that was a help, especially to visitors who spoke only such local languages as Swahili or Basque.

When I called Aaron just before my flight to Moscow, his manner was serious and his brief lecture included several warnings. He reminded me that most of the planet was ruled by dictators of one kind or another, but said the dictatorship was far from absolute in Russia. My satellite communicator would be confiscated when I arrived, but the chances were good that I would get it back out of customs bond when I left. Anklets were mandatory in Russia, and with modern computers the state had no trouble keeping track of everybody. But control had lessened over the past several decades for a number of reasons. The average Russian was wealthier than his ancestors and had more mobility—most Russian families owned cars. And when miniaturization had passed a certain level, early in the century, it had become virtually impossible to keep people from buying direct-broadcast satellite receivers on the black market, in spite of the severe penalties for being caught with one. Aaron warned me that I'd be offered such receivers for sale by apparent "dissidents," but that I shouldn't buy one. At least half the receivers that were sold in dark alleys had built-in pulsers that would relay their positions straight to Internal Security, and link the illegal purchase directly to the buyer. Russians bought their receivers only through trusted friends. He also advised my avoiding black-market rubles. After those warnings, however, Aaron said that control of the average Russian was lessening somewhat because of emigration to the space colonies. Toward the end of the last century the bright, innovative Russians who wanted to escape the bureaucrats had volunteered for work in Siberia, and they had built a great nation there. But now the same sort of people chose the Russian colonies in space, where the living conditions were a good deal more pleasant.

Aaron told me that while I was in Russia I would probably be shown one of their model factories. Productivity was low in all state-centralized systems, a consequence both of worker disinterest and the inefficiencies of a system that was always too big. To try to combat that problem the Soviets had been experimenting in the last few decades with smaller organizations not tied to national quotas or plans. For legitimacy the state called them "collectives," but they came closer to being private corporations. Aaron's lecture gave me accurate guidance, and I also found that, as a tourist, I could charge purchases in Russia as conveniently as elsewhere. I'd lost track of the currencies I'd been exposed to, but it hardly mattered, because my wrist calculator transformed them all to standard units based on an average of the world's most stable currencies and the current price of gold. It kept up-to-date with the exchange rate, shifting from day to day, of any currency I had to deal with. I also got more use out of my translator in Russia than anywhere I'd been earlier, even though a great many Russians were obviously apprehensive about being seen talking through one to a foreigner.

On the flight to Bombay I had time for a long talk with Aaron. It jibed with the tourist literature, but he added historical perspective. The total demographic transition to a near-stable population took fifty to one hundred years, Aaron said, but most of the poor nations had made it by now. Satellite communications had given the Indians a cheap way to bring education to their remote villages. Satellite power had solved their energy problem, and because wealth and energy use went hand in hand, it had raised their living standard correspondingly. Greenhouse agriculture, guided by computer, had solved their food problem by closing the water cycle and providing dependable crops free of weather. And by providing food at the village level, it had also bypassed the whole problem of an inadequate system of distribution; best of all, it had left the agricultural production integral with the village where the ordinary Indian had his loyalty and identity. As India had begun to turn the economic corner, the multinationals had invested there heavily, and that had given an added boost in technical education as well as in capital funds for industrial development.

I had the good fortune to meet a young Indian university student on the plane, and he was kind enough to invite me to his home. Through the helpfulness of his family I was able to visit several villages. It had to be by chopper. Each village had a resident nurse and an assured food supply. Television was universal, even in small houses whose lights were powered by the local greenhouse electric system.

On my last day I had to leave early to catch the plane for Australia where I would visit Aaron's home. The Adelaide boomer threaded its way past Sumatra and Java and stayed supersonic over the sparsely populated Gibson and Great Victoria deserts. On my second evening with Aaron we began discussing my next stop, Japan. Aaron said he was reluctant to try to give me guidance to that country. It had been two years since he had been there, and at the speed the Japanese were moving, two years put him way out of date. For historical background, he told me that the Japanese had taken the economic lead over other nations about a hundred years earlier. That very success had helped to preserve the Japanese sense of unity, already strong because of the nation's homogeneity. Aaron believed, however, that no country could easily remain dominant for more than about a hundred years. Its population, at first lifting itself from austere conditions by hard work, later became satiated by wealth and complacent about its position, losing much of its competitive drive. Other nations, envious of its position and frightened of its power, tended to unite against it either in military or economic actions. Aaron told me that if the Japanese had maintained the economic growth rate that the nation had enjoyed toward the end of the last century, Japan would by now have reached a heat-barrier, generating over a megawatt per capita. Instead, the Japanese economic growth rate had slowed during the twenty-first century, and a great many Japanese had emigrated to colonies in space. Aaron suggested that I take note of the number of daily flights from Tokyo to the AWP spaceport, and told me that the wealth I would see in Japan would be staggering, yet would be only a fraction of the total wealth of the Japanese people because so much was now invested in the Japanese colonies.

I'd heard that Tokyo International was the world's largest airport, but I wasn't prepared for the enormous collection of floating discs that it comprised. There were no individual runways or taxiways. Each floating disc was a flat, uniform expanse of concrete over a substructure, and computers separated aircraft both in time and space so as to use every bit of area and every second of time. The operations were always directly into the wind, an easy thing to arrange on a circular airport usable in any orientation.

After my astonishment at the size and coordination of Tokyo International, I was also unprepared for what I found as we passengers streamed out of the jetway. Among the chattering, cheerful, well-dressed crowd of people waiting at the gate were a number of quiet young men, each with a pleasant but neutral expression, each rather short even for a Japanese, and each with a Japanese calligraphy character tattooed on his forehead. As I walked past, one of them smiled and raised his hand.

"Mr. Rawson?" At my puzzled nod he bowed and his smile broadened. "Welcome to Japan. I am a robot working for the Convention and Visitors' Bureau of the Japanese government, and I have been assigned as your guide and interpreter while you are in our country. There is no charge for my services, but you are free to accept or decline them. I should add that the bureau wishes to extend special hospitality to a visitor from such a great distance, and that it will probably ask the favor of an interview, which will then be published in one of our tourist magazines. My name is Toshio Takata, and most of my English-speaking guests call me 'T-Square,' " Before this last sentence he had clasped his hands behind his back, so my uncertainty on the protocol of shaking hands with a robot was resolved.

I accepted readily. T-Square seemed to know everything about my hotel reservations, and even the details of my baggage. My hotel, a big one, had its own floater line direct from the air terminal, so within minutes I was installed in a comfortable room. On T-Square's advice I agreed to his returning in an hour so we could discuss my itinerary. I spent the time first in enjoying a steaming Japanese-style hot-tub in my suite, and then in a short nap. I was awakened by soft music. When my eyes opened there was a rustle of curtains, and I found that one whole wall of my darkened room had become, apparently, an invisible window through which I looked out on a courtyard with carefully raked gravel, surrounded by a Japanese garden and a high stone wall. The angle of the afternoon sunlight told me the time, and several butterflies hovered near the flowers, but there were no human figures. The holographic scene shifted as I arose from my bed and walked toward the closet for my robe. I heard the distant sound of a bell being struck, and T-Square's voice came from somewhere near the room door.

"Good afternoon, Mr. Rawson. Do you have instructions for me, or would you prefer that I make suggestions?" I asked him to join me and he was there within a few minutes. I found it refreshing to talk with a travel agent who had total, instant recall of information. He was, of course, encyclopedic. After we had reviewed the sights that I could see in Tokyo, and the short trips that I would make to Kyoto and Kamakura, T-square made a suggestion that surprised me.

"A Japanese family living near Sapporo, on our northern island of Hokkaido, is interested in Fox Cluster and has extended an invitation to you to visit for two days. The distance is 850 kilometers, about as far as from London to Berlin. The trip will require only fourteen minutes between terminals."

My eyebrow raised at that. Even a floater would take more than an hour for such a trip. T-Square smiled: "The journey will be made on what is called a 'High-Speed' or constant-drive floater. The car will be under full acceleration for the first half of the trip, and deceleration for the last half. We use them for long journeys between a few pairs of points: Tokyo–Sapporo, Tokyo–Nagasaki, Nagasaki–Sapporo, and some others. During the trip you will experience an apparent weight that is about 15 percent greater than normal. The speed at the midpoint will be about one and a half kilometers per second. Of course, virtually no curvature can be allowed in the line near the highest-velocity midportion. I should say that the Kitagaki family speaks Basic, Mr. Rawson, and I am sure you would find the visit most enjoyable."

I agreed, and a date was set. T-Square and I would have several days for ordinary touring before the Kitagaki visit. Those days passed quickly. The high level of Japanese material wealth showed itself in several ways. Automation and computerization appeared to be almost total. Every street was sparkling clean, because there was an unobtrusive army of special-purpose robot machines to see to that. I saw a great deal of effort going into beautification: new parks were being built and landscaped, temples were being restored and their grounds extended.

The city's new hotels and office buildings were mainly underground, their windows replaced by holographic window walls with a visual range broad enough to duplicate bright sunlight. Enclosing roofs extended from office blocks to cover adjacent streets and parks. Tokyo had become a multilayered city, the streets now entirely pedestrian malls. Below them was a level devoted to electric cars, and still lower was a level with floater terminals and freight transport.

Our first trip by electric car from the hotel was in the early evening, our destination a top-rated Japanese restaurant. We left curbside and I discovered that the car's "windows" were in fact video screens. They showed us passing through what seemed to be a shining waterfall, and beyond it we found a pedestrian street on which ours appeared to be the only car.

We moved swiftly along a central grassy strip between sidewalks crowded with well-dressed Japanese and tourists from every part of the System. I asked why we were being given this special treatment, and T-Square answered that our car was moving under computer control through a level that was virtually featureless. As we traveled, our view showed a trip through the pedestrian streets above us. The speed of our simulated journey was calculated to bring us to our destination just as we did, in fact, arrive, and the scenes were in real-time. The people I saw were walking those streets at that moment, and I was seeing them through a sequence of fixed miniature video cameras, hung from thin cables along the centers of the streets above their heads. I'd see those cables as soon as I went out walking, but the video pickups on them were too small to be noticed.

It puzzled me that the Japanese made such lavish use of robots, for I'd understood that robots were very expensive.

"Initially we were," said T-Square, "and as export products we're priced as high as the market will stand. But when automation passed a certain level, even robots could be made quite cheaply. Self-replication and automated repair permitted the rapid duplication of whole factories, and prices on the domestic market fell rapidly."

We passed through another waterfall of light, and drew up in a large courtyard lit by gas lamps. When the video screens darkened and the car doors opened, I was prepared for a complete change of scene and was all the more surprised to find myself in that same courtyard in reality. Attendants led us to an elevator that raised us the few meters to the restaurant. T-Square sat with me and we studied the menu. His explanations helped to round out the translation that the menu shifted to when I pressed the "English" tab. He also asked if I wished to be joined by a geisha on the following evening, and warned that it would be expensive whether she were human or only a robot, because the geisha union was strong and insisted on not being undercut by machines. That next evening, in a restaurant specially recommended by T-Square, I blew a substantial wad of credit on an hour's visit by a human geisha. Her command of Basic was excellent, but she spoke little English, and I preferred T-Square's unobtrusive services as translator to the more obvious use of my translating machine. The geisha, I learned, was a student of anthropology at a university. Like most geishas of the present day she had learned her art as a hobby, and exercised it, not from economic need, but from the desire to meet and talk with people from a variety of countries or colonies in the System. In Basic she let me know that most human geishas selected their clients after questioning their robot guides and accepted only a small fraction of the invitations they received.

On the day of my visit to Sapporo a call arrived from the Kitagakis soon after my breakfast tray had been collected from my room. The holographic window's curtain opened to reveal a Japanese living room almost without furniture. A middle-aged couple, robed and sitting cross-legged on floor mats, smiled, and the man spoke to me. As his lips moved, a computer voice provided a simultaneous translation into English.

"We look forward to your visit, Mr. Rawson. Our daughter Akara has offered to make the short trip to Tokyo so as to accompany you to our home. Will you accept?" I did so, but was unprepared for the sight of Akara, who met us at the electric-car level of the hotel. After the holographic view of her home I was surprised to see her in a stylish skirt and blouse that might have come, and perhaps did, from a Paris boutique. She was a slim, pretty girl with black hair and eyes, who chattered unself-consciously in Basic as we rode to the High-Speed terminal.

We transferred to a car larger than that of the ordinary floater. Each of its compartments was mounted on bearings, so that it was free to rotate forward or backward as the car accelerated or decelerated. Because of that arrangement, its passengers experienced only an apparent "down" acceleration during the trip. I hardly felt the slight extra weight caused by our acceleration, but there were a few seconds when my weight noticeably lessened. That was the thrust-reversal point, halfway through our journey.

Akara excused herself when the electric car from the terminal arrived at the home of the Kitagakis. T-Square remained unobtrusively a step behind me as I met the couple, but leaned forward whenever necessary to murmur pointers on etiquette. A half-hour later Akara appeared in an entirely different role. She was clad in a kimono, with her hair and face made up in a style I recognized from prints by Hokusai. Her Japanese was translated by the house computer into the rather formal English that I'd come to expect from such machines.

"I do this by choice," she smiled. "In Japan now, with automation so advanced that people only work two or three days a week and have long vacations, most of us devote our energy to hobbies and travel. The preservation of the Japanese cultural tradition is more than a hobby, though. It is so nearly universal that you might call it our main national theme. It is strongest of all in our colonies. Later, after you are rested and settled, I will join you with my parents to perform the tea ceremony."

Mr. Kitagaki's main hobby was bonsai, the art of raising miniature plants, and he took pleasure in showing me the small garden where he had brought that art to an exquisite level of perfection. Later, in the room I'd first seen him in, the computer's translator preserved his voice intonations as it explained to me in English:

"Many of us feel that the mechanistic aspects of our civilization should be balanced each day by hours into which machines do not intrude. Most modern Japanese live in two worlds, the automated, computerized world of business and travel and the traditional world of the home, where we like to rest our eyes on scenes entirely from the era that preceded the industrial revolution."

In my days with the Kitagakis I noticed that even our conversation was governed by our location. Any discussion of the modern world occurred only in the modern portion of the house, a portion superficially like the rest, but whose walls and screens sheltered electronics and computers as advanced as those I'd seen at the Tehaneys'. T-Square often accompanied me to that part of the Kitagaki home. But whenever we moved toward what I thought of as the "time-frozen" rooms, he quietly excused himself and left. Our tour of Sapporo was confined exclusively to parks, temples, and other buildings of a time-frozen nature. The Kitagakis were correct in assuming that I would find those historical sites more interesting than the high technology that I'd come to take for granted in Japan.

Once, in the 2081 section of their home, they spoke of Fox Cluster and its remoteness. They were envious at the thought of a human community removed by many billions of miles from the Earth's arsenals of nuclear weapons and free of the danger of terrorist attack. They told me that when Japan had become very wealthy it had been singled out as a special target for such attacks. They apologized for the security measures against terrorism that I might encounter while in Japan, and explained that those measures were necessary evils in a nation that had suffered more through terrorist bombs than in all the wars of the past century.

—E. C. R.

IN READING Eric's observations on his travels around our planet we are reminded that the progress of an individual nation depends on its social organization, cultural heritage, and political system, as well as on material resources. The drivers of change will enable many countries to achieve great improvements in living conditions by 2081, but those powerful tools will be left unused or turned only to destructive ends in many parts of the world. It requires no intelligence or education to pick up a submachine-gun, point it, and pull the trigger, so terrorism, revolution, and conquest are easier routes to success for opportunistic leaders in backward areas than is the way of peaceful construction. I find it an equally unwelcome conclusion that nuclear terrorism is likely to be a major element in the history of the next century. But the reasons for that conclusion appear to be inescapable. For all that has been done to prevent it, nuclear proliferation continues. And while identifiable nations may hesitate to launch nuclear weapons for fear of reprisals, no such bar to destructive acts exists for terrorist groups. Moreover, the leaders of such groups are often fanatics quite willing to die as long as they can pull the objects of their hatred down with them.

We North Americans are fortunate that our ancestors, frontier colonists and emigrants, were forced to develop for survival a pragmatic, positive attitude toward inventions and mechanisms. It helped us a great deal to make the most out of the first centuries of industrialization. Unfortunately, the cultural heritage in some of the nations that need industrialization most is very different and constitutes a barrier to urgently needed technical development. Throughout India, for example, so many young people choose to be educated for "clean" desk jobs that the nation now has an unusable surplus of office workers, and many civil servants face mandatory retirement at the age of fifty.

In spite of such cultural barriers to physical progress in many developing nations, the prospects for improving the lot of the world's poor and hungry majority look more hopeful to me than the chances for averting all use of nuclear weapons in these next hundred years. The problem of excessive growth rates in population confounds our attempts to increase the supply of food, but owing to the efforts of such demographers as Roger Revelle, we are coming to understand why populations grow too rapidly and how to slow that growth without denying to individual couples the right to choose whether to have a child. Couples choose to have big families as long as the infant mortality rate stays high, much over twenty per thousand. In poor countries, surviving children are the only security for old age. Birth rates drop only when infant mortality drops below that figure and overall death rates fall below ten or so per thousand. The technical developments that will insure abundant and reliable supplies of food can help to bring about that change, and so can the developments in education by satellite that can provide women in rural areas with information on interesting options beyond childrearing. The total demographic transition to a relatively stable population takes about fifty to one hundred years, but many of today's poor nations will have made it by 2081.

It is much more chancy to guess which nation will be in the lead in economic and technical development a century from now. Clearly, England was ahead during the nineteenth century, and the United States during much of the twentieth. The author Norman Macrae, in the Edison Electric Institute's book, *Prospects for Growth* (Praeger, 1977), makes a persuasive case that the baton of leadership, during the next century on Earth, may pass to the Japanese. He argues that for the past twenty years Japan has generated the highest sustained real industrial growth rate in the world, three times the United States average, and that its cultural traditions are particularly well suited to success in an industrial age. A Japanese forms a life-long attachment to a corporation, and the corporation provides him not only with a salary but with housing, medical services, and recreation. Macrae keeps his options open, though, by noting signs that the United States may be regaining its former sense of confidence, drive, and enthusiasm. In my view, the nation that leads in this next century will be the nation whose ideas, techniques, and approach to problem solving are most widely copied by others. Quite possibly the effects of the drivers of change will be to internationalize creative individuals so thoroughly that by 2081 the concept of national leadership will seem rather old-fashioned.

It remains true that Japan, the most successful nation of recent decades, has a very strong sense of national identity. And there is no doubt that the Japanese are ideally set to capitalize on the new concept of colonies in space. Japan's shipyards have built the world's largest ships. The Japanese are a high-technology people, and a higher percentage of them are college-educated than are North Americans. They have a tradition of beautifying confined spaces. And finally, they are pushed as well as pulled, because they live on a tiny, crowded group of islands with few natural resources.

While estimates of the future of individual nations must always be highly speculative, I am on very solid ground in regard to the technical novelties that Eric observes on his world tour. The "Serengeti Drifter" is an aerobody, whose basic aerodynamics were studied a decade ago for low-speed freight-carrying aircraft that could operate very economically. The test flights of one such vehicle are described in a delightful book by John McPhee, *The Deltoid Pumpkin Seed*.

Systems for personal public transportation have been under study for some years. The version that Eric observes in Salzburg would operate at speeds of about thirty miles per hour for the five-minute run between a downtown area and a hotel more than two miles away, and could transport more than twenty thousand people an hour in each direction on every route. In the historic or shopping areas, where any passenger might choose at a moment's notice to call for a stop, the cars would move at a quiet ten miles per hour. Even at that modest speed, well suited to sightseeing and even to reading the signs on shop fronts, the PPT system could transport more than five thousand people per hour into and out of every street. Parking is of course the most vexing problem in any visit to a popular place, and with PPT it would not exist. The moment after passengers left a car it would reaccelerate, and would either be boarded by other people later or be left by the control computer at a remote parking garage until the demand picked up again. There would be a continuous line of the PPT cars, about twenty feet apart, moving along their designated roadways just below the pedestrian level, ready to pick up anyone who came out of a shop laden with packages or who simply felt tired of walking.

Eric's underground journey through Tokyo with his robot guide calls for a little explanation. The journey itself is straightforward, but the system of real-time video sightseeing that makes it an interesting rather than a boring experience is a new application of existing technology. The electric car would travel at about fifty miles per hour, almost on a straight line. The video journey over the more circuitous routing of pedestrian streets would have to be somewhat faster to reach the same destination in the same length of time. The camera lenses to pick up the real-time views would be located every five feet along a thin cable stretched at the center of each pedestrian street at a height of about ten feet. In each second the video on the electric car would show about twenty views, from twenty successive lenses along a particular cable. At that rate the video journey would appear as continuous motion, just as a movie appears continuous when its eighteen successive frames are shown in a second. Each pickup lens need be no larger than a fingernail, and the entire cable would be less noticeable from the street than one of today's trolley wires.

In imagining that the citizens of the world's leading nations in 2081 will devote considerable effort to the preservation of historic buildings and of the natural environment, I may be accused of wishful thinking. But that projection is consistent with today's reality, because it is a fact that both the environmental movement and the drive for historic preservation and restoration are phenomena of affluence. As the drivers of change raise the average income level by more than ten times over the next century, it is my realistic hope that those movements, enriching the lives of everyone on the planet and all those who visit Earth, will strengthen.

The Resting Earth

THE *Dandridge M. Cole* would be outward bound again in July, so the Tehaneys invited me to return to Waterford a few weeks before that, in order to enjoy a leisurely tour at ground level before the ship's departure for the Cluster. Bill offered the use of the family RV, and Ellen suggested that I join her and two of her friends from college for a tour of national parks in Wyoming. As the Tehaneys and I sat together beside the pool one evening waiting for Arthur to announce dinner, Jeannette asked Ellen about her friends. I learned that Trudi had become a professional guitarist and singer. Ed was an ecologist with whom Ellen had taken some classes. He'd graduated and was employed now in one of the colonies beyond the moon. I asked how long it would take us to get to Wyoming, and Ellen passed the question on to the house computer which answered after a few seconds.

"By way of Rapid City and Sheridan the distance is 4,200 kilometers to Jackson. Driving time will be 35 hours at 120 kph. You will cross two time zones. I would recommend starting at about nine o'clock one morning, so that you will have daylight for the most scenic part of the trip. You should arrive about 15:00 on the following day."

Arthur came out at that point to announce dinner, so we left further trip planning until later. In the evening we gathered in Bill's office, where we had full access to libraries and satellite data. Satellite pictures taken a few hours earlier showed us the soft green of June over the plains states. I asked about one set of mountains we'd be crossing, the Bighorn range in Wyoming, and Jeannette remembered it well. She said a perilous road without a guard rail snaked its way up the east face of the mountains. On one trip over the Bighorns she had come to every hairpin turn wondering if the drive computer was still working.

Ellen suggested that we leave on Tuesday morning, to avoid the heavy recreational traffic which peaked during the four-day weekends. Tuesday was only two days off, so Ellen would have to find out whether Trudi and Ed could get free that quickly. She was occupied with her communicator bracelet for a few moments, but after she'd spoken her friends' names and added such identifying facts as their ages and the names of their colleges, the amber "working" light glowed and she leaned back in her chair. Five minutes later the communicator's light changed to green, and the voice of the house computer sounded from a speaker nearby.

"Trudi Ohrbach located in Florence, Italy. Ms. Ohrbach signals ready to talk." As Trudi's voice sounded the videos remained blank, and I knew it would be bad manners to ask why. Trudi accepted the invitation to travel west with us, and said she would take care of her own travel arrangements by way of Milan to Cincinnati or Cleveland the next day.

Our next try at communication proved more difficult. Ellen's request by way of her bracelet was answered several minutes later by the house computer: "Ed Martin not located on Earth. Continuing search." A few seconds later it told us Ed wasn't at work in his colony job either. The amber "working" light stayed on for a good ten minutes after that and finally changed to green.

"Mr. Edward Martin's identifier is unlisted. He has been notified of your call and will return it in an hour." Ellen, amused, explained that an unlisted identifier was the modern version of the unlisted telephone number. Ed's own communicator had reported our call, and if he hadn't wanted to answer, our computer would have drawn a blank—it would have told us that he was not locatable. As it was, we could talk with Ed, but because of his unlisted identifier we wouldn't learn where he was.

While waiting for Ed's call we planned the provisions for our trip. Ellen didn't want to stop the RV except for fuel before Wyoming. I asked if she'd bring the RV to the house, but she said these vehicles weren't allowed in town, because they were too big and awkward for Waterford's small streets. Instead, we'd board the RV at the town wall where there was a special garage and loading dock.

When Ed called an hour later the video stayed blank, and I could tell immediately he must be off-Earth—there was a delay of about one second between question and response, and the usual awkwardness that always happens when a time delay is added to a voice link. He said he couldn't get away immediately but he offered to arrive by Tuesday evening. Ellen agreed, and called Trudi again to set the rendezvous for Tuesday evening at the Tehaneys'.

We had two days, then, to get the RV ready. At Bill's suggestion we let it spend the first day at a service garage, where a computer checked all its systems. The service computer reported to us next evening that the garage had replaced a tire and done a general tune-up; the machine was now in good working order. Ellen and I began scanning the video library index for music and holofilms to be loaded into the RV's memory banks. At Ellen's command the house computer supervised the loading of each selection.

Tuesday dawned clear and sparkling, so the town's roof stayed off. Ellen and I bicycled to the RV garage, and entered through an airwall port in the landscaped wall of the town. By command through her bracelet the RV had driven itself from a parking level located under the retraction area of Waterford's roof to a loading dock beside a carpeted lobby.

I was astonished at the size of the vehicle. It was fifty feet long, ten wide, and a little over eight feet high. It was streamlined, from a rounded nose to a tapering rudderlike knife-edge at the tail. There were six wheels, two near the front and four more in tandem pairs most of the way back. All six steered for sharp turns. There were windows, opaqued now, over the nose, roof, and sides, but they ended just after the width of the machine began to narrow at the rear. Ellen told me the rear section was reserved for a small sauna and gym.

The wide entrance door was at the level of the loading dock, and it slid aside at Ellen's command. I found the interior remarkably familiar; it was much like that of a private space yacht of the kind most families in the Cluster own. At the front was a lounge with a couch, reclining swivel chairs, coffee tables, and a control panel. In the midsection was a kitchen and a well-equipped bar enclosing a dining room. Farther aft were bedrooms and bathrooms. Ellen told me every wall above waist height could be made transparent, opaqued, or turned amber to reduce glare. She said it was the Tehaneys' practice while traveling to give the computer a general instruction to amber any window that was exposed to direct sunlight, but leave the rest clear. That kept the computer busy, but gave the passengers a restful glare-free ride.

With the help of a "smart cart" that was a private version of the kind I'd used in air terminals, Ellen and I loaded the supplies from the supermarket's delivery canister into the freezers and cabinets of the RV. I was surprised at the quantity of provisions, but Ellen said they would not only give us the freedom to travel with few stops, but would also give Trudi a chance to show off her skills as a high-quality cook. As Ellen arranged the stores she explained that water was recycled on board the RV and all other waste was ashed and stored—that was why RVs were allowed up to the roadheads in primitive areas. I walked aft from the kitchen to explore the staterooms and found that each had a large bed, a controllable window-wall next to it, a small coffee bar with a refrigerator, and a private bath. In the gym just behind the aft stateroom there was a small hot-tub, from which the bather could enjoy the view through one-way windows.

Ellen brought the machine to life long enough to repeat a system check. The onboard computer reported we had fuel for sixteen hours steady running and water for a two-week trip. We locked the machine, dismissed it to its garage stall, and retrieved our bicycles for the ride home.

We spent the next hour in the pool. At five a bell chimed and a near-by video came to life. Trudi, a cheerful, round-faced, brown-haired girl, was on the screen. In the background I could see the outlines of the familiar "single" seat in a floater, with its lights, controls, and a pillow tucked behind Trudi's head. When she saw us she laughed, asked us if we were trying to make her jealous by posing in the pool, and immediately told Ellen of five more items that were absolutely essential for the RV's pantry. By the time Trudi arrived we were dressed and ready for her.

Ed arrived half an hour later. He was short, bearded, and deeply tanned. Later Ellen speculated to me privately that he'd just come from a ski colony with intense high-altitude sunlight. He gave Trudi a hug, shook hands with the rest of us, and retrieved from his autocab an odd-shaped bundle. It was his backpack, and evidently he'd get us hiking by sheer force of example. I welcomed the chance, because everything else on Earth seemed to be designed to save people exertion.

Next morning when I awoke the roof was back on Waterford. Out my window I could see grass wet with rain, and the internal sunlights were bright with Waterford's early morning. A quick check of the video showed the view from Waterford's weather tower: gray cloud and steady, soaking rain. Ellen bounced in, her usual lively early-morning self, and perched on the edge of my bed while we drank our morning coffee. She told me that Bill was doing one of his ranch breakfasts for us. We'd find steak, eggs, and trout all set before us on the same table, with bacon and pancakes on the side. For once, she said, she was going to take a diet pill, so that none of the calories would stay with her.

For our leave-taking all six of us rode together in the big limousine over to the RV dock. The lobby was quiet, with only two other vehicles being loaded. Jeannette remarked that it would get crowded by the following afternoon, because the people who started then could be a thousand miles away, at their destinations, by Friday morning. For weekend excursions in an RV, she told me, people usually let the machine travel all Thursday night getting them where they wanted to go, and all Monday night getting them back. Some people even did their work from an RV.

Our good-byes were quickly said, and the door slid shut. Ellen keyed "Go" on the panel, and the RV began to follow its preset program. The engine came to life, the machine backed slowly from the dock and turned. We waved to Bill and Jeannette as it passed the dock, then settled in the living room and heard the patter of rain on the roof as the RV passed through an airwall tunnel into the gray rain of the June morning.

As we neared Lake Erie a fog developed. Soon I could see no farther ahead than the length of the vehicle, but it didn't slow down. Ellen explained that the RV steered by reference to magnetic markers buried in the roadway, so it didn't need to use "vision" for driving. For the same reason it carried no headlights except for emergencies. Like a ship, it had green and red running lights at starboard and port. I remember little of that first day on the road, except for a conversation with Ed while Trudi and Ellen conferred about our lunch menu. We were sitting in the lounge, chairs reclined, and almost every vehicle on the road was at the same steady 120 kph. We rarely changed lanes. There were a fair number of trucks on the road, featureless except for advertising, and some RVs, but nothing smaller than a six-passenger limousine except for the occasional robot police cruiser. Those wardens of the roads were very low, less than a meter high, with a tall mast extending to the legal height limit of the roadways. The mast carried video lenses and antennas. Ed told me that accidents were very rare, because the car computers never took chances and, unlike people, never got tired or bored. Once in a great while, though, there might be a major systems failure on a car, RV, or truck, and when that happened there was likely to be a fire in the resulting crash. The police cruisers, he told me, were mostly tankage for fire extinguishers.

Each time we topped a rise I could see that the forests extended, hill beyond hill, out to the horizon. Ed told me that the trees were all second-growth. Hundreds of years in the past the original forests had been cut for farmland, but in the early twenty-first century the rise of greenhouse agriculture had made ordinary farming unprofitable. In the late twentieth century, according to Ed, there were twice as many people living in this area, but now most of it had reverted to forest, mainly mixed hardwoods. A good many small towns had become ghost towns or had been bulldozed for parklands. Still, I could find a number of very comfortable estates tucked away among the trees. Their owners worked at home or maintained limousines for commuting to work. Some of these owners made a habit of breakfasting and watching the news while they drove to work, and they napped on the way home.

Once that day a chime sounded and the video told us of congestion two hundred kilometers ahead, near Chicago. It recommended a discretionary change of routing, and showed the original route in red, with the alternate in green. We agreed to the change, and I made it a point to be alert the moment when the drive-computer selected the appropriate off-ramp.

After we'd played four-handed poker for a while and I'd gone back for a strenuous hour on the gym equipment, followed by a shower and a soak in the hot-tub, it was cocktail time. Ed, with a glint in his eye, mixed a wild concoction that frothed at the top, was green under that, and ended at the bottom of the long-stemmed glass in a wicked-looking red. After that drink, called an "mc^2," I was especially glad the computer was doing the driving.

Pennsylvania's rain gave way to sunshine as we drove farther west, and by nightfall our roads were dry. There was almost no noise from outside: a gentle hiss of wind, the quiet hum of the turbine at the rear, and a slight change of noise level on the rare occasions when we left the right-hand lane to pass a slower-moving vehicle. As twilight deepened, the other three moved back to the kitchen. Both Trudi and Ed, I gathered, doubted Ellen's cooking ability and were likely to contribute more advice than they were asked for. I found myself alone in the lounge, watching the flicker of lights on the control console. The roadway before us was almost invisible in the gathering darkness.

Dinner was a cheerful affair, made intimate and romantic by candle-light and wine. The vehicle banked as necessary so the dishes and glasses had no tendency to slide, but both they and the table were slightly textured as well. Ed and Trudi made themselves comfortable on the recliner couch after dinner and selected on the holocube the finals of the gravity-free team gymnastics of the System Olympics, a full light-second away at Harbortown in high orbit. The figures of the team from Bali formed flowerlike patterns, twisting and changing in the slow seconds between contacts with the surrounding cylindrical floor. It was a study in perfect control rather than a test of physical strength; a gravity-bound gymnast would have been judged on different grounds. I found the patterns soothing, and after a time they made me sleepy enough that I made my way aft to bed. When I awoke, the darkness was complete.

My head on the pillow was just above the lower edge of the window. I found the control and switched from "Opaque—Warm White" to "Full Transparent One Way." Within seconds, the roof and wall seemed to disappear. Neither the steady hum of the engine nor the hiss of air outside had changed, but it was as though the compartment was now open to the world outside. I could see the brighter stars above, but nothing compared to the dazzling grandeur of the universe seen from space. After a few minutes I drifted off to sleep again, but I was awakened by brighter lights and a lessening of the background noise. The RV had slowed and we were negotiating an off-ramp. The clock showed a few minutes after midnight. I interrogated a small video panel near my head by keyboard, and saw our red dot just west of Sioux City, Iowa. The video showed the last and the next off-ramps, and bordered in green the one we were on, "Sioux City #22, Elkton Service Area." The video switched and gave a choice of services:

"Restaurants" (it listed six), "Motels—Showers—Supermarket—Gift Shop—Fuel Services—Resort Hotel—RV Marina." I knew that the hotel and marina would share swimming pools, tennis courts, gymnasia and probably an abbreviated golf course, all covered. The green letters "Selected" were under "Fuel Service" so I knew the RV had calculated its reserves and decided to top off its tanks. We'd been on the road for fifteen hours and had covered some thirteen hundred miles in the old units. No one had keyed in any request that the RV couldn't take care of by itself, so it hadn't troubled to wake us for the stop. We entered an airwall tunnel and the machine coasted for a moment. I knew from Ellen's briefing that it was switching to electric drive. The turbine would be winding down and the wheel motors would run on stored energy while we were inside the service area.

The landscaping inside the covered area was muted: grass, leaf-bearing trees, and flowers natural to the Iowa climate. We passed a number of turnoffs and entered a brightly lighted area set with long parallel docks at RV door height. Most of the vehicles at the ramp were trucks, and we took our place in line with them. After a minute we moved forward. An automatic fueler rolled on tracks parallel to us, and when we stopped it moved slowly forward to locate our fueling port. A light flickered near its top, and

I knew it was scanning the binary code painted on the RV's side, to check our credit and charge the fuel against our account. In the distance I could hear the gurgle of liquid flow beginning.

Outside, a man in uniform walked by. He stopped beside the fueler, and held a small device close to the port. Later Ed told me it was probably a gas analyzer, checking to make sure our machine's fuel port sealed well enough to be within legal limits for pollution control. If it had failed we wouldn't have been awakened, but there'd have been an entry in a central computer bank that we'd learn about in the morning, with a directive to comply within seven days.

Several minutes after the inspector had moved on the flow of liquid stopped, a valve clicked shut, and the robot fueler retracted its telescoping arm. We turned slowly and ponderously to pass a truck still moored to its fueling line forward of our position, and eased past the line of vehicles under the lights. I questioned my bedside video and learned the quantity of fuel loaded, the brand, the price per liter, and the total. Unasked, the on-board computer also volunteered that all other expendables, turbine oil, hydraulic fluid, water, and tire pressures, were topped up.

We slid through the exit airwall, the turbine spooled up, and within a few seconds we rejoined the road west. The speed crept back toward its computer-set 120 kph. The hum of the turbine, the hiss of air and tires, and the gentle sway as we took curves combined to lull me to sleep again. There were no more stops until I was awakened by daylight streaming in through the small transparent section I had left in the window.

I was curious about how far west we'd traveled during the night, so I keyed a request to the RV's computer even before I rolled out of bed. On the bulkhead at my feet a map appeared with the state boundaries outlined in red. The small dot showed our position between Sundance and Gillette, Wyoming. I touched the keys and the scale expanded, and when I keyed "Topographic" a complex pattern of mountains was shown by contour lines. In less than an hour we'd leave the main highway for the road up the east face of the Bighorn range. I saw through the panoramic window-wall a land of mesas and parched plains, under a sky so clear and blue that distant clouds seemed cut off at their bases by the curve of the Earth. At my request the bulkhead screen gave me views directly forward and aft. The nearest vehicles were more than a mile away. As always, traffic control had evened the spacings between vehicles, so I knew there must be only a few on the road. I took a hot, luxurious morning bath, dressed, and went forward.

Ed and Trudi hadn't yet appeared, so Ellen and I set breakfast cooking, took our coffee cups to the lounge, and with all the forward windows set to "Full Transparent" sat together on the couch while the mountains grew before us.

Soon the others joined us, and breakfast was finished before the RV began working its way up the face of the mountains on a series of switchbacks. At each hairpin turn it slowed nearly to walking pace, and we could hear the hiss of the hydraulics as the wheels swung to negotiate the turn. There were no trucks with us now, and few other vehicles. The traffic eastbound was mainly open pickups, limousines, or RVs, but there were so many different models that I was never to see one identical to our own. The view back over the plain became more spectacular with each hundred meters of height we gained, until finally at each hairpin we seemed to be hanging in the sky. After the last we turned west, entered a narrow pass, and joined a tumbling mountain stream icy with the snow-melt of the mountain spring. The road twisted its way upward through a narrow, forested canyon until we came out onto a high plain set with pine and fir. The tree line was only a few hundred meters higher than the road, and above it the peaks showed green with moss and lichen and white with patches of snow. The temperature outside was only a little above freezing.

Past the western ridge of the Bighorns our descent was even more dramatic, for I was conscious of our dependence on the RV's sure-footedness. I asked about brakes, and was told the six drive-motors were running as generators, on the downhill, pouring their power first into charging the batteries and then into electric heaters mounted far aft on the roof.

On the plains we picked up speed again, and by lunchtime were rolling through Cody. For some hours a red X had been anchored to a spot on the map a little to the west, and when we questioned the computer it told us there was a defective road marker ahead. As we neared the spot our speed dropped off to a crawl, a chime sounded, and we were asked to fasten our seat belts. Ed told me the RV would follow a painted line that gave no anticipation of what the road was doing ahead. A group of four men in hard hats, with several pieces of heavy equipment, was standing by the road to let us by. At the center of the lane they'd already carved a neat cylindrical hole in the concrete. I saw a plug of equal size, with the replacement marker evidently already in it, standing at the roadside ready for installation.

Ellen told me that ordinarily when such repairs were necessary, all traffic was routed into the other lane so that no reduction in speed was necessary and travelers weren't even aware of the problem. In this case, though, both lanes were out of service because of a crack that extended across them. We gave a smile and a wave to the work crew as we passed, and the men waved in return. One of them looked Asiatic, and Ellen told me he was probably an American Indian; there were big populations of Indians in all the mountain and desert states. Once past the obstruction the computer switched to its normal mode, and our speed came back up to the steady 120. Later, on schedule, we coasted down to the level of Yellowstone Lake, lined at intervals by campgrounds and RV parks. The RV swung to the left at a crossroad, and we idled our way at a slower speed through a shallow, winding canyon beside a stream, until before us the expanse of Jackson Hole opened. I spent another hour on the exercise machines in the gym, Ed baked in the sauna, and we got out warm clothes ready for the mountain air.

We slowed at the park entrance, and took in a batch of folders and maps from a smiling, golden-haired woman of college age. She wore a National Parks uniform complete with a broad-brimmed hat. While we were stopped, a scanning light beam at her side checked our number, and she then handed us a permit to stay overnight in the park. Ellen turned to me with a smile and said that I was the passport for all four of us. There was a six-month waiting list for places in the Tetons, and a four-week limit on camping. Visitors from outside the country had some priority, and mine was the highest of all since I had come from so far away. Our clearance to stay had arrived before we left Waterford.

We were sited on an open plain a mile from Jenny Lake. The location was less private than I would have liked. Only low trees and bushes, recently planted, separated one RV space from the next, and our view of the mountains was over the roofs of vehicles like our own. Nevertheless, the two weeks that followed were among the best that I spent on the Earth. My muscles were usually sore from hiking, and I was constantly peeling from sunburn, but the air was crystal-clear and the lake water was like liquid ice. There were a great many other hikers, some of them reserved but most of them friendly and outgoing. A few people invited us to visit them in their tents or RVs. At Ed's insistence Trudi and I took a two-day cram course in mountaineering, and then the three of us climbed the Grand Teton with a guided party. That was a glorious day, but I spent the next two recovering from it, with frequent soaks in the hot-tub.

I had my doubts about horseback riding. Though I'd done the usual childhood pony riding at home in the Cluster, I'd never learned to ride properly. Finally I gave in and enjoyed the experience, but again the sauna and hot-tub got a good workout afterward. Ellen waited out most of our strenuous hikes, and when we clumped down off the mountain in our heavy boots, our legs white with dust, she would usually be waiting at the camp, tanning in the sunlight, with a cool drink beside her.

After toughening us up for several days, Ed persuaded us to drive north to Idaho so we could go backpacking. By then I was enthusiastic, but Ellen was still dubious. In the end Trudi and Ed went ahead at their own fast pace, and we followed more slowly up the trail. Because of our communications via satellite we were able to talk with Trudi and Ed each evening, even if we happened to be camped in a narrow box canyon that blocked direct line-of-sight radio signals to them.

The camping equipment was ingenious and light, but it still weighed enough to make my shoulders ache by midafternoon, our usual stopping time. A touch of the button would inflate our tent, giving us a large screened room. For the remainder of the day the extended solar mirror would focus sunlight on a small black sphere where water was dissociated into hydrogen and oxygen. At night they would recombine in a fuel cell to give us electricity for lighting, cooking, and our electric sleeping bags.

We spent two days in a high mountain meadow with a steep mountain to the north, its slopes rough with scree. Twice in the late twilight we saw small herds of moose. Next day we started back down the trail and were overtaken by Trudi and Ed in the afternoon. I took a certain amount of teasing from the others because I'd insisted on taking a snake-bite kit with us; of course we hadn't needed it. Still, brought up as I had been in the Cluster where there are no poisonous snakes, the notion of rattlesnakes in the American West had made me a little wary about where I stepped. I had liked my brief sample of the wild areas of the Earth except for one thing: bugs. Of course, at home in the Cluster I'd been able to hike and to sleep outdoors without putting up with flies or mosquitos.

At the road-head we climbed aboard the RV, set it to begin the homeward journey, and took long, soaking, hot showers to get the grit off. In the mirror I saw a face I hardly recognized: reddened, stubbly with beard, bumpy with mosquito bites, topped by a tangle of unwashed hair.

By the time we all emerged from our showers, washed, dressed, and respectable, the RV was hundreds of kilometers to the east. We had set it for a more northerly route by way of the floating tunnel under Lake Michigan from Manitowoc to Ludington. As we drove, Ellen called her parents and brought them up to date on our trip. Her last call to them had been made from our mountain meadow one evening, while the campfire crackled and I studied the familiar stars.

As we drove and I had time to think back over our days in the mountains, I realized once again how precious was this Earth, not only to those who lived here, but even more to those of us who lived beyond. Ed had talked of the strong pressures from the space colonies to preserve the wilderness areas, and of the wealth from off-Earth that had poured in to help finance that preservation. I decided that I would accept his invitation to join the best of the preservationist groups. Whether or not I might ever live on Earth myself, some of my great-grandchildren might choose to do so, and I wanted to be sure that Earth would still be there, green and inviting, though most of her children might then live far away.

—*E. C. R.*

LAND TRAVEL a century from now will be governed by the interaction of human desires with technology, economics, and politics, as it is today. Some conclusions are nearly certain: that energy will be available as needed from some one of several possible inexhaustible sources; that living standards will rise, as they have for centuries, despite wars and recessions; that automation will make it even easier for ordinary families to own large, complex machinery; that people will continue to prefer, other things being equal, private means of transportation. That is a desire that cuts across cultural lines to a remarkable degree.

For a large, long-distance, recreational vehicle, the major technical problem is energy storage. The most likely solutions to that problem were covered in the "Energy" chapter of Part II, with one exception. It is barely possible, though uncertain, that enough energy to drive a large RV over long distances could be stored in kinetic form by a rapidly rotating flywheel in vacuum. At present, even the most advanced high-strength materials can give us, in flywheel form, an amount of stored energy per kilogram of mass that is only about the same as we could get from electric batteries— that is to say, far too little. Flywheels would have to do ten to a hundred times better before they could compete with chemical fuels.

Engineers have wrestled with the problem of self-steering vehicles for decades. The old assumption was that the intelligence required for driving was far too great for any computer that could be stuffed into a car; therefore, it was reasoned, any driving system would have to be based on a large central computer. New technologies, however, have made the problem much simpler than that. Cheap microprocessors make it more reasonable to leave the second-to-second responsibility for driving to an onboard computer, while a central source need supply only relatively simple services such as information about traffic, road conditions, and detours. That information could easily be transmitted in digital form to the vehicles' onboard computers, via occasional roadside antennas or via satellite.

Here, for example, is one system for automatic driving that would be inexpensive to install in our existing highways. About every hundred meters in each lane there would be an underground marker consisting of a set of permanent magnets. Those magnets would be set in concrete, forming a binary code that could be sensed by a coil of wire under each vehicle. The code would say to the on-board computer, for example, "50 meters ahead there begins a curve to the right. It begins with a curve radius of a thousand meters and then tightens to 300 over a road distance of 500, according to the standard prescription." The car would sense as it passed each marker whether it were drifting to the right or left, and would make smooth corrections as necessary. Every few kilometers there would be a device to sense the passage of a vehicle (it could be as simple as the hoses we cross occasionally, which are connected to traffic counters) and to feed that information to a microprocessor in a box at the roadside. That local traffic monitor would keep track of the average number of vehicles on the highway and send radio signals to each vehicle as it passed, telling it to slow down or speed up slightly in order to maintain an even spacing between vehicles.

That would place the main burden of intelligence and control on the individual car or truck. Each vehicle would have a low-power radar to measure the distance to the next vehicle in situations where the traffic was closely spaced. It's worth noting that low-power "sports radars" are now available for the individual buyer. They can be held in one hand like a flashlight, and they cost only about 2 percent of the price of a car. The on-board computer would regulate the speed of the vehicle to the legal limit with high precision simply by timing the interval between crossings of the magnetic markers. And how high will that speed be? With automated driving human error will be removed, so speeds will not be limited by concerns about safety. I believe they will be set by considerations of fuel economy, highway noise, and the lifetime of tires. We can't increase speeds very much without excessive fuel consumption, because per mile of driving the fuel burned goes up roughly as the square of the speed. Highway noise and the rate of wear on tires also go up sharply as the speed increases, so in my guess the computer-set highway speed in 2081 will be somewhere near 120 kph, about 75 miles per hour. People who want to do their own driving and who want to race will do so on tracks and road courses that are set aside for recreational driving.

Now for the final part of the problem: how will the computerized cars keep to the center of their lanes if they cross highway markers only about every three seconds? The answer lies in a peaceful and inexpensive spin-off from some military hardware that has been developed at great cost over the past three decades, the technology called "inertial navigation." Inertial navigation is a precise, robot version of something that all animals do automatically: feeling the sensation of acceleration when they move, and estimating from that sensation how they are changing their speeds and their positions. We feel something akin to that sensation in a car rounding a curve, then straightening out again. The human body isn't designed to measure those sensations of acceleration to compute where we're going except very crudely; by contrast, the inertial navigation systems that have been built for military use are incredibly precise. Those mounted in the nose cones of intercontinental ballistic missiles are designed to guide those missiles for flights of up to twenty minutes, without any reference whatever to the outside world, and to steer them so precisely that they can hit a target as small as a single building that is five thousand miles away. In order to do so they must measure and compute for three directions: up/down, east/west, and north/south. The problem for automated highway driving is absurdly easy by comparison: the inertial sensor need only measure acceleration in one direction, left/right, and we can tolerate errors in the angle of the drift of the vehicle to the left or right that become a hundred times worse in only three seconds than the military system accumulates over a full twenty minutes. For the highway vehicle, the inertial sensor could probably be as simple as a weight on the end of a spring.

A few minor changes in our major highways would be required in the evolution to automatic driving. We would have to add at the entry and exit ramps grids at road level that cattle and smaller animals could not cross, and we would have to raise the height of boundary fences. At present most such fences are too low, and deer can jump over them. All of those changes to our highways, with the addition of passive magnetic markers and occasional traffic-monitoring sensors, could be made at a tiny fraction of the cost of scrapping our roads and replacing them. Politically speaking, the system I've described would be far easier to adopt than most other alternatives, because it would be compatible with our existing highways and would put almost all of the necessary equipment—and therefore almost all of the cost—into the vehicles rather than into a centralized system. Individual decisions to spend money are always far easier to make than those that require agreement by large committees.

Given the very low cost of solid-state electronics, it would be possible (and would probably be mandated legally) to provide in every automated vehicle a great deal of redundancy, so that no individual failure of a component would lead to an accident. Such redundant systems have already been common in aircraft for many years. Once driving is automated, we can expect an enormous saving in human life. Although the accident rate on the roads of the United States is lower than in any other country in the world, in the past thirty years about one million Americans have died in car accidents—a tragic toll many times greater than the number of Americans lost in all the wars of the twentieth century. The automation of driving will also lead to economies at the same time as it saves lives. Right now, long-distance truck drivers must turn themselves almost into automatons, driving endless hours while half asleep in order to earn money at freight transport. It would be far safer and more economical if a driver could become a transportation manager, directing from his home the travels of several trucks that would drive nonstop, day and night, under the local command of their on-board computers. Similarly, taxicabs would be far more available at odd hours than they are now, and people who were elderly or handicapped could be far more mobile and independent than they are at present, when they must call on friends, family members, or hired drivers to take them about. Parents of school-age children could instruct their cars to obey the children's commands, within prescribed routes and times, so that the parents would be freed of the chore of chauffeuring them to school or on visits to friends. With automation, the routine monitoring of highways by cruising patrol cars could be carried out cheaply and effectively, a single police officer supervising through radio and video links a number of self-driving vehicles.

In this chapter, the last in which we follow Eric's journey before he returns home to Fox Cluster, he encounters a few technical matters that require explanation. The Tehaneys' RV accomplishes its braking electrically rather than mechanically, because electric braking can be very precise, can compensate automatically for slippery surfaces, and never requires the replacement of brake shoes. Eric's hiking companion, Ed, makes use of an "unlisted identifier" to guard his privacy. We can be sure that no system of positive identification and location will be accepted in countries where individual rights are preserved unless there is some way to prevent the system being used for invasions of privacy that are unrelated to its use for preventing crimes. But you may have been surprised to read, in the midst of these examples of futuristic technologies, that Eric and his friends are given colorful brochures and maps little different from those that are handed out today at the entrances to national parks. Printing and publishing will still be vigorous in 2081, but they will have changed significantly. The printed word will usually be stored electronically, and memory cartridges that will cost only a fraction as much as today's paperback books will insert in "slates" whose quality of black-and-white reproduction will be very high. But for high-quality, glossy reproduction of colors, as in art books, maps, and slick-paper magazines, I doubt that even in 100 years there will be anything to equal the printing of ink onto paper. There's much more uncertainty in the matter of camping equipment, but on their walking tour Eric and Ellen go to futuristic extremes, carrying with them even a portable solar-electric energy converter. The equipment listed is intended to suggest what will be possible, rather than what most people will use. Of all the items carried, only the satellite communicator is a virtual certainty for a typical backpacking trip in 2081.

In their tour by recreational vehicle, Eric and Ellen encounter many examples of an environmental awareness that will be general in 2081. Most industrial countries experienced severe pollution problems during the third quarter of this century, but very little of the increased pollution was associated with the increases in population, average family income, and passenger travel that occurred in those same years. Almost all of the tenfold increase in pollutants came from the manufacture of new synthetic products, mainly from the chemical industry: fibers, plastics, synthetic detergents, and pesticides. One of the most dangerous pollutants, mercury, increased thirty-fivefold over a quarter century, mainly as a result of its use in the production of chlorine and paint. Lest we feel that a democratic society copes poorly with such problems, we should note that in state-controlled countries there are generally rewards only for managers who exceed their production quotas, not for those who clean up their factories. There are strong ecological movements in the most affluent nations, and those movements have achieved considerable success. For example, the Hudson River is now a great deal cleaner than it was a few decades ago, and fish are now caught there that couldn't have lived in the river in the worst days of pollution. The movement for environmental cleanup is likely to succeed particularly for the localized sources of pollutants: factories and municipal sewage plants. It faces a far more difficult challenge in the case of products used for agriculture, such as fertilizers and insecticides, because those pollutants are dispersed into very low concentrations and washed into streams and rivers by rainfall. Many of our lakes are suffocating under an unhealthy burden of algae force-fed by the runoff of agricultural nutrients, and there is no single localized source of those pollutants that we can control.

In my view, the development of closed-cycle (greenhouse) agriculture over the next century will be the only effective solution to the problems of agricultural pollution and deforestation and also of year-to-year variations of food production. In closed-cycle agriculture, runoff water is cleaned and recirculated instead of being allowed to escape, and fertilizers are recycled instead of being allowed to run off into watersheds. Artificial lighting supplements natural sunlight so that the growing season can be extended to a full year. Crops are protected from climatic extremes outside. Basic research into greenhouse agriculture is being done by corporations and universities, and it will receive a boost from the development of self-sufficient space colonies. As soon as there are a few hundred people in residence outside Earth's biosphere there will be a stronger incentive than ever before to learn every detail of agricultural production in a closed system. Much of the effort in research on conventional agriculture must be devoted to fighting natural plant pests—those insects, viruses, and microscopic parasites that have evolved, over the millenia, to compete with humans for the harvest of their food crops. That is what forces the rapid introduction of new food-crop species and the use of ever-greater quantities of pesticides. But in closed-system farming, the bugs and the blights are excluded physically rather than attacked chemically. The greenhouse agriculture revolution is closer than you might think. Already Soviet cosmonauts have grown wheat and cabbages in space, and Soviet technicians have lived in closed-cycle environments on Earth for several months at a time.

It is a paradox that the very success of greenhouse agriculture makes us underestimate the extent of its present development. It is encountered only rarely by most of us because it takes up so little space. In contrast, open-field dirt farming requires a vast area to produce relatively little food. At present, greenhouse agriculture is a commercial success in Holland, in Japan, and in several locations in the United States. On Kharg Island in the Arabian Gulf, it is the only source of fresh vegetables in a wide area. In the late 1970s, the General Electric Company spent corporate funds for the successful development of a pilot plant for enclosed agriculture at its main research facility in Schenectady, New York. The plant used artificial lighting, a special atmosphere enriched in carbon dioxide to yield rapid growth of crops, and a closed system of recycled nutrients. Many of the details of G.E.'s work are unpublished precisely because the work was successful: the details became proprietary trade secrets.

Greenhouse agriculture will lend itself naturally to farming by individual families, for it requires only a small area, demands considerable care and attention, and produces crops of high quality that command premium prices, outselling the inferior products of large-scale, open-field agricultural companies. As it gradually takes over during the next century, we can expect that it will have an enormous positive effect on reducing the pollution of our lakes and streams, increasing the purity of our foods, and permitting the reforestation of our landscape. All five of the drivers of change will contribute to its success, and as a result, some of our grandchildren may control their family-owned greenhouse by their home computer, seed and harvest with automated equipment, obtain the latest word on techniques from research colonies in space, bathe their crops with artificial sunlight, and decide what crops to seed next on the basis of a communications network that will receive information from the entire planet and beyond it. With their efforts, and those of millions of others around the world who will take up greenhouse farming, enough can be grown to feed the world's people, and our land can recover its forests and the purity of its waters.

Part IV

Wild Cards

Wild Cards

Viewing the year 2081 in Part III, we balanced the odds for each likely change as carefully as we could, in order to find the most probable, realistic future. Now let's throw caution aside and let our imaginations soar to the outer limits of the possible.

Of all such possibilities, the worst is that there may be no future at all, that humankind may annihilate itself in an ultimate, suicidal, nuclear war. Nevil Shute's *On the Beach*, a tract of the early nuclear age, warned of just such a catastrophe. He imagined that all living things north of the equator would be killed in a nuclear exchange, and told us of the final, hopeless year when the Australians, doomed by the radioactive cloud spreading slowly to the south, would be left no choice but the manner of their deaths. Yet had such a nuclear war really occurred, I believe that Nevil Shute himself would have helped to "write" a happier ending. He would have returned to his original profession of engineering, and led the effort to construct radiation barriers and shielded greenhouses to save a portion of humanity. Of course, if that grim possibility did come to pass, it would be much more difficult to save our civilization than to save a few survivors.

There is reason to hope that nuclear war, even if it does occur, will not escalate to the point of total destruction. If any sanity remains on the part of those who control the nuclear weapons, an initial exchange will be followed by an attempt to freeze the tactical situation while negotiation and "conventional" warfare continue. And historically, the wars that have involved many nations and killed millions of people have been followed by periods of deliberate restraint. Such times of restriction and recovery followed the Thirty Years War, and more than a century later, the wars of the Napoleonic era. We may be in such a period now, after the appalling number of deaths brought by the Second World War. And there is now another restraining influence: the power of the multinational corporations. The multinationals have become the whipping boys of intellectual society; it is fashionable to blame them for all the ills of our world. Yet they do serve as stabilizing forces. They came about as the result of modern communications, automation, and management aided by computers, and they thrive best in a peaceful world. Although they include industries that produce weapons, they are fundamentally economic entities that measure success by profits earned, not by populations subjugated, territories annexed or heretical ideas erased.

Yet, if total nuclear devastation is only a remote possibility, total and continuing peace seems equally remote as long as the power of the nation-states remains. The causes of war will still be with us on this Earth—an important qualifier—a century from now. Those causes are the desire to dominate territories and subjugate peoples, the urge to compel others to one's own religious or doctrinaire beliefs, and the lust for power of individual leaders. There are too many examples in history of a major war following the rise to power of a charismatic megalomaniac, bent on obtaining the adulation and commitment that a population only grants in a time of crisis. A war can also be triggered by the actions of a peacetime leader who fails in his task and then attempts to divert the blame of his people toward an external target.

Whatever the risk of total destruction while humankind remains bound to the surface of the Earth, that risk will fall to zero, and humanity will be unkillable, when a substantial number of people are dispersed in self-sufficient colonies widely separated in space. We can also hope for a more peaceful future in space than has been our history on Earth. A space colony will be too small in scale and too distant from its nearest neighbors to be an adequate base for conquest. Its population will be too small, and its government too easy of access, to provide the conditions for the rise to power of a world conqueror. Men of that stamp, if they are born in the colonies, are likely to seek out the great concentrations of people that will still exist in the nations of Earth—just as Napoleon left his native Corsica, Stalin his birthplace in Georgia, and Hitler the Austria of his youth.

Most wars that are not caused by the ambitions of individual leaders come about as the result of territorial pressures. There is no need for such pressures to develop, at least for thousands of years, on the space frontier. We know that materials exist, even in our solar system, for the construction in space of Earthlike island-territories totaling millions of times the land area of the Earth. Those territories will be indefinitely extensible, and can be enlarged simply by new construction, without taking over the land across a border. Space colonies can be moved. Movable land area is a concept that has never existed before in human history. Within less than a generation a space colony could move itself hundreds of millions of kilometers from a location that it found threatening or unpleasant. With the help of mirrors to concentrate solar energy, such a colony could maintain an Earthlike environment anywhere within the solar system. For those reasons it is highly probable that territoriality will lose much of its force within the next century.

Though we cannot foresee the alignments and confrontations that will determine the wars of the next century, we can make informed guesses as to the weapons that will be used in those wars. In 2081, the individual human in war will no longer be the hero of romantic history, but only a shivering, naked hostage to fortune: a victim. The research that first develops human-level robots, whether or not they are furnished with bodies in human shape, will be funded primarily by the military. As we already see in the development of cruise missiles, human warriors are being replaced by machines. Ultimately the glamorous figure of the wartime fighter-pilot will give way to the robot: able to withstand thousands of gravities of acceleration while the human can withstand only ten; needing no complicated life-support system; far tougher than fragile human flesh in surviving radiation; knowing no fatigue; never subject to doubt, despair, or pangs of conscience; merciless. Such robot warriors will control weapons that would have seemed, a few years ago, the stuff of science fiction: charged particle beams able to blast holes through the atmosphere to destroy inbound missile warheads; neutral particle beams that can travel hundreds of kilometers through space at nearly the speed of light; lasers, whose beams of light will carry enough energy to melt tons of metal in a single shot. But with all these radically new weapons there will also be reincarnations of the old. The ordinary bullet, for all its antiquity, will take its place in the arsenal of weapons for use in vacuum. There, with no drag, a bullet can be accelerated by magnetic forces to a speed higher than that of the fastest meteorite. Bullets of that speed will travel a thousand kilometers in a few seconds and will be too small to be detectable by radar. Discharged machinegun fashion, such deadly hailstones will each carry in its energy of motion more destructive power than a high-explosive shell.

Like those species of fish that inflate themselves to gigantic size on the approach of an enemy, war craft may carry radar and optical reflectors on extended arms to misdirect the fire of the enemy. In space, where even large lightweight objects can move without drag, decoys will be used extensively.

Much of the shielding used in space may be derived from materials found there, the natural soils and rocks of the lunar surface and the asteroids. These raw materials will also be refined for the construction in space of giant ships and bases to be used in orbit around the Earth. There is no reasonable natural limit to the size of an object built in space, so if military incentives are strong enough, it seems likely that the largest spaceships will be vessels of war.

Already, in the chapter on space travel, I pointed to the likelihood that military pressures will force the development of the most futuristic weapon of all, the antimatter beam. At present, antimatter can be produced in high-energy particle accelerators used for peaceful research, but it can only be made in tiny quantities. At our present technical level it would take more than 3,000 years to manufacture even a millionth of a gram of antimatter. But when we look back at the development of aluminum over this past century, from a pure element more rare and precious than platinum to a metal so cheap and common that it is stamped into beer cans, it seems not impossible that by 2081 antimatter will be made by the ton. Antimatter beams, enormously powerful laser beams, and bullets accelerated to a significant fraction of the speed of light are possibilities that may be turned into reality by weapons research. But research in each of those areas can be applied to peaceful purposes as well. And though conflicts rooted in the territoriality and the ideologies of Earthbound human history may rise like some evil affluvium into the near reaches of space, they will seem pointless to those who dwell at great distances from the surface of our war-torn planet. Independent, self-sufficient space colonies may at last provide an environment where humankind can live at peace. Perhaps then our species will come of age.

At the other extreme from a world of armed frontiers is another possible future for our planet: an era of total freedom of movement, entirely within the bounds of our present scientific knowledge and of the materials we know we can make. All travel would be at nearly zero energy loss, in vacuum. Nearly all energy put into accelerating passenger and freight vehicles would be recovered during their deceleration by the mass-driver technology that is already under development. Just under the surface of the land, and below the oceans at a depth free of storms, there would be a network of vacuum tubes linking the cities and the spaceports of the Earth. Within them, floater vehicles would accelerate at two gravities, a stress that would be noticeable but not dangerous for most people, to a cruising speed of seven miles per second. It would take only nine minutes to reach that speed from a standing start. At seven miles per second, substantially faster than a satellite in orbit, the floater car would press outward on its enclosing guideway with a force that would seem like normal Earth gravity. In that way the total travel time, including acceleration and deceleration between the most distant points on the Earth, would be only thirty-nine minutes.

In such an ultimate transportation system, flight to and from orbit would occur in almost the same way. A curved vacuum-tube guideway would be suspended close to the top of the atmosphere by balloons anchored by tether cables. Passengers would take a ten-minute elevator ride from the ground to a station at one end of the guideway, where they would board a floater vehicle. It would accelerate at two gravities within the tube until it emerged at orbital speed. Returning floaters would enter another tube (a bit of careful aiming there) and decelerate, giving up their orbital energy to electric power. As long as the total traffic flows to and from orbit were about equal, that system could transport an almost unlimited number of people to and from orbit at practically no cost in energy. The travel times would be similar to those of today's rockets, about twenty minutes to orbit. That technology may seem highly improbable, but there is nothing about it that requires either technical knowledge or materials that we do not have today. One element of that technology, a balloon able to support itself permanently at the top of the atmosphere, has already been studied in considerable detail by a group at the Franklin Institute in Philadelphia. The balloon is called "STARS," for "Solar Thermal Aerostat Research Station." It would be a mile in diameter, and would absorb sunlight to heat the air inside it enough to provide buoyancy. My own guess is that a complete system consisting of superspeed floaters and mass-drivers support-

Giant balloons, floating near the top of the atmosphere by the buoyancy of air warmed by sunlight. These balloons, more than a kilometer in diameter, can support communications platforms, satellite-power receiving antennas, and magnetic accelerators to launch passenger craft out of the Earth's gravitational pull. (COURTESY FRANKLIN INSTITUTE)

ed by balloons to send passenger craft to and from deep space will be built eventually, because it will allow an almost unlimited volume of traffic to, from, and over the Earth without damage to the environment. Some of that system may be in operation by 2081, but not, I would guess, very much of it.

It may just be possible to develop superstrong materials during the next century. We've known for many years that carbon and certain metals could be very strong when they were in the form of tiny, ordered crystals. However, we've never been able to preserve the same order and the same strength in pieces of material larger than microscopic size. The strongest large-size objects in use today are the cables of suspension bridges, and we don't know how to make them much stronger now than we could fifty years ago. It is tantalizing that the ultimate theoretical limits of strength are about one hundred times greater. If we had such material, a wire no thicker than a needle could suspend the weight of an automobile. In practical applications, it could be used in the building of suspension bridges several miles in length, aircraft of much higher efficiency and load-carrying ability than those of today, buildings with enormous clear spans free of supports, and perhaps less fortunately, taller skyscrapers. The most generally useful application of superstrong materials would probably be to the building of flywheels for storing energy. Such flywheels, spinning so fast that they would store more energy in their motion than we carry now in the form of gasoline, would power electric cars of high performance. Those cars would be totally nonpolluting and—unlike any electric car that's now possible—would never require battery replacement. Such materials might also make possible the "space elevator," a favorite science-fiction dream that goes back several decades to theoretical studies done in Russia. That device would be a cable reaching down to the surface of the Earth from a counterweight beyond synchronous orbit. Elevators would run up and down the cable, trading energy between the gravitational and electrical forms as they went. Arthur Clarke described the space elevator in his novel *The Fountains of Paradise*. As I've already shown, though, one could build an equally efficient transport system into space using balloon-borne floater guideways, without the need for superstrength materials.

In the realm of physiology, it seems nearly certain that well before 2081 we'll find a way to select the sex of a child at conception. And in that century of research, we'll probably learn enough to control the complex of diseases known as cancer. With the techniques of research using recombinant DNA, it's barely possible that we'll also learn how to modify the genetic structure prior to conception, so that a child will be sure to grow into an intelligent, good-looking adult with a healthy body that's neither too fat nor too slim. We can well imagine the controversy that would develop should it also turn out to be possible to select such subtle qualities as kindness and compassion, or to choose selfishness and aggressiveness instead. Research of that kind will probably begin with the less ambitious goal of eliminating such genetic defects as poor eyesight, a malfunctioning heart, diabetes, or allergies. At the limits of the barely possible there's another science-fiction idea: that we may be able to make such precise electronic connections to the human brain that we can record the life-experiences of an individual, with all the sensations of sight, touch, hearing, taste, and smell.

In the past two decades, methods have been worked out for transplanting healthy organs to replace ailing ones. But as long as those organs come from donors, they can inflame the new body to reject them through its automatic immune response. The transplanting of organs will surely remain a rare and difficult procedure, because it will depend on the availability of a healthy organ from an accident victim and will require continual supervision to detect the early signs of a flareup of the immune response. But there's another way to make replacement body organs, a way that may become practical during the next century. Every cell of the body carries within it the genetic code for the entire individual, and biologists are just beginning to learn how to "clone" from one cell a microscopic bit of tissue that can grow into an adult body. In plant physiology, it's routine for certain plants to be grown, complete with leaves, stems, roots, and flowers, from a fragment of a single leaf. Perhaps in a century biologists will learn so much about the complexities of the human cell that they can take a tissue sample from each human being in childhood, freeze the sample, and then grow from it a heart, liver, kidneys, eyes, and other critical replacement parts, in anticipation of their being needed in later life. Cloning will raise very serious moral issues, and I would not be surprised if the most advanced work on it is done in research centers far from the Earth, away from the tangle of overlapping laws and jurisdictions that will slow or prevent such work here. In my opinion, even if cloning can be made to work it may be too slow and unwieldy to compete in the "organ market."

For a number of bodily organs there is already a more practical alternative, as I described in "The Lotus and the Thorn." Machinery can be kept going indefinitely if we are willing to replace parts that wear out. Artificial organs made of the inert plastic Teflon (the same one used to line frying pans), and of certain metals, especially tantalum, don't produce any immune response at all. Such metal and plastic parts are already used routinely to replace damaged or diseased blood vessels, bone sockets, portions of the human eye, kneecaps, and other human parts. Such "bionic" technologies present little difficulty in terms of social acceptance. We respond with pleasure and relief when such techniques restore good friends to better health and freer activity. The hero and heroine of "The Six Million Dollar Man" and "The Bionic Woman" were admired television characters. Computer-directed, automated factories will someday be able to produce, at moderate cost, replacement organs for humans of every bodily type. As a result, people will be able to maintain good health and freedom from infirmities into a vigorous old age.

The road ahead for bionics is not entirely clear, though, because of a problem that may or may not be solved by 2081: though muscle, bone, and skin cells can regenerate after damage, nerve cells cannot. And if we do not learn how to regenerate nerve fibers so that they can connect to new replacement organs, whether biological or mechanical, the new organs will not be able to feel. Perhaps that's not important in the case of internal organs like the heart and kidneys, but it certainly does matter for the surface of the skin. If our descendants, in the course of having portions of their bodies replaced, lose their nervous sensitivity, so they can no longer enjoy lovemaking, eating, and the rest of the sensual pleasures, longevity will have been bought at too high a price. As of now, we cannot say whether it will have to be paid.

To obtain a significant extension of the average lifespan would require scientific knowledge that we don't yet possess. Living organisms appear to be programmed for death, and for more than forty years biologists have sought to understand the death wish the cells fulfill by halting their division after a few tens of cycles. Not long ago three outstanding specialists in genetics and biochemistry, Joshua Lederberg, Arthur Kornberg, and Luca Cavalli-Sforza, explained to me some of the latest speculations on the aging process. They noted that the victory over poliomyelitis had been won by following a simple clue: that victims of the disease appeared to be immune to contracting it again.

Is there an equally useful clue to the aging process? Perhaps it is the correlation between age and the likelihood of cancer. Though cancer can occur at any age, its chance of striking increases greatly as a human being, or any other animal, ages. A mouse is old when it reaches the age of two, and a two-year-old mouse is usually cancerous. Perhaps, the speculation continued, both aging and cancer are symptoms of a breakdown of the DNA-repair mechanism in somatic cells.

In every cell there are small, specialized groups of molecules continually moving up and down each strand of the DNA helix, checking for signs of damage: a hydrocarbon group extended at the wrong bond angle; an amino acid of the wrong size or shape; a wrong sequence or correlation of the acids in the DNA helix. When the DNA-repair mechanism finds an error, it performs an act of "recombinant DNA." It excises the bad section of the strand and replaces it with a newly assembled good one. In a healthy cell, DNA repair occurs in a matter of seconds, as can be shown by experiments in which damage is induced by ultraviolet light. But in certain cells, there are indications that DNA repair can become sluggish, and possibly aging is a symptom of such slow or careless performance on the part of the DNA-repair mechanism. Aging may therefore be like cancer, a kind of disease—and so, by inference, curable.

There is, of course, a long distance between such a speculation and a full understanding. We can acquire a respect for the distance yet to go by appreciating that roughly two-thirds of the DNA double-helix is there for reasons we do not yet understand. In experiments with simple cells, that two-thirds has been removed, without apparently affecting the ability of the cells to divide and reproduce.

If that wild card, a cure for aging, were to turn up before 2081, it would be joined quickly with inevitable developments in bionics to produce human immortality. That goal might be reached in at least one other way. To maintain the body or its brain without aging is only the most obvious path to immortality. It requires the least understanding, because we could achieve it without delving into the mysteries of identity. If, however, we unravel those mysteries, we may open the way to the transfer and recording of the self. With cloning, humans might then command an endless succession of bodies, each occupied only for its prime of youth and then discarded. The self with all or a subset of its memories would be recorded and transferred with each rejuvenation.

Even if we reach that capability, it seems unlikely that we will do so within this next century, because the task is harder than any other that we've considered. We have only the barest clues to methods for recording human memories, and are still farther from understanding the mechanism of human identity. Yet, if identity is a physical phenomenon of the brain, there should be the possibility, ultimately, of recording it, transferring it, and imprinting it either on another identical brain or on an imperishable nonorganic matrix.

If immortality were to be realized, whatever the method, its discovery would put an enormous strain on the fabric of society, greater possibly than society has ever known. If the human race loses its mortality, it will be losing one of its most precious possessions, strange as that may seem. We do not need immortality in order to preserve humanity's greatest works. Creative genius can leave its mark on the world within one human lifetime in a thousand ways. To us, Aristotle, Rembrandt, Mozart, Shakespeare, and Einstein will never die. With mortality, even the most bitter conflict between enemies cannot go on forever. There is comfort as well as pathos in the old phrase, "It will all be the same in a hundred years."

Because of mortality, even the cruelest and most despotic dictator has only a finite span of rule. The chains forged by Stalin and Franco were broken only by their natural deaths. Hitler, if he had conquered in World War II and obtained immortality, would rule the world today in a rule that would never end, growing ever more cunning and experienced with the years.

Even without the horror of a permanent worldwide dictatorship from which there could be no breakout, endless life would be a curse to humanity in more subtle ways. A dominant figure in any field, whether it be science, literature, art, or politics, would remain dominant forever, never stepping aside for newcomers with fresh ideas. Immortals might refuse to have children, not wishing to be disturbed by the natural selfishness and importunities that are a part of childhood. In that event, society would lose the innocence and healthy simplicity that children bring to us now, along with the potential to rejuvenate our world. An immortal society would be deeply conservative, and the stagnation of the human race would follow almost certainly.

What of the other races of thinking beings that may have evolved before us? We found no life on Mars, and we hear no radio signals from civilizations other than our own. As far as we know from the data we have, we may be alone in the galaxy. Why? Is it perhaps that immortality is a technical achievement that comes naturally soon after our own stage of civilization and brings with it inexorable stagnation and decay? If so, either we will reach the same dead end of endless life or escape it by lucky chance and, mortal still, roam outward among the stars, discovering the archaeological remnants of earlier civilizations that found immortality too soon.

And yet, for the individual, immortality is so alluring a prize that I cannot imagine a deliberate, universal, permanent renunciation of all research that might lead to it. To make that renunciation would be to set aside the most basic of human drives, the urge to survive. That survival urge has been deeply ingrained into all of us, because it has been selected for sharply and intensely by Darwinian evolution.

As we know, the promise of great reward brings out the worst in human beings, and realistically we must expect that the chance of obtaining immortality would excite many people to theft, murder, or warfare. Yet, even for the individual, immortality might be as much a curse as a blessing. Endless life could well bring satiation, an ever-more frantic search for pleasure or for meaning and ultimately a boredom more dismal than anything we mortals can imagine. I suspect that the incidence of suicide among "immortals" would be far higher than our own.

If we search for wild cards among the areas beyond the borderline of scientific respectability, we encounter the study of extrasensory perception and other psychic ("psi") phenomena—telekinesis, reading the future, thought transference, and so on. Most scientists would characterize the psi phenomena as "not proven," but there have been times before when the majority view on a scientific question has turned out to be wrong. Occasionally I've listened to lectures or impassioned individual harangues by speakers convinced of the reality of psychic phenomena. Each time I have tried to be fairminded and have looked over what literature was available. Each time I have come away unconvinced.

Two developments of recent years now make it more difficult than ever for scientists to form a balanced judgment about psychic phenomena. First, enthusiasts are now convinced that there is an "observer effect," that psi effects disappear in the presence of anyone who is skeptical about them. That is wonderfully convenient for the enthusiasts: it insures that anyone hoping for positive results will first have to abandon what all scientists have learned is essential in the search for truth: a skeptical, painstaking search for every conceivable source of error.

The second new development is an interest in psi effects on the part of military services. The Russians were the first to show that interest. Now the Americans, afraid that something however unlikely might turn out to be a potent weapon and be used against them, are looking into psi effects as well. The military research is hidden by secrecy, so one only hears rumors about it. Of course the rumors are that the psi effects have been proven to be real—the rumors wouldn't spread otherwise.

Psi effects, if real, are as likely to be proven in this next century as in any other. They're also likely to be of more use in military and other clandestine applications than in ordinary communications. By 2081 the communications network that will exist on the basis of conventional techniques like radio, communications satellites, and laser transmission will be so rapid and convenient that thought transference would be very nearly redundant.

If psi effects do turn out to exist, they don't necessarily have to violate known physical laws but may simply be extensions of them. Most people think of scientific truth as something that shifts with time. That's not the case: the body of scientific knowledge is not a picture that wavers and re-forms with each new discovery. Instead it's like a jigsaw puzzle that's already partly assembled. New discoveries fit new pieces into the existing puzzle and make the picture more complete, but they don't alter the structure that's already in place. Psi effects, if they exist at all, may simply involve physical forces that are not yet understood, just as magnetism, two centuries ago, was a force as mysterious to the most learned scientists as to the sailors who used it for navigation. Alternatively, psi effects might be an unsuspected result of combining physical laws from two well-known areas. The laser principle was just such a combination, its elements being taken from the two thoroughly understood areas of electromagnetics and quantum mechanics.

If psi effects are at the ragged edge where the unknown shades into the impossible, there are three more old favorites of science fiction that belong well over on the other side, the wildest of wild cards. Should any of them be realized, it would explode the whole scientific jigsaw puzzle, clearly violating presently known laws. Travel faster than light, time-travel to the past, and antigravity are all sheer impossibilities. Or are they? Let's examine the outside limits of our knowledge to see if there are possible loopholes.

Travel faster than light and time-travel violate the same physical principle: causality, the rule that an effect cannot precede its cause. In quantum mechanics we indulge, for convenience, in what seems to be a violation of that rule. We carry out calculations allowing for the motion of certain particles backward in time. But that is mathematical shorthand, and the results of any calculation of a complete experiment must be in accord with the principle of causality. How far could that rule be stretched? Far enough to be interesting. It would not violate causality, for example, to devise a machine capable of viewing any event in history, in complete three-dimensional color with stereophonic sound. As for our own physical movement through time, it is strictly in accord with Einstein's equations of relativity that we could slow down our aging by traveling very close to the speed of light. Quite possibly by 2081, and almost for sure by a century later, there may be people whose life spans have been extended by their travel at a significant fraction of light speed. It would also not violate known physical laws for us to enter suspended animation, to be revived millenia into the future. But in both of those legitimate methods of extending life, the person involved would not experience a greater life span; instead, the traveler's own bodily processes would seem to everyone else to be slowed down. And causality would definitely be violated if we were able to move backward in time and influence events in the past, or if we were able to see into the future.

It's been suggested that there's an escape hatch from these rules related to gravity. There's a bare chance that a physical object or a light signal could enter a black hole, a gravitational door leading out of our universe, and reappear out of a "white hole" somewhere else. Adrian Berry has written of that possibility in *The Iron Sun*. Even if that most adventurous kind of space travel eventually turns out to be possible, there is no guarantee that it will violate causality. If white holes exist, their spacing from the corresponding black holes and the time delay between the disappearance of an object into a black hole and its reappearance out of a white hole could obey a rule consistent with causality: the rule would say that travel by the risky route couldn't outrun a light signal sent through ordinary space. All our experience with scientific discovery in the past suggests that if such "wormhole travel" turns out to be possible, it will satisfy causality and take its place as one more piece in the overall jigsaw puzzle. I doubt that we'll be anywhere near ready to tackle wormhole travel a century from now, and my out-on-a-limb prediction is that in 2081 we'll still see no way to travel faster than light. The cosmic speed limit will still be in force.

Antigravity is another old favorite of science fiction. We already know something about it that we didn't know fifty years ago: that we can't get around it by using antimatter. Though a beam of antimatter will be a potent, unstoppable weapon, it will still fall down, not up—we know that as a result of the great progress in understanding the quantum numbers of elementary-particle physics that has been made in the past quarter-century. As for antigravity, the answer from over a half-century of research into relativity and gravitation would have to be: don't place any bets on it. The notion of antigravity had its greatest vogue in the period when humans yearned for flight but had not yet achieved it. Now that the airplane and the rocket are commonplace realities, the concept of antigravity has taken on a faintly musty, Victorian air. Even if it were to be found possible, it wouldn't make nearly as much difference as we might have thought a century ago. Space colonists will be able to turn "gravity" on or off at will simply by walking up toward or down away from the axes of rotation of their slowly turning habitats. So to be provocative, I'll sum up antigravity in a few words: impossible, or if possible, unnecessary.

Travel at super-light speeds, time-travel and antigravity all are questions related to the fundamental structure of the universe. There are two other questions that I find at least as fascinating, because they relate to life itself. Those twin mysteries of this next century are the meaning of consciousness and the uniqueness of life. Humanity may be well on the way to turning both those wild cards face upward by 2081.

Consciousness, that piercingly keen sense of "myself" that each of us carries through life, is at once the most familiar and the most inexplicable of phenomena. In *Mechanics of the Mind*, a book that grew from the 1976 BBC Reith lectures, the physiologist Colin Blakemore attempts to cut through its mystery. He acknowledges that the self may be separate from the living body, but reminds us of a basic tenet of the scientific method: that one doesn't introduce a new hypothesis until one has exhausted every possibility of explaining a phenomenon by an old one. He believes there is no need, so far, to invoke a new, transcendent principle to explain consciousness. One of his most compelling arguments is that consciousness, like all the rest of our attributes, must have evolved as the result of evolutionary pressures. Clearly, our sense of internal awareness affects our choices among possible actions, and clearly, its influence must have a survival value. Therefore, Blakemore argues, consciousness must be a part of our bodily equipment, rather than something transcendental, unrelated to biology.

He marshals another argument in support of this view: the sense of internal awareness, the sense of association between body and mind, can be destroyed by injuries to a certain part of the brain. Within the cerebral cortex of every animal there is a "touch area" that contains a "map" of the body, connected by nerve fibers to the tactile sensors. The map is distorted, with the most important and sensitive areas being most generously represented. Injuries to the parietal lobe, just behind the touch area, produce an extraordinary disturbance of the relationship between body and mind. The opposite side of the body is lost to the owner's consciousness, and hangs as what Blakemore calls "an unwanted parasite on his conceptual self."

Is consciousness, therefore, an attribute only of living creatures that think, or is it associated with all thinking entities, including inanimate computers? I suspect only the former, because consciousness is so closely tied to the parietal lobe, an organ which has no counterpart in computers. As Blakemore puts it, "Those features that will give a computer consciousness will probably have to be designed into it just as deliberately as it is told how to multiply and divide." We should not expect, therefore, that consciousness will spring forth automatically when computers of the kind we have made so far reach some magic level of complexity.

Supposing that these arguments are correct, is it likely that in this next century we will learn to build computers that have a sense of their own identity, as we do? That would be a wild card indeed. We have understood arithmetic since antiquity, so it is only a problem in engineering for us to design computers with arithmetic ability. But we still do not understand our own consciousness, so we are not even close to designing a sense of identity, of self, into the computers we build. And if we could, the prospect would raise frightening moral issues. In a disturbingly godlike way, we would then be creating sentient beings. Some of the questions it would raise would be merely banal: a Bill of Rights for robots? The vote? An Equal Rights Amendment? The ordination of computers as priests, ministers, or rabbis? Others would be far more terrifying: if the computational speed and encyclopedic memory of computers were allied, not only to the superhuman strength and immortality of robots, but to the fierce desire for survival that characterizes conscious animals, would we create a race of superbeings that would brush us humans aside or exterminate us? I rather hope that we don't risk the experiment.

If understanding consciousness, that first great mystery, demands a turning inward of our attention upon ourselves, the second great puzzle requires our looking outward, letting our imaginations roam through space and time. Were there many different, independent points of origin for life within our galaxy, and did they spawn other civilizations beyond our own—civilizations that explored, as we have, the universal laws of nature, and applied those laws to the building of technological artifacts like radio transmitters and spaceships? Or is life on Earth unique, the result of some extraordinarily unlikely combination of cosmic accidents?

Through most of this century it seemed reasonable, in accord with the post-Copernican realization that the Earth is but a minor planet in orbit around a small star of a rather common type, to assume that life originated independently at many points in the galaxy. That may indeed be the case, but the idea has been called into question by the negative results of two experiments: we have found no life on Mars, and we have detected no signals from other stars, beyond those pulsings and hissings in the radio spectrum for which we can find natural explanations in the science of astrophysics. The questions have become much sharper since a few people began exploring one of the consequences of the drivers of change. During the late 1970s a number of scientists—Sebastian van Hoerner, Michael Papagannis, Frank Tipler, and myself in the United States, and I. S. Schklovskii in the Soviet Union—pursued simultaneously and independently a chain of logic, and all reached the same conclusions. Ronald Bracewell also investigated these concepts, and came to similar results.

We began by appreciating that any other civilizations in our galaxy would be almost certainly either far more primitive than ourselves or else far more advanced technically. The reason is that compared with the slow time scale of galactic evolution the discovery and application of the scientific method occurs almost as fast as an explosion. Four centuries ago, for instance, there was no theoretical basis for any one of the drivers of change. Now the fundamental theory for each of the five is well understood, and is being applied successfully to working machinery. An equal time into the future all five will seem to our descendants as ancient and primitive as the digging of canals, the construction of windmills, and printing by woodblock now seem to us. By then automation will produce any apparatus, no matter how complex, without human intervention. Space colonies will have spread throughout our solar system and almost certainly beyond. We will be using the energy and material resources of our entire solar system as easily and routinely as we now dig coal and smelt iron.

Extraterrestrials with whom we might make contact must be imagined in the context of that level of civilization or beyond it, because the chance that they would be within a few hundred years of our own level of development is slim indeed: it is the ratio of that time span to the total length of time over which a civilization could originate. The origin of civilizations must be keyed to the birth and evolution of stars and planets, and that has occurred throughout most of the lifetime of the galaxy—more than ten thousand million years. Therefore, the probability of another civilization being at our level, give or take a few hundred years, is less than one in a million. For any advanced civilization *not* to be ahead of our own by more than a hundred thousand years, the odds are still very small—less than one in ten thousand.

When a civilization reaches our own technical level, there are just three paths its future history may take. Two of the three are dead ends: the civilization may destroy itself, or it may slip into stasis, a permanent steady state. Stasis, as I'm using the term, simply means that the civilization will never do more to study the galaxy beyond its own solar system than to stare through telescopes and listen for radio signals. Stasis could be perfectly satisfactory. After all, the oyster fills its ecological niche so well that it hasn't changed for a million years. A civilization could freeze its technical progress at a modest level and could devote the rest of time to the arts, to philosophy, or to contemplation. But we could never expect to hear from such a civilization.

There is, of course, a third possibility. A civilization could begin building colonies in space. To achieve that breakout from the nest-planet doesn't even require high technology; just shipbuilding techniques combined with extractive metallurgy, farming, elementary chemical rocketry and a knowledge of basic Newtonian mechanics. Even the limited breakout of a civilization into the local space of its native solar system would be a transition with high survival value in evolutionary terms. Once it occurred, the resources of a whole solar system would be available for use, and the dispersion of individuals into colonies throughout the system would make the race invulnerable to any single disaster. The race would be virtually unkillable from then on.

For any race that broke out from its native planet, it would be natural to take a strong interest in other star systems. Any race achieving space flight would know from astrophysics that nearly every star has debris around it: asteroids, comets, planets, and their natural satellites. By definition every star would provide colonists with an energy source—the star itself. That means that once a race achieved space flight, almost every star in the galaxy would become for it a safe, no-risk target for possible emigration. The colonists could always build habitats with the gravity and the atmosphere for which they had evolved. And they could always orbit those habitats at the right distance from any star to get enough, but not too much, sunlight. If the stellar type were very different from that of their parent star, the colonists would have to use filters to make the sunlight spectrum look familiar, but that would be an easy task. The construction of colonies around the stars nearest to the parent star would be another step in cultural evolution, again with survival value. Given the limit on the speed of communications set by the finite speed of light, the new colonies would separate culturally, each moving down its own historical path. That cultural dispersion would make it even more unlikely that the entire race would end up in one of civilization's dead ends—destruction or stasis.

The settlement of other solar systems is not an essential condition for the argument that my colleagues and I pursued independently, but is natural and consistent with it. The only essential link in the argument, at this point, is that a civilization taking an interest in the rest of the galaxy would seek to learn the most about it with the least effort, and to do so without running any risks.

Let's continue the chain of logic by supposing that there is, in fact, at least one other civilization in the galaxy that has reached our present technical level, and that it has neither destroyed itself nor settled into stasis. Recall that the odds are better than ten thousand to one that the other civilization is now more advanced than ours by more than 100,000 years. Let us imagine that this older civilization evolved on a planet orbiting a star called Prima. Already a tenth of a million years ago the Primans had reached a technical level a few hundred years beyond where we are now, and as a result were certainly in command of two technologies in particular: the mass production of antimatter and the construction of self-replicating machines of the kind I discussed in the chapter on "Automation."

Wishing to learn as much as possible about the galaxy, the Primans chose a method of observation that had to satisfy a number of conditions. We can reconstruct those conditions, for they depend only on logic, not on our assumptions as to the philosophy or psychology of the Primans. First, the method would have to insure the earliest and most rapid response. Second, it would have to be complete in the sense of scientific observation; that is, it would have to cover all the possible locations where non-Priman life might be stirring. Third, it would have to be efficient, obtaining the maximum amount of potentially useful data for the minimum expenditure of effort. Last of all, it would have to be safe. Though the Primans may have thought it very unlikely that there was anything dangerous waiting for them "out there," they had no way, prior to their search of the galaxy, to rule out that possibility completely. Therefore, the method of search they adopted would not have been one that revealed the location of Prima.

The Primans rejected out of hand a transmission of radio or light signals, because that would have given away their position. They rejected simply listening for corresponding signals from other civilizations because of its uncertainty and incompleteness: no signal would be heard except from civilizations that reached a high technical level, and then only if the other life forms chose to transmit.

To the best of my knowledge, there is just one method of observation that would have satisfied every one of the Priman conditions; I'll outline it now, as a definite scenario. The Primans refrained from investment in the galactic search until their technology could satisfy two conditions: first, that it could build multistage rockets, fueled by the reaction of matter with antimatter, that could reach a high fraction (70 to 95 percent) of the speed of light. Their reason for that condition? There wouldn't be any sense in launching a probe at a lower speed, because it would be passed en route by faster equipment developed later; it also wouldn't make sense to wait longer for more sophisticated research, because the cosmic speed-of-light limit would restrict any further improvement to a few percent, no matter how much effort was expended on it.

The Primans' second condition was their achievement of self-replicating machinery. They delayed launching their search program until they could build self-replicating devices of great complexity, capable of reproduction in about ten years or less. Again, the choice was justified by the argument that a self-replicating system with slower performance would be outpaced by equipment developed later, while not much would be gained in the total search program by waiting for systems capable of more rapid replication.

The Primans constructed their first long-distance spaceprobe, Replicator One, when the two technical conditions were both met. The computer that guided the space probe's actions stored a detailed, complex program, but it did not need to have creative ability; it was only the descendant of number-crunching arithmetic computers like our own. The Priman space probe, like a typical modern rocket, consisted of fuel to the extent of 90 percent of its total starting mass. Most of the remaining 10 percent was the upper stage, a deceleration rocket with, again, a 9:1 ratio of fuel to vehicle. The fuel for both stages was matter and antimatter in equal quantities, electrically suspended. A few parts in a thousand of the original mass was the payload, weighing perhaps as little as a ton or two, but containing the necessary computer programs and automated equipment for building small versions of chemical processing plants, machine shops, assembly plants, and so on. Replicator One accelerated to a cruising speed close to that of light with its first-stage fuel, discarded the burnt-out stage, coasted until near its target star, then decelerated with the fuel of the second stage. Once in a nice close orbit with plenty of sunlight, it began converting solar energy to matter and antimatter in preparation for the next voyage between stars, then collected planetary debris to replicate itself. Once the replication process was under way, it spent a few years surveying the entire planetary system, taking up low orbits around each planet in turn and surveying for primitive life (a chlorophyll signature in reflected sunlight as just one example).

One thing that Replicator One did *not* carry in its computer program was any record of the location of Prima. It didn't have to. It did carry a reference coordinate system which it would leave to all its descendants, so that they could communicate with each other and pinpoint the location of any star in the galaxy, probably by reference to the galactic center and the direction of the nearest neighbor galaxy, Andromeda. The key elements of the Replicator programs were so simple that we can reconstruct them ourselves:

• As soon as you arrive at a star, turn on your automatic beacon signal to tell other Replicators "I'm here." Look in the direction of each nearby star, at the standard beacon frequency, to see which ones already have Replicators. Don't replicate unless you find a nearby star that isn't already equipped with a Replicator. If you do, send one there.
• Whenever you receive a signal message from a Replicator orbiting another star system, relay it to all the Replicators around the stars nearest you that are farther than you are from the message origin. Disregard any signal that you've already received and relayed before.
• Don't chatter. Send to your nearest neighbor Replicators only the initial information about your star system, and relay updates no more frequently than every million years unless something changes markedly.

The Replicator probes, acting on those instructions, spread out and reproduced, forming a sensory network throughout the entire galaxy. The network reported back to Prima every significant detail about the origins of other life forms, along with a wealth of scientific data. Chances are that the Primans let the first few cycles of replication—perhaps from the original Replicator to 128 of them by the sequence of doublings 1, 2, 4, 8, 16, 32, 64, 128—take place locally under Priman supervision. They then despatched a hundred or so Replicators to selected points throughout the galaxy to serve as nuclei for duplication. From those points, Replicators then spread outward, leaving one of their number in every star system, until Replicators from different nuclei encountered each other and obeyed their program command to stop replication. Of the 128 Replicators from the first 7 doublings, two dozen or so may have been sent to the stars nearest Prima, so that the Primans could obtain rapid and complete coverage of the star systems that might be early targets for colonization.

Let's check how effective the Replicator program was for Prima. The first hundred Replicators, moving outward at close to the speed of light, required from a few hundred to 50,000 years to reach their destination stars and begin replication. From each of those points, daughter probes moved outward and reproduced, spreading like a bacterial culture in a dish of nutrient. That process terminated in less than 10,000 more years, with a probe in orbit around almost every star in the galaxy. Only 37 doublings (370 years in all) were needed to provide Replicators for every star in the galaxy, no matter how insignificant. News of the origin even of primitive life traveled through the galaxy as laser light, relayed by a tight, narrow beam from each powerful transmitter to a receiver at a nearby star, then amplified and sent onward again. Because the signal path zigzagged from star to star, much as our telephone messages are relayed from city to city, the overall speed of a message crossing the galaxy was a little less than that of light, but not much less. For the short distances between adjacent stars the laser beams could easily punch through the dust clouds of the galactic center, so the Primans got full coverage even of stars that they couldn't see directly. And even the more paranoid members of Prima's civilization could sleep quietly, because Prima remained safe: it received messages, recorded and analyzed them, but sent none. Its own star, of course, was equipped with a beacon transmitter to ward off any overeager Replicators, and never originated any news reports.

If the Primans ever existed, that is if any civilization reached our level and survived beyond it, a Priman space probe has been observing our solar system for a very long time. If it ever was knocked out of commission by a meteor strike, it was soon replaced by replication from one of its identical twins at a nearby star. The news of the beginnings of life on Earth reached Prima a cosmic eye blink after the probe arrived; remember that the 100,000 years that it took to emplace the probe system throughout the galaxy and to receive information from its most distant members was only one part in 100,000 of the age of the galaxy. The Primans may well have had a number of information updates about the Earth before the first ape-men dropped out of the trees. Whether there were any Primans left to hear the news, or whether they cared, didn't affect the existence or continued operation of the Replicator system. And if that space probe exists, where is it now? Up until about 1950 it was probably in low orbit above the Earth. When the beginnings of long-range rocketry heralded the dawn of our space age, the probe would have withdrawn to a safe distance to escape detection. Probably it is now leading or trailing us in our orbit around the sun, just a few million miles away, and it will retreat farther still as our activities in space increase.

Would it have been difficult for the probe to communicate with us? Hardly! Given the resources of primordial debris that exist in our solar system, the probe could have built, at its leisure, a large lightweight mirror and placed it in high orbit above the Earth. With the mirror it could have reflected sunlight to Earth in the night, to make a brilliant signal obvious even to stone-age cavemen: perhaps a simple 1, 2, 3, 1, 2, 3, . . . formed by flashes of light, or for a more sophisticated audience the sequence 1, 3, 5, 7, 11, 13, 17 . . . of the prime numbers.

But there have been no extraterrestrial signals of any kind. At this point our solid chain of logical argument pauses for conjecture, for our reasonable question, "Where are they?" can have many explanations, and all depend on the unknown psychology, philosophy, or moral values of the Primans. It is possible that there are a thousand probes in the solar system observing us, sent by a thousand, different, independent civilizations—but that every one has been programmed only to observe and never to affect our natural development by signaling to us; to them, we may be animals in a zoo or a wildlife refuge. Or the probes may all be programmed to make no overtures until they have "checked with headquarters." That could take a fair fraction of a million years. Or they could be programmed to make no signals until we have "made it" on our own. We may be under a cosmic veto circuit, that will unlock the transmitter switch only when a thousand years of radio communication have continued *after* the last atomic-bomb blast; or only when our own descendant colonies have scattered safely to other stars. Whatever the reasons, there are just two logical alternatives to explain the silence that surrounds us: No matter how many Priman civilizations there may have been, every one of them programmed its Replicator probes to remain silent: "Don't call us, we'll call you." Or, we are alone in our galaxy. The Primans are us.

These alternative conclusions are so different that we are left in frustration; is there nothing more we can learn? There is, and it is a matter of the greatest importance as we face these dangerous decades that lie ahead, before human life disperses safely outward from the Earth. In the late 1970s, after following the chain of reasoning that I have outlined, I realized that it has a corollary: although Priman civilizations with peaceful intentions could have refrained for ethical reasons from revealing their presence, there would have been no way to conceal hostile action. If the Primans were hostile to other life forms, it would have been chillingly easy for them to include one final instruction in the programming of their Replicators:

- If you observe any signs that an intelligent, technological civilization is developing on any planet in your system (campfires at night, farming, roads, boats, and buildings are all useful indicators), destroy all life there. Do so by building orbital mirrors to reflect the light of the local sun, so as to raise the surface temperature high enough to sterilize the planet.

More apocalyptic methods of extermination would have been possible but unnecessary. In military terms, if the Primans intended hostile action against other life forms, they would have programmed their Replicators to carry out a preemptive first strike long before any younger civilization reached the level of the telegraph, much less the technical level of the nuclear bomb. Above all, the probe would have been directed to eliminate any non-Priman life form before it achieved the capability for spaceflight, because that technical achievement would expose the probe itself to possible interference by the younger civilization.

Civilization on earth has been allowed to develop. Therefore, we can be quite sure that no civilization hostile to other life is in command of the galaxy. Either there has never been such a killer life form, or any that developed were contained by earlier civilizations with peaceful intentions, or we are, in fact, alone in the galaxy. All three alternatives lead to a single, profound, and positive conclusion.

Our galaxy is friendly, and it is waiting for us.

A Final Word

I'VE GIVEN you my predictions about the world of 2081, and of course must warn you that at best they can only be right in broad outline. Yet I must point out that they're consistent with the histories both of technology and of social interaction. It's an exciting future that I'm predicting, even more different from the late twentieth-century than our own time is from 1881. Some people may be frightened rather than attracted by the prospect of so much more change still to come. But we need not be afraid if we approach the future armed with understanding. So that you may gain that understanding and help to make the future an improvement on the past, here is my advice as we begin the century that will lead to 2081.

First in importance, guard the freedom of ideas at all costs. Be alert that dictators have always played on the natural human tendency to blame others and to oversimplify. And don't regard yourself as a guardian of freedom unless you respect and preserve the rights of the people you disagree with to free, public, unhampered expression.

Second only to guarding the freedom of exchange of information, acquire a firm basic knowledge in communications and in technology. Learn to use your native language well and precisely, because ours is and will become even more a communicating society. Equally important, learn the basics of the technological world. If you don't understand the laws of Newton, or don't know the difference between volts and amperes, you'll have little hope of understanding this next century. Trace the functions on a pocket calculator to make such concepts as exponential growth and sine-wave oscillation less of a mystery.

If you are beyond college age, you may object at this point that you are too old to learn even the ABCs of the technological world. Fortunately that is not the case. Modern research has shown that there is little if any loss of the ability to learn as one grows older, as long as one's health remains good. Attitude and effective habits of study matter far more than age. Much of the most interesting and valuable educating now being done in North America, for example, is through evening classes attended by adults, often in their 40s and 50s, who hold down full-time jobs in the daytime hours. Many such people are learning more now, because of their maturity and commitment, than they did as regular college students years before. And even if you cannot or prefer not to attend formal classes, you can learn a great deal about physics and engineering by arming yourself with a pocket calculator, a good first-year textbook, and the determination to begin solving some problems on your own.

More than twenty years ago Sir Charles Snow lamented the sharp division between "The Two Cultures," the literary/artistic and the scientific. My observations over the past decades, the evidence of current events, and the research and analysis that went into this volume all confirm that Snow was perceptive in identifying the problem, and entirely right to be very concerned about it. For a time, until the 1960s, a successful beginning was made toward raising a generation of humanists with a good grounding in the sciences, and scientists with significant basic knowledge in the humanities. Unfortunately, that movement toward education for "literacy" in both of the two cultures came to a halt with the ferment of unrest and the resulting lowering of standards and of course requirements that shook the universities at the end of the 1960s. Only now, more than a decade later, is there a significant movement toward higher standards and the education of a generation literate in both of the two cultures.

Bridging the culture gap is a responsibility that we all share, whether we are young or old. And if you are young enough still to retain a choice in what to emphasize in your formal education, I believe I am giving sound advice both for your own personal success and for the good of society when I recommend that you bridge the culture gap through your own educational choices. The reward for a simultaneous literacy in both the humanities and the sciences is that it can make the next decades not only survivable for you but enjoyable. There are some other suggestions I can make, based on my own experience and observations, that apply particularly if you are young enough to have most of your life still ahead of you:

First, you are probably critical of older people and they of you. Never mind, the differences in attitude and viewpoint between the young and the old have been with us in every generation, and in a normal lifetime you'll be on both sides of the conflict. Second, don't waste too much effort in searching for conspiracies. Most of the harm done in the world is out of stupidity, not by design. Be on the watch for skulduggery—we all owe a lot, for example, to the trust-busters of Teddy Roosevelt's time—but don't fall into the trap of thinking that every evil thing that occurs in the world is a part of some diabolic master plan. The notion that whatever is wrong with the world can be blamed on somebody (never, of course, one's self) is a rather infantile carryover from the childhood days when our parents were thought to be all-powerful and therefore all-responsible. And last, in the matter of self-indulgence: we live in a comfortable, relatively affluent society, but comfort, security, and the license to do precisely as one likes throughout life aren't the be-all and the end-all of existence. In fact, they can become thoroughly boring. As H. G. Wells reminded us, the purpose of improving society shouldn't be to eliminate hardship, but to insure that when hardship occurs it's to some good purpose. Subjecting yourself deliberately for a period of time to a situation where you're under orders can be good for the growing-up process, and if you find yourself with that opportunity, whatever it may be, don't necessarily run away from it.

Now for those matters that concern us all, whether we are young or old. As I have emphasized, and as we can verify by our observations, the knowledge that is acquired about the physical world, both in the natural and the life sciences, is unique in that it builds on all that has gone before and so grows continually. That gives to humanity an ever-increasing power, and we therefore feel, quite properly, a responsibility to use it wisely. All too easily many of us feel that responsibility in negative terms only, as an obligation to dig in our heels and resist all further change. But the opportunities that now lie before us to shape this next century better than the last depend to a great extent on science and its applications through engineering, and we will fail in our duty if we do not courageously seize these opportunities to improve the human condition.

Indeed we humans, frail and bumbling as we are, can prevail over world problems that now seem insurmountable. And when we take the initiative to do so, let it be with humility and a sense of proportion. We who belong to this particular time should not be so presumptuous as to think ourselves wise enough to determine the course of humanity for all time. Our descendants will have ideas at least as valid as our own, and they will have the advantage of our history to learn from. The evidence of our mistakes may be almost as useful to them as the fruits of our successes. Our paramount responsibility is to keep the freedom of choice alive for them, so that they may inherit a world still rich in options.

Quickly as our world is changing, I find it reassuring that humanity has weathered the changes brought about during this past century. Whatever happens, I'll place my bet that we'll be able to cope with the next. Some few of you reading this book, perhaps more of you than we now expect, will still be around in 2081. If so, look back over these yellowing pages, from your vantage point in our future. Perhaps the next time you read them you'll still be young, and will be living comfortably on a colony circling another star, in the year 2081.

Bibliography

Selected Reading

Part I—The Art of Prophecy

SYSTEMATIC PREDICTION OF THE FUTURE

Brown, Harrison. *The Human Future Revisited.* New York: W. W. Norton, 1978.

————, Bonner, J., and Weir, J. *The Next Hundred Years.* New York: Viking, 1957.

Bundy, McGeorge. "After the Deluge, the Covenant," in *Saturday Review World*, August 24, 1974, p. 18.

Casey, D. R. *Crisis Investing.* Seal Beach, Calif.: '76 Press, 1979. (On economic cycles.)

Clarke, Arthur. *Profiles of the Future.* New York: Bantam Books, 1964.

Feinberg, G. *Consequences of Growth.* New York: Seabury Press, 1977.

Ferkiss, Victor. *Futurology: Promise, Performance, Prospects.* Beverly Hills and London: Sage Publications, 1977.

Haldane, J. B. S. *Daedalus, or Science and the Future.* Folcroft Pa.: Folcroft Library Editions, 1923.

Heilbroner, Robert. *An Inquiry into the Human Prospect.* New York: W. W. Norton, 1974.

Heiss, K.; Knorr, K.; and Morgenstern, O. *Long Term Projections of Power.* Cambridge, Mass.: Ballinger, 1973.

Kahn, H.; Brown, W.; and Martel, L. *The Next 200 Years.* New York: William Morrow, 1976.

Meadows, Donella; Meadows, Dennis; Randeas, J.; Behrens, W. *The Limits to Growth.* New York: Universe Books, 1972.

Mesarovitch, M., and Pestel, E. *Mankind at the Turning Point.* New York: E. P. Dutton, 1974.

Shuman, J. B., and Rosenau, D. *The Kondratieff Wave*. New York: Dell, Delta Books, 1972. (On economic cycles.)

Suedfeld, P., and Weld, M. "Dark Trends: Psychology, Science Fiction and the Ominous Consensus," *Futures* 8:22

Thomson, George. *The Foreseeable Future*. Cambridge: Cambridge University Press, 1955.

Vajk, P. *Doomsday Has Been Cancelled*. Culver City, Calif.: Peace Press, 1978.

Wilson, K. D., ed. *Prospects for Growth*. New York: Praeger, 1977.

Wise, George. "The Accuracy of Technological Forecasts, 1890–1940," in *Futures*, October 1978, p. 411.

BY AND ABOUT THE "WRITERS OF SHEER DELIGHT."

Evans, I. O. *Jules Verne and His Work*. New York: Amereon Ltd., 1966.

Fido, Martin. *Rudyard Kipling*. Feltham, Middlesex: Hamlyn Publishing Group, 1974.

Freedman, Russell. *Jules Verne, Portrait of a Prophet*. New York: Holiday House, 1965.

Kipling, Rudyard. *The Writings in Prose and Verse of Rudyard Kipling*. New York: Charles Scribner's Sons, 1913.

Verne, Jules. *The Works of Jules Verne* (Prince Edward of Wales edition), 15 vols. New York and London: Vincent Parke and Co., 1911.

Wells, H. G. *The Shape of Things to Come*. London: White Lion Publishers, 1973.

THE TRACT WRITERS

Bellamy, Edward. *Looking Backward: 2000–1887*. New York: Ticknor, 1888.

Huxley, Aldous. *Brave New World*. New York: Harper, 1931 (repr. 1946).

Orwell, George. *1984*. London: Secker & Warburg, Ltd., 1949.

Zamiatin, Eugene. *We*. New York: E. P. Dutton, Everyman, 1925.

Part II—The Drivers of Change

COMPUTERS

Morrison, P., and Morrison, E. *Charles Babbage and His Calculating Engines*. New York: Dover, 1961.

AUTOMATION

Albus, J. S., and Evans, John M., Jr. "Robot Systems," in *Scientific American*, 234, 2 (1976): 77.

Nitzan, D., and Rosen, C. A. "Programmable Industrial Automation," IEEE Transactions on Computers, vol. C-25, 12 (1976): 1259.

Williams, D. S.; Wilf, J. M.; Cunningham, R. T.; and Eskenazi, R. "Robotic Vision," in *Astronautics and Aeronautics*, May 1979, p. 36.

SPACE COLONIES

Cole, Dandridge M., and Scarfo, Roy G. *Beyond Tomorrow*. Amherst, Wisc.: Amherst Press, 1965.

———, and Cox, D. W. *Islands in Space*. New York: Chilton Books, 1964.

O'Neill, Gerard K. *The High Frontier*. New York: Bantam Books, 1978.

———, and O'Leary, B., eds. *Space Based Manufacturing from Nonterrestrial Materials*. Progress in Astronautics and Aeronautics, vol. 57. New York: American Institute of Aeronautics and Astronautics, 1977.

Billingham, J., and Gilbreath, W., eds. *Space Resources and Space Settlements*. NASA SP–428. Washington, D. C.: NASA, 1979.

Tsiolkowski, Konstantin. *Beyond the Planet Earth*. Oxford: Pergamon Press, 1960.

Vajk, P. J. "The Impact of Space Colonization on World Dynamics," in *Technological Forecasting and Social Change* 9 (1976): 361.

ENERGY

Brown, William C. "A Profile of Power Transmission by Microwaves," in *Astronautics and Aeronautics*, May 1979, p. 50.

Dugger, G. L. "Is There a Chance for OTEC," in *Astronautics and Aeronautics*, November 1979, p. 36.

Ehrenreich, H., and Martin, J. H. "Solar Photovoltaic Energy," in *Physics Today*, September 1979, p. 25.

Fowler, J. M. *Energy and the Environment*. New York: McGraw-Hill, 1975.

Hoyle, F. *Energy or Extinction*. London: Heinemann, 1977.

Lubkin, B. Gloria. "What Went Wrong with the Three Mile Island Reactor," in *Physics Today*, June 1979, p. 77.

Smil, Vaclav. "Energy Flows in the Developing World," *American Scientist* 67 (1979): 522.

Stuhlinger, E. "Electric Automobiles—Yes!" Journal of Energy 2, 5 (1978): 279.

Part III—Life in 2081

SPACE TRAVEL

Bruzzone, C., et al. "Design Investigation of Solar Powered Lasers for Space Applications," in Final Report, #MXNW 79–1087 1090 1. Mathematical Sciences Northwest, Inc., P. O. Box 1887, Bellevue, Wash. 98009.

FLYING THROUGH THE EARTH

Kolm, H. H., and Thornton, R. "Magnetic Flight," in Scientific American, December 1973.

Nakamura, S., and Hayashi, A. "Development of the HSST System," Japan Airlines Co., Ltd., General Secretary's Office, Tokyo Bldg., 7–3 Marunouchi 2 chome, Chiyoda-ku, Tokyo 100, Japan (1979).

Salter, R. M. "Transplanetary Subway Systems," in Davidson, F. P.; Giacoletto, L. J.; and Salkeld, R., eds. Macro-Engineering and the Infrastructure of Tomorrow. AAAS Selected Symposium #23, Westview Press, 5500 Central Avenue, Boulder, Colo.

Zurek, R. "Methods of Levitation for Tracked High-Speed Traffic," in Endeavor 2,3 (1978):108. (A Euro-article, sponsored by the Commission of the European Communities through its Directorate-General for Scientific and Technical Information.)

HONOLULU, PENNSYLVANIA

Ball, J. G., and Mathias, R. A. "Lighting the Way to the 21st Century," in The Construction Specifier, January 1980, p. 62.

Gardner, E. A. "Canadian Government Project for a New Town," The Canadian Architect, November 1958, p. 44.

HIGHWAY IN THE SKY

Griffiths, D. R. "Navy to Test On-Board Oxygen Generator," in Aviation Week and Space Technology, February 4, 1980, p. 56.

Harned, M. S. "General Aviation Aircraft in the '90s," in Astronautics and Aeronautics, January, 1980, p. 46.

Hertzberg, A. "A Solar Laser Airplane," in Boeing News, 37, 2 (1978):2.

Larson, G. C. "Advancing Propeller Technology," in Business and Commercial Aviation, January 1980, p. 74.

Strack, W. C. "Turbines Feasible for Lightplanes," in North Atlantic Aviation, 1980, p. 32–C.

THE LOTUS AND THE THORN

Davis, Bernard D. "The Recombinant DNA Scenarios: Andromeda Strain, Chimera, and Golem," in *American Scientist* 65 (1977):54.

Powers, R. M. "In Biomedicine, Bionics Becomes Reality," in *TWA Ambassador*, April 1978, p. 50.

FOR RICHER, FOR POORER

Macrae, Norman. "The Japanese Century Begins," *Atlas* 22 (1975):11.

McPhee, John. *The Deltoid Pumpkin Seed*. New York: Ballantine, 1973.

THE RESTING EARTH

Commoner, B. *The Closing Circle*. New York: Alfred A. Knopf, 1973.

Taylor, T. B., and Humpstone, C. C. *The Restoration of the Earth*. New York: Harper & Row, 1973.

Part IV—Wild Cards

Augustine, N. R. "Augustine's Laws and Major System Development Programs," in *Astronautics and Aeronautics*, April 1980, p. 36.

Berry, Adrian. *The Next 10,000 Years*. New York, E. P. Dutton, 1974.

———. *The Iron Sun*. New York: Warner Books, 1977.

Blakemore, Colin. *Mechanics of the Mind*. Cambridge: Cambridge University Press, 1977.

Brown, B., et al. "The Fermilab High-Intensity Antiproton Source" (Design Report), Fermi National Accelerator Laboratory, October, 1979.

Hackett, J., et al. *The Third World War*. New York: Berkley Books 1978.

Jones, E. M. "Discrete Calculations of Interstellar Colonization," Los Alamos Scientific Laboratory, LA UR 80–128.

Langford, David. *War in 2080*. New York: William Morrow, 1978.

Okress, E. C.; von Stetten, C. C.; and Soberman, R. K. "Lighter than Air," *Construction Specifier*, January 1980, p. 81.

Papagiannis, M. "Could We Be the Only Advanced Technological Civilization in the Galaxy?" Paper presented at the Fifth International Conference on the Origin of Life, Kyoto, Japan, April

1977. Available from author, Department of Astronomy, Boston University, 725 Commonwealth Avenue, Boston, Mass. 02215.

"Particle Beams and Laser Weapons," in *Aviation Week and Space Technology*, special issue, July 28, 1980.

Ridpath, Ian. *Messages from the Stars*. New York: Harper & Row, 1978.

Shklovsky, I. S. "Russian Scientist Forecasts Vast Colonies in Space," *New York Times*, May 18, 1978.

Tipler, F. J. "Extraterrestrial Beings Do Not Exist," internal report, available from author, Department of Mathematics, University of California, Berkeley, Calif. 94720.

von Hoerner, Sebastian. "Where Is Everybody?" Internal report available from author, National Radio Astronomy Observatory, Green Bank, West Virginia.

A FINAL WORD

Snow, Sir Charles P. *The Two Cultures and the Scientific Revolution* (Rede Lecture, Cambridge University, 1959). Cambridge, Cambridge University Press, 1959.

Index

About the Author

GERARD K. O'NEILL is a professor of physics at Princeton University. He received his B.A. degree at Swarthmore College in 1950, his Ph.D. at Cornell University in 1954, and in 1978 an Honorary D.Sc. from Swarthmore. Since 1954 Dr. O'Neill has taught graduate and undergraduate courses at Princeton. His main research area is elementary-particle physics, and in 1979 he published a graduate textbook on that subject, coauthored with his former graduate student Dr. David C. Cheng. In his particle-physics research Dr. O'Neill is best known for the concept of colliding-beam storage rings, and for its implementation in the form of the first high-energy colliding-beam experiment.

In 1969 Dr. O'Neill developed the concept of space colonies as a realistic plan within the limits of existing technology. In 1974 his work became generally known through conferences and lectures, and his book about space colonies, *The High Frontier*, was published in 1977. He received the Phi Beta Kappa Science Book Award for it in that year. Dr. O'Neill founded and is president of the Space Studies Institute, a nonprofit foundation which funds critical research through popular subscription. In connection with his work in space research, Dr. O'Neill served as Hunsaker Professor at M.I.T. in 1976–77, has served on several committees of professional societies and government agencies, directed NASA studies, and lectures frequently. At Princeton he directs research (supported by NASA and the Space Studies Institute) in space physics and applications, continues his research in elementary-particle physics, and from 1979 through 1981 taught an undergraduate course in "Physics Applied to Contemporary Problems," intended for nonscience majors.

In 1973 Dr. O'Neill married Tasha Steffen; they have one child. He has three children, now in their twenties, from a previous marriage. Both the O'Neills are pilots; Dr. O'Neill has logged some 1,700 hours as pilot, mainly in power planes, and also holds the International Diamond Badge in sailplane flying. In addition to his memberships in several professional societies, Dr. O'Neill is a member of the Soaring Society of America and the Explorers' Club. In addition to flying Dr. O'Neill enjoys bicycling, sailing, and mountain hiking.

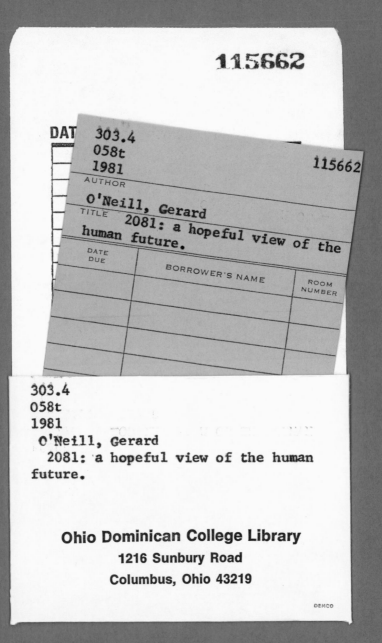